Indecent Exposures

INDECENT EXPOSURES
Twenty Years of Australian Feminist Photography

CATRIONA MOORE

ALLEN & UNWIN
in association with the POWER INSTITUTE OF FINE ARTS

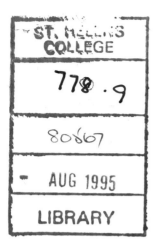
First published 1994
Allen & Unwin Pty Ltd
9 Atchison Street, St Leonards NSW 2065 Australia

National Library of Australia
Cataloguing-in-Publication entry:

Moore, Catriona.
    Indecent exposures: twenty years of Australian feminist photography.
    Bibliography.
    Includes index.
    ISBN 1 86373 162 8.
    1. Photography — Australia — History.   2. Feminism — Australia —
    History.   3. Women photographers — Australia — History.   4. Feminism
    and art — Australia — History.   I. Title.
778.99305420994

Set in 10.5/12pt Garamond by Graphicraft Typesetters Ltd.,
Hong Kong
Printed by Kim Hup Lee Printing Co Pte Limited,
Singapore

While every effort has been made to trace photographers and copyright holders whose
work is used in this book, any further information is welcomed by the author and the
publisher.

This publication was assisted by the Australia Council,
the Federal Government's Arts Funding and Advisory Body,
and by the Power Institute of Fine Arts.

To the memory of Carol Jerrems, whose photographs of Australian women profiled significant role models in my political education and to those women who in 1974 had the foresight and initiative to establish the Women's Art Movement in Australia.

Contents

Colour section appears between pages 98 and 99

Acknowledgements

The information contained in this study has been drawn from the experiences and artwork of many women photographers. I am indebted to these women for sharing their personal, professional and political work with me. Important documents were also obtained from the Australian National Gallery, the National Gallery of Victoria and a number of valuable yet under-funded resource centres such as the Sydney Women's Liberation Archives, the Victorian Women's Art Register and the NSW Artworkers' Union.

I would like to thank the University of Sydney Fine Arts Department, in particular Dr Terry Smith and Dr Tony Fry for their help and support with the initial research for the book, and the Power Foundation for its assistance with the illustrations.

Special thanks are also due to Peter Botsman and Jo Holder for their advice and support, to Anne-Marie Willis and Ann Stephen for their useful comments on an earlier manuscript, and to Fiona Moore for her invaluable assistance with the final draft.

Introduction:
Feminism and art history

Histories

Curatorial and market consensus has it that the golden years of
feminist photo-media have passed. By the end of the 1980s, art movements from the 1960s were starting to make a comeback. A neatened
version of fluxus and arte povera styles seemed more sensitive to the
burgeoning New Age spirit. The nineties promised to be an affirmative, healing decade after the social turmoil of the seventies and the
too-clever-by-half deconstructivist eighties. Or so the story goes.

Such dismissive accounts remind me of an earlier case of
terminal 'decade-ism' back in 1983, when the University of Sydney
hosted the symposium, 'What Ever Happened to the Art of the
Seventies?' By the end of that seminar, many of the participants
were privately thankful that the moral authority of radical politics
had lost its influence.

New intellectual and aesthetic engagements were needed. The
Left had been caught on the back foot since the fall of the Whitlam
Labor Government and had simply not done enough homework.
In the arts it was no longer good enough to simply make pro-
feminist, pro-community, anti-racist or anti-institutional gestures.
Unfortunately the tactical, analytic and political import of those
radical positions were buried in the rubble of 1970s pluralist soup.
Specific projects and positions were historicised as part of an era,
rather than a political strategy.

Could we write a more useful history of the last two decades,
avoiding either the plaintive cry of 'foul!' or unwarranted pats on
the back? Most Australian photography books simply recover
vintage prints, celebrate photographic pioneers or assemble visual
documents of Australian nationhood. Surprisingly few projects

address photographic history in a critical manner. When they do engage with critical theory and cultural studies, they scrutinise photography's ideological function and provide an account of photographers' role in history.

Texts like Anne-Marie Willis' *Picturing Australia: A photographic history* comb commercial, industrial, medical, legal and commemorative uses of photography to chart the forces shaping Australian social and cultural life, encompassing broader issues such as colonialism and modernity.[1] Social history projects such as these seek to unravel the origins of our current situation, presuming that our understanding of the present is informed by knowledge of the past. This kind of investigation has intensified the traditional pedagogical function of history, broadening the field of art history to include a variety of photographic material.

Feminist art history has been a key player in these developments. One argument developed in the 1970s was that the recognition of women as historical agents was needed to correct art history's omissions and mystifications. Accordingly, we added more progressive objects and areas of study to Australian art history. However, the mix didn't quite gel. The simple restoration of women's work in history did not necessarily alter the placement and status of visual documents. Feminist history needed to be strategically developed for maximum effect within the pedagogical and market arenas in which the discipline operated. We discovered that the historical archive is itself not a neutral space of knowledge, for the workings of libraries, museums, art schools, publications and conferences all exert competing pressures and requirements.

More conventionally formalised feminist projects found a comfortable niche within these contexts. Most aspects of feminist photography, however, lay completely outside the aesthetic and institutional ballpark. This indicated a need to formulate and assess feminist photography within a political and interdisciplinary rationale. Our aim was not a more inclusive and gender-sensitive *art history*, for feminist writing is governed by considerations of its political value, and not its contribution to art historical method.

What is now needed is a reconsideration of the relation between historical writing and feminist cultural politics. How is feminist photography best documented within existing pedagogical frameworks (art history, art training, women's studies)? How is it formulated within photographic exhibitions and collections, and how do such forms of categorisation and accumulation affect the employment and practice of women photographers?

Why is it necessary to register these qualifications? After two decades of feminist art and criticism, isn't it important to document feminism's emergence, development and influences before it disappears into the recent art-historical past? But this is precisely the point. Feminist photography can be neatly fitted within a continuity of historical or stylistic moments, as posited in either leftist or conservative art histories. This dispatches it all the more speedily into the ever-expanding archive of Australian photography, leaving the conditions of that archive unquestioned. The singular nature of feminist photography within the archive would also pass unnoticed; it would merely be regarded as a correction and supplement to existing frameworks. The specific political value of diverse images and practices are too easily categorised as '1970s pluralism' or '1980s post-feminism'. These convenient labels unify diverse objects and social relations so that art history can be comprehended as a *discipline*, a continuous space of knowledge. Past and present are linked through some underlying analytic figure—a stylistic tradition, the ethos of an era, or even the repressed voice of woman as a universalised Other.

This form of historicism has often been used by feminists to validate current institutional demands and art practices. It does have a negative aspect, however, expressed in unnecessarily essentialist or even moralistic views on women and their artwork. Once we make assumptions regarding women's proper interests, attributes and capacities, feminist art history uncritically guarantees its own existence.[2]

A static conception of patriarchy as a determining frame for historical analysis may also lead to the uncritical celebration of women artists. Here patriarchal relations are seen to form the 'motor of history', giving rise to women's struggles for autonomy, employment and expression. While clearly patriarchal relations *do* comprise important historical formations, they take no generalisable or determinant form. When evaluating feminist politics, we need to avoid reconstructing a past which fits into but does not question present frameworks, and we need to review our own practice. Once we do away with streamlined conceptions of politics and power, we can start to appreciate divergent forms of resistance under differing historical and cultural conditions.

Feminisms

Feminist photography is not a single entity. There are at least as many strategies available as there are tendencies within the Women's Movement. Yet the search for alternative representations of women has usually been based on a widespread belief in fundamental connections between language, aesthetics and sexual difference. At the very least, feminists have claimed a 'crucial difference' between the perspectives of men and women that may also be expressed in visual terms. This proposition became the basis for distinctions between feminist photography and the broader category of photography by women, as Julie Ewington has argued:

> 'Women who want to be women?' Rather, women who ARE women, who recognise rather than mis-recognise themselves, who embrace femininity rather than opting out to hide out in a successful suit, assuming masculine positions to achieve masculine status.[3]

Is it simply a matter of recognition or choice? If feminist photography reflects or realises an *a priori* political consciousness, how did this consciousness come about in the first place? I believe that our heroine is not a historically stable subject whose experience, perception of the world and mode of working necessarily produces feminine imagery. Nor has she slowly matured and passed on her ideology and expertise to a younger generation. Are there any gains to be made in essentialising feminine authorship and influence as a criterion of evaluation? In many instances, this is precisely the kind of historical gambit now in need of critical assessment.

I find it more useful to accept the feminist photographer as a recent, unstable and still marginalised authorial category, organised around certain institutional requirements and the priorities of feminist politics. Instead of setting her up as a point of origin and evaluation, it's time to rethink the discursive function of this novel photographic subject.

The women discussed here have no *a priori* biographical or political character. These are forged along the way, in the course of a series of important discursive and institutional struggles. Feminist photographers 'emerge on a field of battle and play their roles, there and there alone'.[4] They have helped define and clear a space on the rocky terrain of cultural value, knowledge and power. Along with other artists, they have constituted a radical ethics, or more specifically, an 'etho-poetics', as John Rajchman described parallel strategies in women's writing (or *ecriture feminine*).[5] Feminist photography, like *ecriture feminine*, has sought to invent femininity as an etho-poetic practice. The feminist photographer is the subject of ethical invention and intervention. Her rites of passage have involved the politicisation of the social and the destabilisation of sexual identity. These three themes—the subject, the social, the sexual—have been chosen as points of departure for this book.

Chapter 1 examines consciousness-raising techniques that were developed in the context of aesthetic training and political organisation. The exercise of communality and nurturing behaviour—capacities historically associated with women—were reformulated in the early 1970s within a radical conception of sisterhood. In this way, women became the subject of a feminist etho-poetics. I then discuss photographic interventions within the social. By this I mean work on the sexual division of labour and women's traditional exclusion from the public sphere of work, power and community decision-making. Feminist photography has largely avoided the traditional dichotomy between the public and private domains. Instead, a broad range of projects on the family, community and labour relations have raised crucial questions about women's augmented yet conditional social responsibility and power. The sexually-differentiated body has represented a third common denominator for feminist cultural politics. The latter part of the book charts important shifts that have taken place in the attempt to provide alternative representations of women's bodies, sexual identity and desire.

By the end of the 1970s, feminist photographic strategies began to drift away from an experiential, emotivist politics. In their place emerged more specific, anti-humanist analyses of relations of power and knowledge within a narrower cultural sphere. In the early 1990s, more critical uses of the semiotic and psychoanalytic methodologies that dominated the 1980s have emerged. The politics of the image have again shifted ground. In purely formal terms, the photographic print or series has stretched to wrap-around installation work. The feminist photographer now invents herself as a questioning aesthetic subject from within the mainstream of the museum and the market. Where are the political and ethical dimensions of feminist photography now located?

In describing these changes, I aim to construct a tactically useful history of feminist photographic strategies. If power is conceived as a historically contingent matrix of force relations, feminist photographic practices may be located as technologies of self-transformation as well as strategic interventions within arenas as diverse as art history and industrial relations. These photographic battles can be examined in context, and tactical shifts assessed. What projects have worked? What aims and strategies have we discarded along the way? Where are we headed at present? These questions guide my description and evaluation of feminist photography as a political practice.

1 The feminist artist

A novel subject

The feminist artist emerged as an experiential character in the wake of the New Left, anti-institutional and lifestyle politics of the 1960s. Autonomous forms of feminist cultural analysis, art practice and ethical conduct were delineated around the slogan, 'the personal is political'. Women artists and writers were implicated in a programme of personal, political and professional transformation. The shop-worn stereotypes of female student, camp follower, hobbyist, artist's wife, muse and model were countered by a radical image of feminine creativity.

A (still unresolved) crisis in the avant-garde lent an urgency to early feminist explorations. Along with community arts, performance and aspects of conceptual work, feminism reacted against the 'Americanized' styles of Pop, Colourfield and Minimalism. The 1960s and early 1970s had seen the weakening of traditional art techniques, widespread use of industrial procedures, and an emphasis on narrowly-defined formal problems. One artist and writer observed in retrospect that this meant '(t)he artist's prerogative to determine a meaning of his or her work had been eroded, indeed it had been surrendered almost willingly'.[1] Feminism emerged from this perceived late modernist crisis as part of a renewed insistence upon personal and social responsibility. This call for direct social engagement by artists in many ways echoed the critical, humanist ethics of earlier avant-garde movements.

Feminist etho-poetics involved more than the simple adoption of an ideology or set of responsibilities. It drew upon a bevy of aesthetic and personal techniques through which women could learn who they were, what they could become, and how to achieve change.

1

Photographic skills were learnt and taught as practices of collective self-exploration. In women's studies courses, consciousness-raising exercises, lectures, publications, skill sharing and exhibitions associated with the Women's Art Movements, women learnt a repertoire of gender-specific visual codes and behaviours. These 'technologies of the self' employed a female cultural norm as a critical tool, as a basis for political judgment and as a principle for regulating individual conduct.

Relevant here is the later work of Michel Foucault, well known for his theorisation of the function of power and discourse in modern Western society.[2] Whilst many feminists acknowledge the utility of Foucault's work on the exercise of power, the regime of sexuality and modern forms of subjectification, his genealogy of ethics is specifically masculine. Women simply cannot accede to the status of ethical subject within the historical, civic and philosophical arenas Foucault outlines. Instead, many philosophers have looked elsewhere—in particular, to feminist culture—to trace the contours of a new feminine rationality or ethics.[3]

Feminist art workers took their cue from the Women's Liberation slogan 'the personal is political' when characterising a specific female aesthetic. It ushered in a wealth of previously ignored social objects and relations (women's work, family, health and sexuality) as relevant to art practice and as valid art subjects. The camera could be used to identify these areas from a personal–political perspective. Self-portraiture, health imagery, work on the family album or photo-documentary studies of women at work helped to frame specific feminine experiences as the prime material for women's conduct.

Corresponding images of feminine creativity and women's culture were promoted by challenging existing art practices, materials and formal conventions. Women-only workshops, discussion groups and exhibition/community projects gave participants an opportunity to reconceive art's traditional functions to entertain and instruct. The historical role of art—to provide a creative balance between intellect and emotion—was intensified within the consciousness-raising context. Art could express personal fantasies or desires. It could also translate or generalise these in critical and political terms. Art was the perfect mechanism for the ethical work of self-clarification. It could guide women's conduct according to an image of radical femininity. It helped women transform themselves into the ethical subject of their own actions.

The personal is political

In 1973, Sydney writer Barbara Hall canvassed the attitudes towards women artists of selected Melbourne and Sydney commercial galleries:

> Most of the responses were like Max Hutchinson's (Gallery A): that he had trouble persuading buyers to take the work of women artists, that they felt they weren't worth as much as the work of male artists.[4]

A year later, Hall returned from North America after contacting New York and West Coast women's art groups and viewing the West-East Bag, the first North American slide collection of women artists' work. A meeting was called, attracting about thirty women, and regular meetings continued with what eventually became a core group of seven. These two events set the agenda for the Sydney Women's Art Movement (or Sydney WAM): support, education and the promotion of women artists' work. The group also highlighted discriminatory structures and practices in the visual arts industry through a regular newsletter, public talks, exhibitions, workshops, questionnaires, submissions and demonstrations.[5]

Sydney Women's Liberation had been in existence since December 1969, but few members of Sydney WAM had previously been involved in organised feminist politics.[6] Some were involved in Marxist organisations, and their interest in cultural politics had grown from a concern with American political and cultural domination. Others had contributed to Post-Object Art activities. All had been politicised by the anti-war movement. In Sydney, as elsewhere, feminism in the visual arts emerged in parallel to other Women's Liberation activities, as Barbara Hall later noted:

> We were upgrading a lot of devalued factors—ourselves, our social status as women, our powers of intuition; and flexing our outrage when we learnt where we were. The art movement did not spring from within the Women's Movement and what I think this has meant is that we operated more often from springboards which were moral in origin rather than ideological.[7]

Metaphors of importation and influence thus do not in themselves explain the emergence of feminist consciousness in the visual arts. Women's Liberation and the Women's Art Movements developed in tandem:

> We used to talk about and around two subjects constantly in the early sessions of the WAM: 'an evolving women's or feminist or feminine aesthetic', which came from the American arts feminism scene, and that the 'personal is political', which was a theme from the Women's Movement proper.[8]

The belief that the personal is political formed an influential nexus between feminism and art. It not only opened up a new terrain for cultural politics, but also provided the means of recogsing these new issues, and suggested the form of their treatment. Problems that did not fall within the conventional syllabus of both aesthetic and political programmes were articulated in transgressive and personalised terms. It was a substantial list, including women's domestic imagery and traditional arts, vaginal imagery, female sexuality, non-traditional art materials and media. New subjects, objects and techniques, along with forceful calls for equal representation, space and employment opportunities for women artists, stunned contemporary art audiences.

Even the more progressive alternative exhibition spaces had largely ignored women's work. As Barbara Hall later noted:

> In Sydney the art hippies at the Yellow House waged a stupid and unwinnable rivalry with the new misunderstoods, the conceptualists and post-object artists—all male of course—at Inhibodress, a collective in name only. Women occasionally exhibited or performed in either space (the late Philippa Cullen for example) but were seldom noticed by critics. If you were a woman artist or performer, people looked around for your boyfriend.[9]

Despite the liberal rhetoric of late modernism and its offshoots, women were not getting jobs in the new art colleges, and their work, when noticed, suffered at the hands of a Clement Greenberg-inspired formalist criticism. Sydney WAM claimed that child care, domestic labour, lack of resources, work space and professional confidence were also contributing to the high dropout rate of professional women artists. Corresponding connections drawn between women's artwork and their personal lives, feelings and social placement suggested integrated systems of support. This meant creating autonomous forms of organisation, women-only workshops, seminars, consciousness-raising sessions, exhibitions and community projects. Making art was seen as a pathway to women's personal and political self-realisation. In many ways, these personal–political prescriptions dovetailed with what Ian Burn has called the 'self-externalisation, or avant-garde "humanism"' of Conceptual Art.[10] However, using art as a means to draw together women's fragmented social experience implied a social collectivity which challenged the liberal individualism of the formalist canon, the lone conceptualist gesture and the 'do your own thing' counter-cultural ethos.

Feminine aesthetics and the confessional

Self-examination with the camera involved learning a repertoire of feminine imagery, feelings and responses. Specific visual and verbal forms, such as diaries or family album work, personal testimonies, questionnaires, image analysis and related interpretive commentary, and the practical exercise of 'doing the circle' in which everyone had their say, became central techniques of self-clarification. The Women's Art Movements, women's studies courses and art reviews became spaces for what was in effect a self-regulated confessional. Informal rules published in the second *Sydney Women's Art Movement Newsletter* suggest a common procedure:

1 Select a topic.
2 Go around the room, each woman speaking in turn. Don't interrupt, let each woman speak up to fifteen minutes, and then ask questions only for clarification.
3 Don't give advice, don't chastise, don't be critical.
4 Draw generalisations after everyone has spoken or before that go around the room and talk again.
5 Draw political conclusions—if you can.
6 Keep the group below ten women.
7 In order to develop trust and confidence don't repeat what has been said in the group.
8 This is not a therapy–encounter or sensitivity group situation.[11]

Exhibitions associated with Sydney WAM, such as *Fantasy and reality*, *It's great to be an Australian woman*, *Experiments in vitreous enamels* and *Self images* similarly encouraged women to reconstruct their identity in public through the identification of specifically feminine character traits, matrilinear family portraits and the exposition of fraudulent, media-generated self-images. In some ways these practices followed traditional paths. For many years, the self-portrait has assumed the privileged status of pathway to a hidden, existential and transformative truth about the human condition. But whose condition? Feminist confessional practices gave a political inflection to this preoccupation with the self as Other. Who was this new subject looking in the mirror? Women gazed into the lens of the camera and felt themselves to be 'ready-made', pieced together from alien forms. Unsatisfied, they looked to their mothers, sisters and lovers in the impossible search for a more authentic self-reflection. A decade later, this strategy of 'looking hard' would be inverted. Feminists would come to work around notions of the feminine self as a vector of competing, often contradictory discourses.

In the mid-1970s, however, feminist art revolved around an image of creative self-realisation which demanded new forms of conduct. The very nature of the feminist art confessional—the family album, the group photo-documentary session, the skill-sharing workshop—specified forms and attributes such as emotional honesty, nurturance and collectivity as an ethical ideal. The feminine essence-as-standard became a criterion for interpreting and regulating both art and conduct. Unfortunately, at times these etho-poetic techniques also carried with them an echo of nineteenth century feminist discourses on women's moral superiority and social responsibility.

A model student?

Women's studies was another important site of invention and intervention. Feminist electives initially functioned as a corrective supplement within the tertiary art curriculum. Photography was also something of a special case in the art school. Although professional training in the medium had been offered at selected Institutes of Technology for a number of decades, few women travelled this road. Sue Ford, for instance, was one of only two women photography students who graduated in 1962 from the Royal Melbourne Institute of Technology. The training she received there was technically and vocationally oriented.

Six years later, Prahran College of Advanced Education in

Victoria employed the fashion photographer Athol Shmith to introduce a fine art photography course within its Art Department. Carol Jerrems, perhaps the best-known woman photographer in Australia from the 1970s, took up photography when it was first offered at the College. When comparing prints by Ford and Jerrems from the late 1960s, key differences in photographic training are apparent. Ford's innovative experiments with codes of glamour and modern landscape were formulated within a different set of professional references to Jerrems' 1968 fine art folio. The fact that the National Gallery of Victoria purchased Jerrems' *Alphabet*, a rare achievement for student work, indicates the divergent paths of commercial and fine art training in the new colleges of art and design.

Male lecturers dominated the new photography departments, so many women attended women's studies electives or WAM activities for studio and art historical tuition. Others were self-taught, learnt from friends or had taken up the camera as an extension of work in other media.

By the mid-1970s, however, the art colleges became a powerhouse of feminist instruction, support and politics. By blending the *atelier* model, the technical school and the progressive principles of elementary art education, an earlier, skill-based training was modified to fit the pedagogic ethos of modernism. Feminism found a precarious niche here, in the experimental, student-centred modern art curriculum. Yet relations between 'the modern' and 'the feminine' have always been ambiguous. In this case, women's studies was at best accepted as a correction to perceived discrepancies between bearings and actualities. The most progressive School philosophy or pluralistic course structure may bear little relation to what actually takes place in the tutorial or workshop. At most, they form evaluative markers with which to identify problems and sketch ideal outcomes.

WAM surveys of tertiary art education drew attention to the fact that, historically, the majority of art students and arts–crafts teacher trainees are women.[12] However, men comprised most of the teaching staff, especially in tenured positions, at senior levels and in studio areas. Feminist criticism of staff discrepancies soon broadened to address questions of assessment, teaching methods, curricula and resources. The new tertiary art education was failing to meet fundamental educational requirements of the majority of its students.

Sue Ford, *Carmel and Trish*, 1962. Gelatin silver photograph, reproduced in Ford, *A sixtieth of a second: Portraits of women 1961–1981*, Experimental Art Foundation, Adelaide, 1987, p.20.

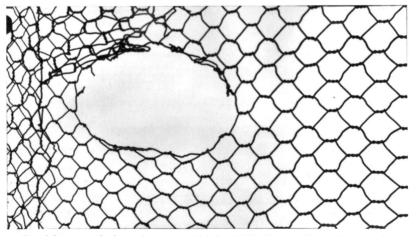

Carol Jerrems, *O*, from the series *Alphabet*, 1968. Gelatin silver photograph, 19.7 × 11.1 cms. National Gallery of Victoria, purchased 1971.

If so many art students were women, then gender was an important planning component. Bonita Ely, co-organiser of the Victorian Women's Slide Register, argued in her 1977 survey that the lack of female role models and exposure to women artists' work contributed to problems on campus and the high dropout rate of women professionals. Ely and others called for staffing policies and teaching methods which were sensitive to the experiences, interests and artwork of women students:

> [They] may want to express something very personal in their work. If they've had a baby, if they've had a miscarriage they may want to make a statement about that. If they've become involved in the cycles of nature and would like to express a very personal affinity through their menstrual cycle they could very well be made to feel embarrassed about such work and find that experience has to be sublimated or sidestepped.[13]

Women's work was ignored or misunderstood by the blinkered perspectives of male lecturers, as Ely also noted:

> Confronted by work that is made of pink satin and lace, they cannot understand what it is. When confronted by a ten foot steel girder structure they know what THAT is. These 'blokes' who are in jobs of authority and who can't see half the work that is going on around them, should not have those jobs, they're unfit to teach, they cannot teach.

In demanding that art education address the questions of women's experience, feminism actually intensified the ambitions of the humanist, post-war education agenda. The integration of personal and professional identity, a wholistic approach to learning and the encouragement of student cooperation was integral to women's studies courses.[14] These courses formed a corrective model to keep the comprehensive tertiary institution realisable. This is why the most commonly accepted model—the single semester women's studies elective—was never accepted as anything more than a voluntary supplement to existing programmes.

Why was the introduction of elective courses championed by feminists and adopted by the Colleges? For a start, they were strategic and achievable. Affecting recruitment, seniority and staffing was extremely difficult without Equal Employment Opportunity legislation. The limited resources and bargaining power of women students, part-time teachers and supporters lent itself to narrowly focused activity. While demands for change in staffing quotas appeared unrealisable in the short term, the School's elective structure and liberal philosophy allowed room for the incorporation of a Women and Art course without undue or protracted conflict. The humanist orientation of the tertiary institution could be realised in a women's studies elective, thereby marginalising the feminist constituency at the same time. The art school could simultaneously supplement its authority and dictate the terms of resistance.

But there was more to it than that. The pioneering American programmes popularised by Judy Chicago, Miriam Schapiro and others suggested an alluring, *wholistic* model of autonomous feminist art education. If gender was pertinent to staffing, curricula, assessment, teaching methods and studio atmosphere, then how could these elements be separated in institutional reforms? What would be the point of exposing students to histories of women's art, if they then had to return to an unsympathetic studio, taught by male staff? Feminine aesthetics demanded a fully integrated pedagogic environment. This was provided in the women's studies 'hothouse'.

Here women could invent an alternative place, taste and tradition. Practical skills and art materials held ideological lessons. A family snapshot or intricate d'oyley pattern were documents of social negotiation. Students elaborated on earlier cultural patterns, with subversive handiwork and agit-prop domestic labour. The work was analytical, collectively produced, and socially engaged. It challenged institutional obsessions with spontaneous expression, individual vision and fine art. It was therefore difficult to assess in traditional terms.

Paradoxically, women's studies exemplified the tradition of non-didactic 'self-discovery' on which modern art education is based. In the women's studies elective, the 'personal is political' meant learning from intimate experience, without the sublimating operation of a modernist aesthetics which had mediated personal and social matters within the accepted realm of Modern Art. Women were taught to resist imposed conventions and rules— except, of course, for those norms embodied in the idea of 'women's culture' itself. Students thus learnt to identify and practise specific feminine skills, processes, and imagery as a mode of self-expression. Convention and rule were seen to give way to the fullness of an authentic feminine voice, and the student's work could be evaluated and corrected according to norms that she would freely acknowledge as her own.[15]

The woman student could not become a 'model student' however, since the experiential basis of women's artwork fell outside the institutional repertoire of 'self-expression'. The problem was that women tended to invent the wrong kind of self, and from the wrong set of materials. At art school, one could learn how to stage the self through limited tropes of cultural alienation or madness (Van Gogh's ear), penetrating vision (the eyes of Picasso) and gestures of self-actualisation (Pollock's muscular arm). It was unfamiliar with the alienation of domestic labour or suburban neurosis. It could not cope with self-realisation through central core imagery, tampon installations or mothering performances. Feminine self-expression looked messy, formless and embarrassingly confessional.

Students working in a non-experiential mode also faced institutional incomprehension. The interdisciplinary mix of art theory and studio practice enabled women to recognise their position within language and meaning. This also countermanded institutional norms of self-expression. Feminism challenged the apparently neutral etho-poetic mantle of the artist and resisted the anti-intellectualism of the studio.

Complaints of feminist over-didacticism, theoreticism and obscurity are a perennial art school whinge. The theoretical impetus of feminism has continued to contradict the pedagogical priorities of modernism. The British art historian Griselda Pollock locates this antagonism in an unmistakable gender and generation gap, between the female student majority and the male teaching majority:

> [The teachers'] sense of art and culture was formed at a different moment from that of their current students. Confrontation with deconstructive practices is hard to accommodate to their paradigm of art and its appropriate terms of assessment (such as does it move me?).[16]

Pollock notes that this argument should not be reduced to the traditional romantic narrative of 'academics versus radicals'. It is not a simple case of staff trained and socialised 'within one form of modernism or another [or] that these folk find it hard to adjust to radical post- or anti-modernist art'. The art school is a far more complex terrain of struggle, and gender has proven a major complication within it.

Despite its pedagogical innovations, women's studies has remained a correctional supplement to the studio curriculum. Feminist courses remain peripheral and tenuous, fought for anew each semester by largely untenured women staff and students. The elective status of many women's studies courses make them vulnerable to staff changes and fluctuations in course funding. Notwithstanding its influence in the art history and theory, the tendency is for women's studies to be taken as one form of specialisation. This allows other theoretical and studio areas to remain unaffected by feminist initiatives. The core component of art theory and practice in some schools has, for instance, remained a narrowly-conceived history of modernism.

Interpreting feminine aesthetics

Despite the continuing resistance of the art school, few would deny that feminist criticism has unsettled accepted notions of artistic quality, value and expression. Art's universal truths were, however, initially debunked from equally generalised feminist perspectives. Following North American precedents, many Australian writers and artists held that feminine aesthetics traversed class, cultural and historical boundaries. Sexual difference and women's exclusion from public culture became the basis for broad aesthetic interpretation. Artists and critics assumed that feminine aesthetics would be easily apprehended and relevant to all women. In this, feminist aesthetics claimed to anticipate and embody a general feminist consciousness. One positive outcome of this spurious and Eurocentric assumption was, however, the insistence upon accessibility and audience involvement as evaluative criteria.

Art criticism was the third most influential institutional space of feminist invention and intervention. The critic's gentle guidance could help the artist, art student and female spectator to develop a heightened feminine sensibility. Her own aesthetic response was thus an early target for experiential self-correction. She learnt to scan art processes, products and her own responses for the signs of femininity through which women could recognise their present experience and future bearings.

The feminist critic learnt to identify and interpret cultural discourses which departed from the debilitating roles marked out for women within the given structures of sexuality, work and consumption. Her strategies have trodden a fine line between prescribing a feminine aesthetic code and offering scenarios in which the images and practices of femininity are open to change and do not reconstitute oppressive paradigms.

This personal–political agenda was initially set by American writers such as Lucy R. Lippard, whose 1975 tour has been cited in most accounts of the Women's Art Movement in Australia.[17] Lippard's tour was well timed. International Women's Year also witnessed the publication and widespread discussion of Judy Chicago's *Through the flower*. Lippard's own book, *From the center: Feminist essays on women's art*, was an eagerly anticipated 1976 publication. In Australia, Lippard talked of the difficulties faced by the feminist critic. The parasitical nature of art criticism within an exploitative art economy was deeply problematical. Feminist art and criticism were in danger of complicity with the very terms and structures of a market they sought to criticise. How could critics promote women's work, yet avoid the bourgeois and masculinist values underpinning the Australian contemporary art market? Themes of regional heroism versus international innovation, the pressure on artists to make history within a narrowly conceived modernist lineage and a restrictive formalist code had dominated post-war art criticism in Australia. Was the feminist critic a contradiction in terms? Many believed so. Lippard registered this ambivalence in emotive terms:

> I started writing for (women) ... because I found that women artists wanted to be in the magazine. It was important for women to be there to show ... but on another level, I still feel these institutions are bad places for women—and for men. So women should have a piece of the pie, but the pie is poisonous.[18]

Lippard had reviewed the implications of her status and promotional power as a basis for defining a critical practice. The traditional role of the critic as consumer guide, artists' advocate and cultural exemplar was maintained, albeit recast in more progressive terms. Feminine aesthetics demanded more detailed empirical research, a responsive eye, and a partisan pen. As the Melbourne critic Janine Burke put it:

Feminist art criticism is defining a sensibility that has existed in women's art despite time, style or period, and that sensibility is now emerging more clearly, more strongly, more urgently and more beautifully than it ever has before. The role of feminist criticism in relation to this should be a supportive one... [19]

The critic's own taste, specialist knowledge and writing style was retrained. Criticism was harnessed to the ongoing life process of feminist ethics. As Lippard had testified:

The Women's Movement changed my life in many ways, not the least being my approach to criticism. It may not show too clearly from the outside; I'm still working on that. But from the inside, from where I live, there is a new freedom to say how I feel and to respond to all art on a far more personal level. I'm more willing to be confessional, vulnerable, autobiographical, even embarrassing, if that seems called for.[20]

The ideal of a feminist 'freedom of speech' provided Lippard and other writers with a measure and means of ethical action. The traditional pedagogic role of the critic as embodiment of taste and vision was intensified. Burke recounted the story of her own 'becoming', in the Lippard manner:

Starting out as a cut-and-dried-formalist... I was deadly serious about certain kinds of art which had prescribed responses, certain histories and certain directions...
Eventually I became disenchanted with the predictable nature of the art I wrote about and identified with... Perhaps the most exciting feature of this gradual change was by becoming involved with women's art I discovered that a range of art that I had once dismissed as low-brow and trivial I could now respond to, enjoy and admire. My writing style subsequently relaxed and became more personal, humorous and unencumbered by jargon—rather like much of the art I enjoyed.[21]

Burke's conventional apprenticeship, her discovery of feminism and gradual self-improvement as a critic capable of 'the full response' is an exemplary narrative of etho-poetic self-fashioning. Criticism now emphasised personal growth and political consciousness by linking art to life, particularly the lived experience of the artist and her audience.[22] By the end of the 1970s, however, the testimonial mode was also read problematically, as the tyranny of the self as subject of art criticism. The story of the critic's progress had become unnecessarily linked to individual career aspirations.

Feminist criticism intervened more successfully in debates over the priorities of radical art. In particular, feminism's ambivalent relation to Conceptual Art was actively promoted. The marginality of women's cultural voice, and the broader social and political analyses in feminist artwork gave it a definite edge over other avant-garde tendencies. Barbara Hall noted in retrospect that Post-Object Art had been largely male dominated. Moreover its radical potential had foundered on an insufficient resolution between politics and aesthetics. This, Hall argued, effectively weakened the movement's resistance to commercial pressures. Arguments around objectives and content were reduced to narrow questions of media and form. The media and forms used by feminist artists, on the other hand, were intrinsically linked to broader social and cultural issues.[23] This last claim was certainly true, and market resistance to the materials and forms used in most feminist work has not eased in ensuing years. In the middle to late 1980s, museums and collectors started purchasing Conceptualist pieces from the 1960s and 1970s, partly due to contemporary Neo-conceptualist trends and an appetite for theoretically informed work. For a number of reasons, the more culturally transgressive feminist projects from this period have not, however, appeared on the curatorial shopping list. In this sense, we could say that in the 1970s, feminist criticism did its job only too well, keeping the personal–political interpretation of feminist work firmly on track and away from the 'poisonous pie' of commercial viability or 'high art' academicism.

Current perspectives

In the early 1980s feminism claimed an 'epistemological break' with the past. The temporal and conceptual disjunction between 1970s and 1980s work has been commonly conceived of in two ways. In the first instance, differences are recuperated within streamlined accounts of generational influence. Alternatively, earlier work is rejected out of hand for its theoretical and aesthetic unsubtlety. Unfortunately, neither response opens up current scenarios and strategies to the same level of criticism. In the former case, present successes are celebrated for bearing the fruits of earlier struggles. This common curatorial argument simply pastes over too many cracks, and leaves current institutional inadequacies unquestioned. Celebrations of 'how far we have come' ignore the ongoing under-representation of women and their work in our galleries, art schools and major contemporary exhibitions. A similar myopia can be found in current practices which simply reject the 1970s and confuse theoretical and aesthetic sophistication with the market and museum push for conceptual novelty and finely crafted objects. In fact many projects from the mid-1980s used aesthetic and philo-sophical markers of sexual difference which had been first mooted in the 'dreaded decade' of personal experience and consciousness raising. Moreover, some of the more unnecessary regulatory mech-anisms associated with 1970s feminist aesthetics are still firmly in place, despite shifts in time, place and contents.

Notwithstanding the above qualifications, a number of stra-tegic shifts *have* taken place since the 1970s. Against the idea of a generalised feminist politics, based on an essentialist conception of 'what women are', or 'where we are now', this chapter has docu-mented the initiation of particular etho-poetic practices. Through techniques of self-examination, consciousness raising, skill sharing and aesthetic interpretation, women in the arts could become the subject of their own artistic practice. In hindsight, many discourses and mechanisms adopted in the WAMs, feminist art education and criticism have been useful, while it should be acknowledged that some aspects of this period are no longer politically progressive, or had no sustained impact. Other practices and images have merely reinscribed oppressive forms of self-discipline, or therapeutic or moral codes historically associated with bourgeois femininity.

The forms of power exercised in collective self-examination, consciousness raising and the inculcation of feminine cultural norms in the 1970s included self-clarification, exemplary behaviour, emulation, nurturant, sisterly conduct and the avoidance of criti-cism or competition. The correlation between these organisational mechanisms, art practices and technologies of the self gave the field of feminine aesthetics a distinctly moral flavour. It carried with it the faint echo of nineteenth century artistic and feminist discourses. The emphasis placed upon the artist's experiential, personal and social engagement also reiterated the ethical work of the historical avant-garde. As the art historian Linda Nochlin observed, the term 'avant-garde' was first used to designate radical or advanced activity in both the social and artistic arenas. She cites the French utopian socialist Henri de Saint-Simon, from the 1830s:

It is we artists who will serve you as avant-garde ... the power of
the arts is in fact most immediate and most rapid: when we wish
to spread new ideas among men, we inscribe them on marble or
on canvas ... What a magnificent destiny for the arts is that of
exercising a positive power over society, a true priestly function,
and of marching forcefully in the van of all the intellectual
faculties ...[24]

This traditional 'moralising idealism' of the artist, as Ian Burn
calls it, was harnessed to a second set of attributes. These had first
emerged within nineteenth century feminist discourses on women's
emancipation, moral superiority and social responsibility, particularly through the work of 'social purity' feminists in Australia and
England. Arguably, these radical understandings of female character were later enshrined in the terms and prescriptions of sisterhood, consciousness raising and feminine sensibility.

By the early 1980s, many feminists realised that the regulatory
practices associated with the ideals of 'sisterhood' had their draw-
backs. It became difficult to criticise artwork or exhibition projects. However, the simple fact of women making art and looking
at art which reflected their own experiences as women was not
automatically progressive. 'Women's art' was in danger of becoming exempt from rigorous criticism by women. Moreover political
sisterhood demanded an unnecessary regulation of behaviour. The
extraordinary attention given to questions of sisterly conduct did
not appear to have secured group cohesion or purpose within the
Sydney WAM, for instance. As is often the case with small and
under-resourced groups, members suffered from over-commitment
and burnout; and, in 1976, internal disagreement over priorities of
agitation for affirmative action versus individual consciousness raising eventually split the group.

Subsequent critical and industrial strategies have modified
earlier understandings of personal–political action. Both the aims
of building a generalised women's culture and personal consciousness raising have been dropped from recent art writing and equal
opportunity actions. It is no longer assumed that connections
between industrial demands and feminine aesthetics are politically
viable. From the early 1980s, feminists found it more practical to
campaign for anti-discrimination and affirmative action measures in
purely industrial terms. Gains made in the area indicate that affirmative action does not necessarily introduce the conditions for a

'women's culture' in the art world. In most cases, more conservative art institutions would not countenance affirmative action principles if cast in these terms.

Regulatory mechanisms associated with earlier conceptions of sisterhood (for instance 'doing the circle') have also been dropped as an organisational priority and political tactic. As a result, feminist art organisations do not discuss forms of appropriate feminine practice, identity and behaviour. Many of us now find ourselves juggling potentially contradictory political frameworks of sexual difference and equal opportunity. While the former has become an accepted subject in artwork, conference papers and art theory classes, affirmative action remains a struggle at the institutional level.

In art education, we find that many of the strategies developed in the 1970s women's electives are still pertinent. Interdisciplinary connections made between art history, politics and art practice, and the critique of existing disciplines now needs to be extended. Existing course structures need to be more flexible and distinctions between studio and historical or theoretical studies broken down. The move towards 'studio theory' in some institutions may be on the right track; however here questions of equitable staffing and content need careful attention. Overall, our priorities are now long-term and structural, and the isolated women's studies elective can no longer serve as a token of institutional responsibility. Feminist cultural analyses need to be incorporated into overall curriculum planning, teaching and administrative practice.

Current developments in women's studies in the humanities and social sciences revolve around two preferred models. The first conceives of women's studies as a distinct field of interdisciplinary study with its own staff and administration. A more relevant model for application in the visual arts comprises a disciplinary and inter-disciplinary course structure. The retention of disciplinary studies facilitates critiques and transformations of existing disciplines, as well as providing an interdisciplinary construction of new knowledges. Against an unchanging conception of women's culture, Foucault and Deleuze's metaphor of knowledge as a toolbox suggests principles of strategic utility, exchange and reproduction. Tools may be fashioned for specific purposes from new or old materials. This has certain implications for the principles, skills and knowledges developed in practical art training and the discipline of art history.[25]

Feminist criticism has undergone careful and continuing consideration. The promotion of women's work involves very material battles over employment opportunities, the museum acquisition budget, the wall space of the gallery and the practical and fine arts curricula. In this, feminist artists and critics have rejected the simple acceptance of dominant evaluative criteria, for if masculine status were attributed to women's work, the value of feminist critiques of art history and criticism would be questionable. Instead women's work has been consistently promoted in a way that raises pertinent questions regarding the gender of the artist, and the nature of her work.

While it is important to write women into history at every opportunity, many of our critical strategies which determine that writing have changed. Large contemporary or historical surveys of women's work are no longer championed as the best means of supporting feminist arguments. Careful distinctions are made between feminist projects and 'art made by women', and the latter is no longer simply celebrated as intrinsically progressive.

From the late 1970s feminist criticism again set a radical ethopoetic agenda through the popularisation of psychoanalytic and semiotic texts. At times a prescriptive fit ensued between feminist art and writing, but this loosened by the end of the 1980s as artists reasserted powerful textural, material and historical elements in the representational equation. Semiotic and psychoanalytic analyses were seen to be often hampered by their linguistic base, fostering reductive aesthetic outcomes. In the 1990s some artists have returned to earlier feminist researches on style, decoration, surface and materials. The 'politics of the image' that dominated the 1980s has broadened its iconographical base. Photo-media work is now often combined with photographic installations, painting and mixed media projects which engage with broader historical, textural and institutional politics. Many writers have in turn gone on to pursue an autonomous set of problems within the fields of cultural studies, philosophy and aesthetics.

But this is to anticipate future arguments. Here I have simply introduced feminist aesthetics as part of a broader institutional crisis of artistic subjectivity. The importance given to the problem of 'self' in the excercise of sisterhood, consciousness raising, art training and art criticism gave focus and direction to the complex web of practices by which the individual artist, writer and student could form herself as the ethical subject of feminist action. In the last twenty-five years, however, these constitutive practices have undergone a number of modifications. The following chapters document the development of feminist aesthetics as it has been elaborated in relation to the social and the sexual.

2 Family, community, shop floor: Reconstructing the social

Chapter 1 examined how strategies of affiliation, education and promotion aimed to constitute a socially responsive, avant-garde identity for women artists. It asked what forms of personal and social engagement were outlined in feminist photographic projects. The following chapters review the photography and politics that emerged from 1970s initiatives. The second theme of women's experience documented in this book—the idea of women claiming the public arena—dominated feminist campaigns for affirmative action, equal pay, child care and community services through the 1970s. While these priorities remain in place, feminist analyses have increasingly challenged simple demarcations and affirmations of the social. Feminist photography has played a part in shifting these political schemas, relating women's domestic labour, community involvement and paid work in ways which could not be explained through recourse to the simple dichotomy of public and private.

The photographs documented here have primarily intervened within an interlacing field of social relations and administrative techniques associated with domestic maintenance, women's central role in supporting and regulating community identity, and campaigns waged for equal pay, improved working conditions and job opportunities. 'The social' thus includes notions of personal and familial relations, and not just the economic or public sectors. As Deleuze and Donzelot have argued, the social is a hybrid administrative, protective and regulatory space.[1]

This 'modern hybrid' first emerged through late eighteenth century measures to contain social problems of poverty, family life and a healthy workforce. Today these mechanisms have become associated with 'a general solidarity and the production of a lifestyle...a showcase of development, whose defence comes before all else, something to be offered to the world at whatever cost'.[2]

This was also the space where nineteenth century feminists built a political platform for equal rights. What the suffragette did not realise was that women's emancipation was based on a massive investment in, and subservient position within, the social. For example, women formed a major point of support for the intensification and modernisation of family life. Women's augmented domestic and political power were interrelated:

> It is on condition that we perceive in this increase in woman's domestic power not only the support of all the 'social' professions that would give her a new access to public life but also the springboard she needed for the recognition of her political rights. How are we to assess the importance of militant feminism in the nineteenth century if we ignore its alliance with social philanthropy?[3]

Recent feminist analyses of the social have constituted a pivotal point of resistance and destabilisation, beginning with the simplest formulations of the housewife's subordination. As Deleuze has argued, the social ushered in new 'desires and powers',

> the new requirements of control, but also the new possibilities of resistance and liberation...'Having a room of one's own' is a desire, but also a control. Inversely, a regulatory mechanism is haunted by everything that overruns it and already causes it to split apart from within.[4]

What knowledges of the social have been constituted and popularised by feminist photography? How did the idea of 'the personal is political' blur the perceived boundaries between public and private? Women's community work and participation in the paid workforce were seen to be organised in accordance with their servicing role within the family. Familial duties were in turn revealed to be as rigidly structured as the workforce which they serviced. The home—that complex of sexual, emotional, tutelary and economic relations blithely designated by Christopher Lasch as a 'haven in a heartless world'[5]—was photographed as the site of unpaid labour, social alienation, potential violence, and contradictory ideological and economic pressures.

By the late 1970s, photographers found socialisation models limiting. Projects on the family and women in the workforce could no longer simply rely on generalised schemas of gender, socialisation or the opposition between the public and private domains. More specific investigations of the discourses and practices of modern mothering and the discipline of women's work emerged. Related debates on the political efficacy of photo-documentary are discussed further in Chapter 3.

In documenting the strategies which developed unevenly across the related fields of family life, community relations and women's participation in the workplace, a central, evaluative question is posed. How did these photographs destabilise the circumscribed domestic powers and 'humanising' potential assumed by women within modern, social configurations of rationality and progress?

Feminist photography and women's re-education

The internalisation by women of debilitating social roles was an early focus of inquiry. Gender stereotyping became a cornerstone for consciousness-raising projects. The camera could help women identify and reject their conditioning through the juxtaposition of contending (patriarchal and feminist) value systems. The 1974 publication, *Media she*, provides an example of this de-gendering strategy. Its analysis was passionate if simple.[6] Collaged newspaper and magazine clippings logged key agencies of socialisation. The mass media's portrayal of the family, the community and the workplace were seen to offer a singularly unified ideological picture, in which false consciousness and feminine stereotypes were posited as a general problem. This presumed a clear alternative against which to measure such representations.

In reducing women's social identity to a question of dominant values, the politics of socialisation made use of a behaviourist model of interaction between the individual woman and her social environment. The unified force of the media, the family or the workplace were seen simply to determine women's lives. This conception of socialisation separated the individual subject from the social, effectively reducing the latter to a domain of patriarchal values.

Margaret Higgs, *Woman*. Reproduced in McPhee and Edgar, *Media She*, Heinemann, Melbourne, 1974.

If individuals were influenced by media representations, however contentious, then they could be re-educated by looking at alternative images. This liberal assumption, which underpinned *Media she*'s constitution of women as free agents, cleared a space for a photo-documentary alternative, reproduced at the end of the book. Responsible, realistic images of women by women were the key. In answer to *Media she*, photographer Margaret Higgs took her camera to 'places where women are found in great numbers going about their lives with a dignity which bears little relation to the media female'.[7] The belief that a picture tells a thousand words underscored untitled and uncaptioned photo-documentary images of female stoicism, dignity and social responsibility. These were presented for identification and self-reflection.

Did they work? The strategy of providing positive images as prompts for recognition, self-examination and social responsibility became commonplace in the mid-1970s. It defined feminist photography's subversive parameters (such as the role reversals reproduced in a chapter titled 'Media he?') and its oppositional 'real women'. The camera must be trained on real women, controlled by women, and must be an acknowledgement of the 'self' of women. But what *was* the 'self' of women? In *Media she*, simple techniques of montage, role reversal and photo-documentary yielded a symbolic character, struggling and exploited, and thus showing her true self. A strategy of political education based around a fixed set of social stereotypes was simply producing equally essentialist and moralist images. As Meaghan Morris noted in a 1975 essay on feminist cinema:

> It is easy to forget that ... a stereotype is also a way of seeing things — an intellectual invention, one which is highly useful at times, but which operates by selecting only what suits you. As a tool of analysis, looking for stereotypes can reveal similarities between films, but it can also mask differences.[8]

Photographers increasingly drew back from realist strategies. The photo-documentary excess constructed in *Media she* as 'women's essence' was no longer seen as something expressive in itself, but as inherently connected with the production of knowledge. In fact, many feminist photographers had adopted a self-conscious and consensual approach to photo-documentary from the outset. Early 1970s projects by Carol Jerrems, Ponch Hawkes,

Ruth Maddison, Micky Allan and Sue Ford marked an important step in destabilising traditional documentary affirmations of women's social identity.

The contradictory experience of domestic labour

Since 1963 Melbourne photographer and film-maker Sue Ford has orchestrated a more complex view of women's personal–political experience. Her early work evoked the contradictory emotional investments that maintain family life. Photo-documentary studies and studio tableaux from 1963–74 explored the psycho-social dimension of domestic life. These prefigured later analyses of the family that moved beyond social role theory to explore possible tensions between the psychological and the social that have accompanied recent shifts in family forms.

Ford's studio portraits and fashion work gave way to an involvement in experimental film-making and art photography in the early 1970s. Ford used both media to evoke the frustration and isolation felt by many women raising children in this period of so-called sexual revolution and alternative lifestyles. Her photographs departed from the psychological and sociological stereotypes of *Media she*, as well as Friedan, Oakley and Garron.[9]

Through techniques of montage and superimposition, surrealist juxtaposition and disorienting spatial effects, Ford's housewife became 'Alice' in an unnerving and alienated domestic Wonderland. Her modern mother was literally consumed by consumer products, and distortions of scale and distance between objects assumed a malevolent will. In turn, these household horrors were played back as the hallucinatory projections of her 'housewife's neurosis'. Another series of prints, taken in association with Ford's 16 mm experimental film, *Woman in a house* (1974), reformulated contemporary psychological prescriptions of maternal preoccupation: the isolated young mother appears dwarfed within an agoraphobic, child-centred zone.

This 'domestic contradiction' of pleasure and pain formed the punch line for a later series of witty prints by Sydney photographer Ailsa Maxwell. *Domestic deviations* (1981) parodied the housewife's false consciousness as a perverse realm of domestic fantasy.[10] The modern, multi-gadget home provided a host of labour-saving devices and convenience items for the housewife's auto-erotic pleasure. The corporate dream of domestic efficiency, incorporated

Sue Ford, *Annette Stevens*, 1963. From the series *Woman consumed*, gelatin silver photograph. Reproduced in Ford, *A sixtieth of a second*, Experimental Art Foundation, Adelaide, 1987, p.30.

Ailsa Maxwell, *Riding bare-back*, 1981. Gelatin silver photograph. Reproduced in Brereton (ed), *Photo-discourse*, Sydney College of the Arts, Sydney, 1981, p.56.

in the post-war promotion of consumer durables, had represented a
new phase in forms of domestic labour and experience. Women's
added (yet invisible) labour, and their augmented (yet conditional)
domestic and economic power as consumers and equal 'partners in
leisure' had placed new demands on women in the post-war period.[11]
Housework was reconstituted as a skilled occupation within the
technologically-advanced home. Madison Avenue had translated
the work involved in shopping, cooking, cleaning and maintaining
the modernised household into the language of consumer pleasure
and wish-fulfilment. Maxwell directed 'the joy of housework' as a
parody of auto-erotic sadomasochism.

Other projects explored the paradox of women's domestic presence and power, and yet her simultaneous absence—the mother's
inability to express her own needs and desires within home economics. Maxienne Foote's 1980 series *Monday to Monday* elaborated
this contradiction at the heart of modern family life.[12] Foote rushed
through a week overburdened with familial obligations. The narrow
public/private, work/leisure dichotomy, by which economists could
calculate earnings forgone as a result of unpaid activity, was revealed to be misleading. *Monday to Monday* demonstrated how the
contradictory demands, pressures and pleasures that make up a
woman's week are not so easily disaggregated into productive,
reproductive or leisure activities.

Foote was not alone in evoking the complex physical, sexual
and emotional facets of the 'double day'. Women's domestic labour
and ambivalent emotional investments in family life were given
a new visibility. The family was not seen as a unified entity (the
private sphere), but as a complex field of psycho-social relations
(economic, medical, welfarist, pedagogical). Photographic accounts
of women's labours of love, and their invisibility within traditional
economic calculations, provided a critique of the Marxist theory of
labour value and circulated alongside broader feminist debates on
domestic labour. Domestic labour, central to the reproduction of
capitalism, remained invisible within public calculations and representations. Moreover, work in the home was seen to be directly
related to women's restricted job opportunities.

Women's paid work

Early feminist photographs of women in paid work concentrated
on the poorly paid areas of manufacturing and the service sectors,

Maxienne Foote, from the series *Monday to Monday*. Reproduced in *LIP* 1980, p.67.

where women (and particularly migrant women) have been employed in large numbers since the Second World War. From the outset, feminists steered clear of photo-documentary homages to heroic labour, productive capacity or craft skills, as in traditional photographic responses to the application (and social costs) of scientific management. Indeed, feminist photographic analyses from the early 1970s revealed how women's work was of a very different order.

Campaigns for equal employment opportunity, equal pay and decent working conditions were supported through photographs in the feminist press. The political isolation of the Women's Movement in its early years partly explains the personalised approach to industrial issues in the Sydney newspaper *Mejane*, whereby the experiences of working-class women were introduced to a largely middle-class feminist audience. Throughout 1971 *Mejane* profiled selected jobs: in the home, hospital, factory, office, school and professional cleaning. Photographic slogans by Beverly Garlick imagined the subjective experience of particular jobs. As she later noted in an interview, 'I remember standing outside Bradmills for hours, trying to get the right shot. I didn't think of going inside. I didn't think about approaching the management.' Garlick's political inexperience was partly responsible for her personalised approach, resulting in an image of oppressive women's work that cut across class, culture and age differences. Schematic tableaux and montages demonstrated the parallels between women's work in the office, factory and home. The serialised servitude of the secretary as hand-maiden or surrogate wife generalised an experience of domestic oppression. Similarly, women's contract cleaning was pictured as an extension of domestic labour in an early formulation of the 'double day'.

These early constructions of women's work were printed as campaign material in support of the 1972–73 Federal Government's equal pay legislation. This legislation was unfortunately soon used by employers to rationalise retrenchments, job reclassifications, non-granting of over-award payments and similar ploys, effectively maintaining lower rates of pay for women's work.

In the 1974–75 recession, thousands of Australian manu-facturing jobs were lost, and women workers were among the first to be laid off. At the same time, women were making some inroads in part-time work in the growing service sector. Early contacts were forged between feminists and women working on the shop

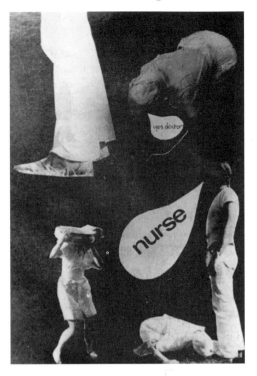

Beverly Garlick, untitled
photo-montage. Reproduced in
Mejane No. 4, September 1971,
p.6.

floor as the Women's Liberation press began to report industrial actions. Uninspiring and technically weak photo-journalism replaced early experiments with montage and directorial techniques in the feminist press. One under-developed photographic strategy linked women's unemployment with concurrent pressures to get women back into the home. A well-organised conservative cry of 'the family in crisis' was an important rationale for cutting back social service spending. At the same time, women workers were castigated for taking scarce jobs that should have been their sons'. Documentary photographs of women pushing prams past the dole office had limited explanatory power in this context. While anti-discrimination legislation was enacted in some States from 1975, the recession caught feminist industrial campaigns on the back foot. Ineffectual campaign imagery in this period fuelled the need for more acute photographic analyses of the sexual economy of work.

Women workers and industrial power

Photo-documentary representations of women workers in the mid-1970s were largely restricted to the feminist press. Here the camera focused on a dwindling manufacturing sector, stressing individual resilience in the face of oppressive work practices. The 1975 booklet *But I wouldn't want my wife to work there* is typical of the period, highlighting the sexual segregation and archaic working conditions in overcrowded Melbourne clothing sweatshops.[13]

The alienation of industrial work has long been a preoccupation of both management and workers' associations. Trade unions in Australia and abroad emerged at a time when work was increasingly becoming an object of science, in which the worker was only one calculated variable among many. Photographs by Hine, Bourke-White, Tudor-Hart and other photographers highlighted this schism between the economic and the social aspects of modern production, from the workers' standpoint. Concurrently, modern management also claimed to reduce the authoritarian presence of the boss and foreman. The major theorist of scientific management, Fredrick Taylor, advocated the calculation of what he called 'optimum conditions':

> ... of adaptation of man to machine, taking proper account of safety margins instead of resorting to fraud to bypass them, (so that) discipline could be made to subsist in the machine itself, rather than behind the worker's back. Autonomised and freed from the bonds of authoritarian organisation, work could become able to deliver higher productivity and wages would remain the sole object for union negotiations.[14]

Under this regime of power and knowledge, the isolation, pace and discipline of the assembly line itself became a major source of industrial disputes, go-slows, absenteeism, industrial accidents and worker dissatisfaction.

Documentary photographs have emphasised the social costs of scientific management. Nearly a century later, however, the major protagonists are migrant women rather than Anglo-Celtic tradesmen. Feminist photo-documentary did not, however, simply record a time lag in the conferring of protective rights on women and migrant workers. The social sciences had dramatically altered the field of industrial relations in the post-war years.

The post-war expansion of industrial psychology provided the conditions whereby the human factor could be reintegrated into the organisation of work. The idea was to bring together the social and the economic in the interests of greater efficiency and lesser cost. The old science of aptitudes, based on a barrage of psychological tests developed for the army (and later for industry) was replaced by concepts of alienation, motivation and human needs, just as the more routine and dirty jobs were filled by migrant and female labour.

When applied to women workers, issues of motivation, responsibility, job satisfaction, the alienation of the assembly line, and human needs were cloaked in nineteenth century conceptions of female nature. Managerial claims that women had an aptitude for repetitive work involving patience, manual dexterity and passivity were key obstacles to promotion. Traditional assumptions of femininity, weak industrial protection and lack of juridical rights restricted women's participation in modern images of industrial rationality and worker solidarity.

Photographs showing women working in non-traditional areas aimed to counter this historical legacy. Helen Grace's posters of women apprentices were prominently displayed on metropolitan buses, trains and trams in 1979, proclaiming 'It's No Longer a Trade Secret: Women Can Do Anything' in a variety of community languages. Apprenticeships in non-traditional areas were suggested by a diagonal file of young women workers in colour-coded overalls, covering a range of skilled trades. Ponch Hawkes' photographs for the *Women and work kit* (1979) sponsored by the Victorian Education Department were also directed towards young women.[15] These kits profiled women working in a range of occupations such as carpentry, mechanics, dentistry, gardening, systems analysis and marine biology. They were also widely distributed through primary and secondary schools. The strategy was to construct an image of dynamic concentration and job satisfaction. Pamela Harris' diaristic narrative from 1975, *Black-jacking a tank*, also pays homage to non-traditional labour. Her pencilled, diaristic entries and quiet, snapshot approach to the sweat, dust and searing heat experienced by the women who work in far-flung outback areas departed from both traditional depictions of industrial labour and the iconography of the Australian bushman. This series is a surprise inclusion in the Australian National Gallery Photography Department. Few projects dealing with women and work from this period are housed in public collections.

Ponch Hawkes, from *The women and work kit*, 1979. Reproduced in *LIP* 1980, p.9.

The formal, conceptual and political challenge of producing dynamic images of ordinary women performing non-traditional jobs, without recourse to the stereotypes of heroic masculine labour or female oddities, has largely remained with us. The projects discussed here framed women workers as glamorous and adventurous, yet as employing knowledges and skills which any woman could take up.

From positive images to social contradictions

The Art and Working Life projects, co-sponsored by the Australia Council and Trades Unions from the early 1980s, have been a central vehicle for critical debates on photo-documentary and positive imagery. As with community arts, many feminists involved themselves in Art and Working Life projects as an important component of their studio work. The programme provided artists with a structure for political engagement at a time when Women's Liberation was becoming organisationally fragmented.

Art and Working Life projects have provided artists with many conceptual, aesthetic and political challenges. They have to fulfil not only the requirements of the sponsoring unions, but also satisfy the conceptual and aesthetic demands of the artistic community. It is a tall order. Initially at least, the workers and their representatives preferred photo-documentary celebrations or images with a high information content. At the same time, artists and art audiences wanted projects to address more complex aesthetic problems. The often stormy relation between the artistic avant-garde and political organisations has a long and well-documented history, and Australian trade union officials remained comfortable with more familiar tropes of expressive realism. As project officer Deborah Mills explained:

> Initially unions tended to promote fairly romanticised and nostalgic images that effectively obscured women workers. But through a number of more recent projects undertaken by feminists working as artists, unionists and trade union officers, the role of women has begun to be revealed in a more significant way.[16]

Earlier images of women working in non-traditional areas had understated the tensions and difficulties experienced by women workers moving into new job areas. In the 1980s this strategy was no longer adequate. Feminist photographers involved in Art and Working Life projects subsequently aimed to evoke the shifting social roles and pressures imposed on women workers across a range of occupations. The historical devaluation of women's trade union involvement prompted the 1985 resource and exhibition project, *And so ... we joined the union*. This extensive photographic and oral history project aimed to dispel common myths about women being apathetic and conservative union members.[17] Three Melbourne photographers (Ruth Maddison, Carolyn Lewens and Wendy Rew) were commissioned by the Victorian Trades Hall Council Information and Resource Centre to work with unions to locate and re-present archive material, and photograph women unionists at work.

And so ... we joined the union is a representative transitional project. Many of the images pay simple homage to union members working in difficult and often stressful jobs. Others present more complex arguments about the shifting demands and pressures placed on women at work. As one reviewer described Ruth Maddison's revealing profile of Pentridge prison officers:

When more and more areas of employment are becoming available to women, they have to learn to *perform new roles*, in the theatrical as well as the sociological meaning of the expression, and there is tension, anxiety and uncertainty about their ability to *perform*.[18]

In front of the camera, the officers try to maintain a tough yet feminine front. The resultant images show a complex institutional presence. They depart from earlier celebrations of women workers with tools in hand, demonstrating specific tasks and skills, reminding us that the power, responsibility and competence of the prison officer or union official are largely invested in appearances. Maddison's camera emphasised the contradictory pressures involved in these occupational performances. Potential images of overt violence, ideological conflict or disharmony are difficult areas to register in union promotions. Her profile of Julie Ingleby, industrial organiser for the Australian Theatrical and Amusement Employees Association, used the cinematic conventions of point-of-view editing to isolate the union organiser in centre frame. Facial expression and body language betrayed the strain experienced in maintaining a dogged political presence in the face of an apathetic or hostile membership. This political and psychological drama was economically scripted in the caption below:

> After an 8am Saturday morning drive to Kilmore, and a difficult meeting with Turf Club workers, Julie Ingleby, organiser for the Australian Theatrical and Amusement Employees Association, says 'You win some, you lose some.'

And so ... we joined the union tried to extend a positive image of unionism to include women workers, and re-drew the industrial boundary to introduce new gender-specific problems and areas for union negotiation. It also had to be mindful of the aesthetic demands of divergent audiences. The work thus oscillated between a consensual approach to documentary, where the photographer and her subject both consciously worked on pose, action and information in the photograph, and made use of more explicit theatrical tropes. Images of women at work had never fitted comfortably within the heroic, photo-documentary mould. Images were needed which would not simply reinvest in the social and which avoided homogenised pictures of the workforce—images that identified and analysed gender-based and job-specific problems.

Ruth Maddison, *Untitled*, 1985. 3 gelatin silver photographs, each 13 × 13 cms. Collection of the artist.

New directions in feminist photography were mounted from this point. Yet from the mid-1970s a parallel challenge to the representative claims of photo-documentary had emerged around images of women in the community. This tendency drew upon traditions of family photography and other domestic arts as an extension of oral history and a tool of community empowerment. These feminist strategies of social 'reconstruction' affirmed women's cultural production and social responsibility. What challenge, if any, did this photographic strategy mount in relation to the social?

Reconstructing the social

Women have played a major part in community arts, both professionally and voluntarily. Community alliances and empowerment dovetailed and extended the feminist principles of sisterhood, collectivity and decentralised organisation. The aim of many women-centred projects was to recover or invent an autonomous, collective identity for women, yet such affirmations required a critical edge. Conventions of photo-documentary, domestic photography and studio portraiture were alternated with these ends in mind. Photography became a form of community development, set within and against the shifting contours of the social.

The notion of a 'community of women' raised certain complications. As women's subordination is socially organised, the use of organic or essentialist coordinates to signify female collectivity was counterproductive. The fragmented nature of the Women's Movement reinforced this perception. Thus the slogan of 'heterogeneity within collectivity' directed images like those found in Carol Jerrems and Virginia Fraser's *A book about Australian women*.[19] This ambitiously titled yet strictly sub-cultural publication sought a culturalist rationale for women's collectivity. It united women artists, film-makers, writers, musicians, activists and public figures under the flag of moral integrity, social responsibility and individual creativity.

The art-historical dispersion of Jerrems' photographs in museum collections retrospectively casts her heterogeneous collectivity of Australian women as part of a broader 'portrait of a decade'. Archival sedimentation has also thrown into sharp relief the traditional parameters used to reformulate women's social identity in the 1970s. Jerrems' collectivity within heterogeneity was moulded through the mixed virtues of bourgeois photographic portraiture, family photography and the social concern of photo-documentary. Personal testimonials edited by Virginia Fraser complemented Jerrems' style of theatrical intimacy and social revelation.

On the one hand, *A book about Australian women* showcased a pantheon of feminist stars. A sense of historical importance guided this compilation portrait, published on the eve of International Women's Year. Jerrems' image of young, predominantly white middle-class women artists, writers, musicians and activists drew upon the liberal recognitions and aspirations of the modern photographic portrait. This genre has provided a theatre of self-expression and social status since the invention of the daguerreotype. As a technology of self-formation, portraiture has played no small part in a liberal image of modern society, where in Mill's formulation, 'human beings are no longer born to their place in life, but are free to employ their faculties, and such favourable chances as offer to achieve the lot which may appear to them most desirable'.[20]

In Jerrems' casebook, self-realisation was often marred by 'unliberal' social intrusions. Her artists and activists employed their faculties in suburban loungerooms, kitchens, community centres and in street demonstrations. Many cradled children as well as paintbrushes or microphones. In Jerrems' view, favourable chances and desirable lives are hard-won collective gains. Mill's principle of self-development and equal participation in civic life has never proved so persuasive in the case of women. Mill and Wollstonecraft saw the autonomous development of intellectual, moral and emotional potential as a basis for individual virtue, and as a complement to civic virtue. This model of individual development was eloquently expressed in the modern biographical portrait. Second-wave feminists like Jerrems observed that women's social duties and status within the family are not generalisable in the same way.[21]

A pervasive sense of masquerade in Jerrems' portraits further destabilised the public demonstration of individuality as locus of intention, character and creative self-improvement. In *Wendy Saddington, Warringal Park, Melbourne, 1973*, both photographer and sitter work on the look of modern identity. Saddington's face forms a graphic mask, with her sharp features framed in an unnerving asymmetry. This mask floats on the surface of the print as an intricate tonal pattern. Tight composition, high contrast and tonal balance makes the eyes the expressive epicentre of the

Carol Jerrems, *Wendy Saddington, Warrigal Park, Melbourne*, 1973. Reproduced in Jerrems and Fraser, *A book about Australian women*, Outback Press, Melbourne, 1974, p.100. Australian National Gallery.

Carol Jerrems, *A Redfern hotel, Sydney '73*. Reproduced in Jerrems and Fraser, *A book about Australian women*, Outback Press, Melbourne, 1974, p.115. Australian National Gallery.

portrait, yet the gesture looks purely performative. In place of an expressive image of self, the photograph reflects only the stylised surface of femininity: enigma, desire, affect.

Jerrems' photographs of Koori women also slipped from the theatre of bourgeois self-realisation to the hybrid social domain of the informal snapshot and photo-documentary. Her further differentiation between profiles of individual activists and photo-documentary groupings of lesser-known Kooris highlighted the class-based and culturally specific nature of second-wave feminism. Nineteenth century British photographic portraits of suffragist leaders at the rostrum or on the march were similarly accompanied by a photodocumentary concern for working-class women and their children. In this way, suffragist photographers constructed an image of moral leadership and social responsibility.

Class and racial distinctions between portraiture and photo-documentary have historically promoted women as natural solvers of social problems by right of their perceived tempering nature and educative power over children and men. Our State archives and museums are slowly accumulating photographs by women which have helped to forge a network between the home environment and a growing constellation of 'social' professions. Many photographers from the late nineteenth and early twentieth centuries are valued by feminist art historians for working in adventurous zones as authentic documenters.[22] It could be said that women photographers in the Australian outback, the Native Mission, urban slum, army barracks or hospital, or even those women who patiently documented the minutiae of family life, have formed part of the mobilisation of women by the church, medicine, nascent welfare organisations or promotional feminism as the lynch-pin of a 'bio-politics', empowering women as physical and ethical models. These photographers were one means by which the private sphere acquired a public rationality.

The consensual nature of women's photo-documentary work, which British art historian Val Williams also traces in current feminist community practices, has remained an efficient and non-coercive form of community sponsored surveillance, regulation and welfare measures 'far removed from the patriarchal systems of mission and borough'.[23] Photo-documentary methods provided effective channels through which desired codes of individual conduct, hygiene, motherhood and social responsibility could be transmitted.

Did Jerrems' portraits depart from this historical investment in the social? Not really. However, nagging social documentary elements intruded into her individual portraits, and vice versa. Her 'Australian Women' failed to perform authentically within an expected liberal ethos of self-development and sovereignty.

Sue Ford also documented her family and friends through the 1960s and 1970s. Her subcultural portraits focused on the physical, emotional and lifestyle changes that take place over time. This extensive project was exhibited in the 1970s as *The time series*. Ford's 1981 exhibition, *A picture book of women*, later edited and published as *A sixtieth of a second: Portraits of women 1961–1981* (1987) could also be seen as an informal element of this broader project; however, its more marginal institutional status has effectively separated the two bodies of work.[24] *A picture book of women* and *A sixtieth of a second* were both autobiographical and collective. Vignettes of Ford and her friends were organised as a process of personal, subcultural and social change. These images were also a far cry from Mill's ideal of autonomous self-development. As in Jerrems' family album, photographic portraiture and social documents maintained an uneasy balance.

Reconstructing the family album

The fine line between deconstructing the social and reinvesting in it became increasingly blurred in projects which relied solely on family photography. From the early 1970s photographers used the family snapshot to revalue women's social role. They modified contemporary sociological and psychological studies on the family to account for the labours of love performed (and often enjoyed) by women in the home. The stereotyped figure of Anne Oakley's 'housewife' was rejected in favour of a more active image of domestic negotiation. Photographic celebrations of matrilinear solidarity and mother-love complicated the simple cry of 'abolish the family'. As Vivienne Binns, coordinator of the extensive community project *Mothers' memories, others' memories* (1979–1981) noted:

> ... people live within certain roles and within certain restrictions but they also can be assertive, can be inventive, can be creative in the way they conduct their lives ... in fact the things that control us are not actually what happens but are things like stereotypes.[25]

Ponch Hawkes, *Sheila and Janie*, from the series, *Our mums and us*, 1976. Gelatin silver photograph, 17.8 × 12.6 cms. Gift of the Phillip Morris Art Grant, 1982, Australian National Gallery.

Feminist photographers reframed the family album to provide an emerging feminist subculture with alternative forms of familial and community identification. As Ponch Hawkes observed of her widely circulated 1976 series, *Our mums and us,* 'a lot of us seem to be trying to see our mothers as more than just parents these days—I'm interested in those changes'.[26] This series also worked within the genres of family snapshot, studio portraiture and photo-documentary. Physical resemblances and filial gestures were framed as an instance of cross-generational sisterhood. The family became fractionalised (mothers and daughters as a separate sphere) and then extended (as 'sisters').

The private realm was put under public scrutiny. The family album was hand-coloured, transcribed in other media, re-edited with handwritten narratives or contextualised with other domestic knowledges, objects, traces, fetishes. These projects aestheticised the album and in turn brought the kitchen sink to the empty white expanse of the gallery. Here informal display and domestic contents sent shivers down the spine of mainstream critics.[27] Ruth Maddison's *Christmas holiday with Bob's family, Mermaid Beach, Queensland, 1979* is one of a number of 'family album' projects that met some resistance in domesticating the gallery.[28] Maddison's installation of delicately hand-painted photographs, paced along an imaginary mantlepiece, paid homage to the last Christmas spent with the family before the death of her mother-in-law. The traditional ceremonial function of family photography, and the inclusion of a hand-worked, cloth-covered occasional table, flowers and two sofas, worked a reverse play with the hallowed emptiness of gallery space. In 1976 Marie McMahon fetishised the ornamental family photograph by silk-screen printing on vitreous enamel. Her cluttered installation, part of a pathbreaking Sydney WAM show titled *Experiments in vitreous enamel*, also effectively feminised the gallery (see colour section). In 1978 Melbourne painter and photographer Micky Allan actually moved in to the gallery for the duration of her exhibition, *Photography, drawing, poetry—A live-in show*.[29]

One of the most well-documented 'memory cycle' projects involving family photography and other media was the Sydney-based community arts project, *Mothers' memories, others' memories* (1979–1981), coordinated by Vivienne Binns.[30] Photographic displays by Grace Oldfield, Helen Vertoudakis, Lynne Broad and other participants recounted autobiographical and biographical narratives about women in their families using photographs, postcards and captions, amongst a treasure-trove of handiwork and other domestic memorabilia. More recently, Tasmanian photographer Grace Cochrane collaged and montaged family snapshots to weave stories and memories around the minutiae of everyday lives.[31] The extended country family of pets and farm stock were woven into an idealised serial of family life and the close-knit country community.

These projects, which span the decade 1975–1985, testify to a persistent interest in family photography. In all cases, relations between female family members were assembled as a continuum of warmth, identification and support. The fractionalised, female family became a self-enclosed haven, where the woman artist–chronicler played the traditional daughter's duty of cleaning up the house and setting family memories in order.[32] The performative, ritual aspect and nostalgic power of family photography was intensified and extended in a mechanism of social maintenance.

The empirical delights of the family album has at times mitigated against critical analysis. While women-identified family forms were mooted, the retention of a child-centred maternal identity meant that the alternative family relations heralded by feminine aesthetics often unwittingly celebrated historically circumscribed familial duties. By simply validating the mother's cultural and social role, many projects could not come to terms with the fact that her labours of love formed non-coercive yet oppressive mechanisms for regulating women's lives and the family.

Ordering the family album has long been a form of feminine tutelage: it is one of the exercises of modern mothering. When captioned, hand-coloured or exhibited along with crochet or lacework, these photographs did not *automatically* produce critical knowledges about the modern family: in some cases they simply formed the latest modification in a long line of domestic regulations associated with women. The family album has contributed to the historical weakening of the husband's and father's authority. It has helped to augment the mother's power and liberalise family alliances within the psycho-social terms of modern mothering (nurturance, family and community maintenance, sisterhood). Many feminist photographic reappraisals of the family album reinforced a strictly social code that has bonded the wife and the child into 'the theme of the big sister–little mother'.[33] This strategy did not necessarily dislodge women's social role as locus of child-centred creativity, nurturance and protection.

As a social intervention within the gallery circuit, however, this work was unquestionably challenging. Along with nappy installations, tampon mobiles, washing performances and central core imagery, family photography raised thorny issues of originality, female spectatorship and contemporary formal paradigms. These projects flew in the face of prevailing aesthetic parameters —a challenge which remains largely unacknowledged. The nexus between categories of the domestic, the real and the experiential that provided a point of departure for this work has condemned it to a marginal art-historical status. The art world is still not ready for unsublimated motherhood. Feminist work on this area has had to divest itself of subcultural associations before it could enter the kingdom of contemporary art. Motherhood regained a subversive yet acceptably aesthetic status in the early 1980s, when suitably formalised in art-historical tropes and theorised in psychoanalytic terms.

Women in the community

On the community arts circuit, oral history and snapshot photography were employed along with more traditional photo-documentary interventions. These aimed to recover a sense of collective identity and community empowerment. This rationale was often complicated, however, by the use of community arts projects in the reclamation and rehabilitation of working-class or marginalised female populations.

The common concept of empowerment has linked community arts and radical social work practice. It is derived from a juridical model of power and sovereignty that dominates both fields. In the 1970s it also motivated the radical feminist and libertarian rebuttal of social, political or educational institutions. These were regarded as bureaucratic, hierarchical and unresponsive to individual needs. In this period, the concept of empowerment was also aligned to a liberal perception of 'community' as a homogeneous and participatory system. In liberal schemas, structural inequalities were attributed to notions such as 'modern urban society' rather than seen to be endemic to capitalism. In both cases this misrecognition of the social sponsored solutions couched in technical rather than political terms. In the words of Ros Bower, a major force behind the establishment of the Community Arts Board of the Australia Council, community arts were 'a defence against the threatening impersonality of the big metropolis'.[34] Art reinforced community identity and individual sovereignty:

> Cultural or artistic animation enlivens every individual who is touched by it; awakens sensibilities; stimulates communication with his fellows. A passive, inert community can be easily duped. It is apathetically resistant to change. It does not produce or support leadership.[35]

Bower's community arts paradigm of local networks and enlivened individuals was in many ways a variant of Mill's 'community of citizens'. In both cases, power was conceived as an agency of sovereignty, as invested in the individual or in a body of citizens. Despite its institutional rationale of freedom, will and empowerment, it is easy to see that the social framework of community arts has itself helped to shape the contours of 'the community'. Again we are in the realm of art, ethics and civic virtue. Community arts programmes 'touch every individual' with subtle techniques of consciousness raising, good example and social rehabilitation in forms which go beyond simple ideas of the State.

Community arts projects have on the whole utilised, rather than analysed, women's traditional social role. They have supported women's pivotal position as voluntary providers and consumers of a range of community services. It also comes as no surprise to see projects targeting specific areas of social security and equilibrium. These are areas which have, however, always been perceived to be in crisis, or subject to attack or disruption, as testified by the endemic social problems of the 'prison crisis', 'welfare crisis' or 'the family in crisis'. They have provided a new field of responsibility for middle-class and working-class women within the emerging social professions, and the community arts worker has been a recent addition to the list. Indeed, community arts is arguably the most 'feminised' field in the visual arts.

Liberal and welfarist models came under heavy criticism in the 1980s. Many projects were criticised for simply providing cheap recreation activities, welfare services, civic enhancement and public relations for local government. The cost-effectivity of community arts was largely due to a heavy reliance on women's voluntary labour.[36] Many issue-based projects have, however, had some success in organising community actions and producing effective and imaginative campaign materials. The *Prahran Neighbourhood House women's photography project* (1985) is one example, providing eye-catching panels for use in publicity and funding submissions.[37] The project was coordinated by Melbourne photographer Carolyn Lewens and five other photographers from Lewens' Technical and Further Education (TAFE) women's photography course. They documented the activities of the Neighbourhood House, which serviced the nearby Housing Commission estates. The photographers worked under the editorial direction of the Prahran women, covering different themes such as child care and after-school activities, the budget cooking class, portraits of Neighbourhood House workers, camps and picnics and the home environment. Personal

Panel from the *Prahran Neighbourhood House Women's Photography Project*, 1985. Co-ordinator: Carolyn Lewens.

accounts of support offered by the Neighbourhood House in the face of domestic isolation and often hostile male partners were also mooted.

Family life and community involvement were linked in a fairly traditional image of women's social responsibility and voluntary labour. These images were selected and edited by the women themselves, in what could be called an 'exercise in sovereignty' through the production, selection and exhibition of exemplary self-images. This form of small-group community training had its precedents in feminist consciousness raising. The project constructed a positive image of women's socialising role in the face of poverty, family breakdown and paternal authoritarianism. Indeed, tapping and reinforcing women's familial socialising role is an important ingredient in successful community arts projects. As Andrea Hull, ex-Director of the Community Arts Board observed of a potential 'target' community:

> The machismo nature of a mining town tends to dominate behaviour patterns for both men and women. There is a paucity of meaningful activities for kids between fifteen and twenty and both boys and girls tend to drift into the acceptable adult pursuits of beer drinking, smoking, driving, riding trail bikes; and the predominance of single men means regular outbreaks of twelve and thirteen year old pregnancies at the Aboriginal settlements down the road.[38]

Have these community arts projects echoed the 'reclamation work' of nineteenth century feminism? Some projects identify women as both in need and as potential volunteer allies. Community arts forms one of an 'archipelago' of State and charitable agencies which encircle dysfunctional populations. Communities targeted by project officers and funding bodies are those in special need: youth, the unemployed, the disabled, isolated areas, multicultural or working-class communities. At the same time, feminist community photography has formed a platform for women to negotiate cultural traditions, social services and family controls. Consciousness and confidence raising is often successful within these terms.

Increasingly, community arts has been recognised as a form of social intervention. In-house training now emphasises the ideological and class-based position of the community arts professional. Special-interest and issue-specific projects are given preference over geographically based communities, and priorities of cultural activism dictate goals of self-determination rather than social integration.

It is difficult to specify the direct result of these recommendations, for the effects of policy often lie outside the expectations of planners. The policies of funding bodies effect a cameo for what may become formulated as desired ends, and yet may have little influence on the day-to-day operations of community arts.

Projects at the Norma Parker and Mulawa women's prisons in 1982–3 indicate some of the difficulties faced in reforming the liberal community arts agenda. In particular, these projects revealed the futility of applying notions of women's culture or community to an involuntary institutional population, where individual survival is paramount, and where concepts of sovereignty or empowerment have little meaning.

Norma Parker is a medium-security women's prison housed in the old Parramatta Girl's Training Centre in Sydney's western suburbs. Its low security grading enabled inmates to participate in four-day workshops at the gaol as part of the 1982 New South Wales Women and the Arts Festival. The workshops met with mixed response. Co-organiser Jan Birmingham attributed the uneven attendance to perceptions among some inmates that collage work was like a kindergarten activity and that to be asked to do it was to be treated as a child. Moreover, the theme of the workshop, 'Connections and Separations' was seen to be 'disturbing and intruded into personal lives'.[39]

Follow-up workshops held at Mulawa in 1983 were run along similar lines. Mulawa is a maximum security facility housed within a men's minimum security gaol at Silverwater, also in western Sydney. Here, however, the arbitrary nature of prison surveillance hampered the proceedings. Prisoners were not allowed to use the cameras themselves, due to the Superintendent's fears about blackmail, security and bad publicity; and inmates had to direct shots for the tutors to photograph. Polaroids were used on account of their familiarity and immediacy and because prints could be counted (inmates were not allowed photographs in their cells).

The Mulawa women were asked to develop imagery based around their own lives. Each workshop began with a round-table discussion on the theme of 'Labels and Other Images' using slides from Jan Birmingham's family album and the mass media. The women were encouraged to talk about their self-image, their children and families, and their experiences and feelings about life in prison.

Consideration needs to be given in applying consciousness-raising techniques in this context. The influence of psychology within the prison system has meant that 'the personal' has become a strategic political site. The institutional sponsorship of rehabilitation programmes had provided a conditional vehicle for gaining entry to Norma Parker and Mulawa in the first place. However, arts programmes must come to terms with the institutional nature of this sponsorship. Confessional techniques for self-examination and attitudinal change may not necessarily be progressive, for the prison has increasingly been organised around the examination of individual conscience.[40] Within this institutional 'seminar of conscience', the notion of 'labels and other images' prompted work that affirmed individual worth and friendship in adversity. Other montages dealt with personal confusion and distress. In the first instance, a photographic collage by Ana Louisa Ankers, titled *Laughter—My Hidden Contraband* demonstrated inventive photographic direction, despite the paucity of available materials. However, this simple affirmation of individual identity against brutal depersonalisation necessarily structured 'the personal' within a strict moral and psychological field.

The emphasis placed on experiential self-scrutiny foreclosed the articulation of specific grievances or political engagements that had marked earlier feminist interventions in the NSW penal system.[41] These consciousness-raising workshops instead reiterated the institutional discourse of moral rehabilitation. The character of the masochistic female victim formed the template for a limited repertoire of photographic motifs. Within this traditional prohibitive discourse, addiction, incarceration and death form the symbolic parameters of lives. Alternatively, utopian symbols of beauty, dreams of escape, future hopes, friendships, and positive self-perceptions were affirmed. This confessional strategy unfortunately worked in a comfortable, symbiotic relationship with the prison system, perpetuating conceptions of individual fault and pathology by focusing attention on defects in prisoners.[42]

In this case, emphasis on moral rehabilitation and emotional adjustment required more critical calculation on the part of the organisers. Within the pragmatic context of prison reform, the projects at Norma Parker and Mulawa tried to set a positive precedent for future workshops. The organisers deliberately tried not to threaten prison officials or structures, and to provide a 'feather in the cap for the Department of Corrective Services'.[43] But this cautious approach did not secure its intended outcome. The low-key, rehabilitative approach taken by the organisers had little influence on the arbitrary nature of corrective services' decision-making, and no follow-up programmes emerged. In hindsight, it seems that institutional obstructions had more to do with the logistics of security and incarceration than with the actual politics or content of the workshops themselves.

Community projects have remained largely invisible in art history, due to their consciousness-raising flavour, subject matter, institutional or subcultural locus and aesthetic conservatism. A few feminist artists retreated from the community circuit in the early

Ana Louisa Ankers, *Laughter—My hidden contraband*, from *Work by the women of Mulawa*, 1983. Co-ordinators: Jan Birmingham and Joyce Agee. Reproduced in *Labels and other images, Caper 21*, Community Arts Board, 1984, p.5.

'Yvonne', *Habit*, from *Work by the women of Mulawa*, 1983. Coordinators: Jan Birmingham and Joyce Agee. Reproduced in *Labels and other images, Caper 21*, Community Arts Board, 1984, p.16.

1980s for these reasons. The strategy of social reconstruction—in particular, the construction of a consensual, collective female identity—has given way to more critical deconstructions of the social field. The latter projects have paradoxically been mounted from within the studio, gallery and academy. The 'field'—that amorphous territory of the community arts professional—was relegated to the 'too hard' basket by many artists and theorists. This retreat parallels a move away from experiential and empirical explorations of the family album. When the archaeological minefield of domestic and community maintenance was later reopened in psychoanalytic readings of the maternal, the artists were not really dealing with the same grandmothers, aunts, mothers and daughters. Family life in the 1980s was couched in anti-familial and anti-humanist terms. The following chapter will unravel the threads of this 'epistemological break'.

3 Deconstructing the social

Debates concerning the truth value and political efficacy of realist aesthetics gained momentum during the late 1970s. Photo-documentary images of women at work in the home, community and work place rubbed shoulders with more complex analyses of representation, work and femininity. These paralleled British debates on narrative cinema and documentary photography. Many writers and photographers took up the political and theoretical impetus of pre-war modernists John Heartfield, Sergei Eisenstein, Walter Benjamin and Bertolt Brecht. Following British and French precedents, semiotic and psychoanalytic analyses supplanted character and content-based criticism. Whilst this Althusserian-inspired theorisation of representation and ideology was making its mark, Foucault's analyses of power and subjectivity were also gaining limited interest among feminists, and early translations of French feminists Julia Kristeva, Luce Irigaray and Hélène Cixous were finding an audience.

Helen Grace's work is a good example of this intersection. Her work with the British feminist photography group the Hackney Flashers prompted the establishment of Blatant Image, a collective involving Grace, Sandy Edwards, Virginia Maddison and Lynn Silverman. Blatant Image hosted a series of discussions, articles and group projects from 1979 to 1982, most notably the large photomural commissioned by the NSW Women's Advisory Unit.

Grace and others' photographs for the 1979 Women's Employment Rights Campaign (WERC) booklet, *Women and unemployment*, documented an uncanny similarity in the regulation of women's blue and white collar work.[1] This congruence lay in women's assumed industrial passivity and manual dexterity, which is actively produced within specific techniques of production management and architectural design. These photographs documented the open plan factory and office as a managerial visual field, gridded by individual work

54

Untitled and unattributed photograph, reproduced in *Women and unemployment*,
Panacea Press, Sydney, 1979, p.23.

benches and work stations. In both manufacturing and secretarial
work, restricted movement, vision or contact with co-workers inversely maximised efficiency checks. The camera as a mobile, proprietary 'eye' recorded how the sexual power relations between the
male boss and female workers is an integral part of work discipline.

Grace extended these observations in a photographic segment
of Ann Game and Rosemary Pringle's 1983 sociological study
Gender at work.[2] In the hospital, Grace brought her camera up close
to register the precision with which dress codes demarcated personnel according to rank, salary, sex, professional conduct, training
and responsibility. The modern hospital is organised as a 'complex,
coherent corpus combining a form of experience, a method of
analysis, and a type of teaching', as described by Foucault.[3] These
functions are specified by an extended medical and paramedical
network of authority, differentiated through quasi-military insignia
and subtle dress codes. Appropriating the photographic techniques
of modern management (security surveillance, quality control, the
time-and-motion study), Grace documented the organisation of
work in its meticulous management of individual bodies, tasks and
behaviours. Her study reveals how the regulation of time (the

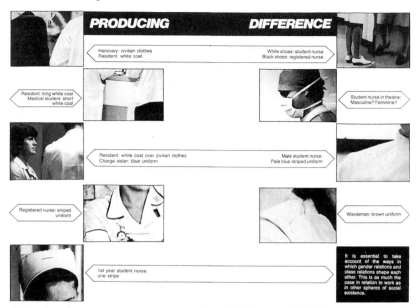

Helen Grace, *Producing difference*, reproduced in Game and Pringle, *Gender at work*, George Allen and Unwin, Sydney, 1983, facing p.62.

bundy-clock, work schedule) and space (the medical examination, factory and office architecture, work space design) enables the invisible and constant surveillance of individuals and the minute breakdown of tasks according to ergonomic, psychological and vocational calculations.

The shift from the literal identification of women at work to more complex arguments about tasks and roles crystallised the divergent priorities of feminist, trade union and art audiences in the early 1980s. Stylish curatorial packages and solo shows had replaced Women's Art Movement and community projects and alternative spaces as the prime sites for aesthetic debate. Art audiences and funding bodies demanded more conceptually and aesthetically 'advanced' projects. Artists working with Trade Unions and in community arts sought to maintain the conceptual and aesthetic relevance of this area of cultural politics within an increasingly market-oriented art world. The Lidcombe Workers' Health Centre project, *Re-presenting work* (1983) is an example of this response.[4]

Helen Grace's signature-style industrial photography techniques were cloaked in a dynamic poster design by Ruth Waller. The question, 'Who photographs work?' revealed the workplace to be already saturated with photographic technologies which commonly go unnoticed. The security ID pin, advertisements for drugs in medical journals, management photographs advertising new technology or efficient production systems, and glamorous images of secretaries advertising nail polish were some of the examples 're-presented' in answer to the question. The panel argued that photography in the work place is generally used to enforce the status quo.

A representative weekly 'calendar' also addressed the issue. A time-and-motion study of the working week isolated individual workers and tasks. This methodical compartmentalisation of time, tasks and bodies was contrasted to a smaller scatter of informal colour snapshots recording convivial weekend activities (the arena of amateur photography). This indirect appeal for workers to render visible their working life was punctuated by panels of prints from the 1950s Chullora Rolling Stock Camera Club.

Breezy design packages such as *Re-presenting work* did not, however, completely breach the institutional and aesthetic gap between feminist, union and mainstream art audiences. As a site for disputation over realist conventions, Art and Working Life programmes, like community arts, were losing their perceived critical edge to gallery-based feminist and Neo-conceptual work. In art world terms, community based projects coordinated by Sydney photographer Dennis del Favero have been more successful, as they are specifically designed for museum exhibition and fine art reproduction.

Domestic Science

Helen Grace's *Xmas dinner* series showed the ways in which a historical regimen of discipline and productivity is applied to the home. Again she used time-and-motion photography to gauge the 'relations of production' of the Xmas family ritual. The meticulous, invisible tasks performed by women in the home were logged as if on the shop floor. Routine domestic activities were documented as potentially unsafe and unsatisfying work practices, involving social and psychological pressures as well as physical and chemical hazards. When used to gauge levels of family maintenance, this efficiency index also revealed the sheer volume of women's work.

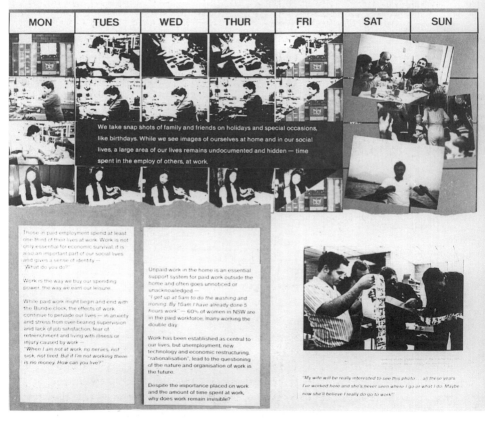

Helen Grace, detail from the panel, *Re-presenting work*, Sydney, 1983. Poster design: Ruth Waller.

Helen Grace, from the series *Xmas dinner*, 1979. Gelatin silver photograph, 11.8 × 9 cms. Kodak (Australasia) Pty. Ltd. Fund, Australian National Gallery.

On the other hand, the wit of *Xmas dinner* lay in its public and technical language. This industrial format undercut the supposed cheer and cosy intimacy of Christmas celebrations, usually captured in family snapshots. The notion of job satisfaction takes on new meaning when (mis)applied to the home. Grace's segmented schedule of tasks and rituals scrutinised a singularly cheerless 'festive' occasion. As writer and curator Julie Ewington remarked of the series:

> This work has been controversial since its first exhibition, precisely because of this dreadful ambiguity at the heart of the ritual. It reveals that if men are public ceremonial leaders in our society, women are its functionaries.[5]

The industrial coordinates that Grace brought to *Xmas dinner* departed from the crafty, family album emphasis of the *Mothers' memories* project in which it first appeared. Most of the other exhibits celebrated the eloquence of the family album and women's undervalued social responsibilities. Grace's snapshots were not 'eloquent' in this sense. They took their cue from the Brechtian dictum that, in itself, a photograph (of a factory, for instance) may reveal little about the relations of production that constitute the modern factory or industrial capital. Likewise, the family snapshot is singularly silent in relation to the domestic labour that reproduces Christmas dinners or the modern family. As Grace's caption to the series explained:

> The sepia toning is intended as irony. There is nothing romantic about domestic labour nor is it particularly heroic. Attempts to sentimentalise the work of women serve to conceal the real relations of production and reproduction of which domestic labour is an integral part.

The maternal body as a site of cultural transgression

The family album took another turn in the 1970s, in applying rudimentary psychoanalytic concepts to the maternal relation. Helen Grace's political economy of *The lovely motherhood show* (1981) and Laleen Jayamanne's autobiographical meditations on *The holey family* (1979) were early explorations in this area. These projects have remained relatively isolated within contemporary feminist debates and overlooked in later attempts to trace the origins and influences of 1980s art photography. This is partly because these projects were shown in the unselected theme shows *Mothers' memories, others' memories* (1979) and *The lovely motherhood show* (1981). These feminist and community projects rarely feature in histories of 1970s and 1980s art.

Grace and Jayamanne's work departed from the purely experiential coordinates that dominated shows like *Mothers' memories*. They jostled Marxist political economy with French feminist critiques of the Freudian school, against a backdrop of 'personal–political' autobiography. The resulting formal and conceptual fragmentation in the work testified both to a perceived lack of fit between Marxist, psychoanalytic and feminist discourses, and to the transitional nature of these projects.

The lovely motherhood show investigated the theatre of motherhood through a disjointed series of nursery mobiles, wall panels and a mock family album. The plot took shape between intersecting economic processes, the interventionist measures of obstetrics, pediatrics, cultural discourses on motherhood and the highly regulated (yet 'ever-failing' and thus potentially transgressive) subjective knowledges of the mother.[6]

The modern figures of mother and child are showcased within a lucrative reproductive industry. The *deus ex machina* at work in

Grace's hybrid psycho-social theatre was introduced as a momentous narrative, 'In which our heroine, driven by unconscious desire, embarks on the path of True Womanhood...' Initial disjunctions between competing discourses on motherhood and political resistance established an uneasy and unresolved exchange between feminism and Marxism, in which the body of the mother was set against the narrow humanist project of political economy. The maternal body also posed a problem for a feminist material analysis. As an object of knowledge, it confounded simple delineations between social and non-social, conscious and unconscious experience. In her family album, Grace speculated:

> It is not only that the maternal body is the site of a splitting, as Kristeva puts it, but rather that it is the site of a complete breakdown of divisions. The external world becomes internal, the 'unified' subject becomes two. How in this situation can you present a 'personal', 'individual' account of experience? Who is speaking?

The heroic adventure embarked upon by the mother was thus not simply one of conscious choice, unconscious desire, or economic, social or ideological administration. Rather, all these practices have instituted the knowledges, responsibilities and pleasures of motherhood.

The mother was initially observed as a pathological medical subject within the hospital, to be later enlisted as the closely monitored, paramedical ally of the pediatrician and the baby care industries. At the same time, Grace observed, these industries employ women workers 'in such a way that they cannot possibly be the sorts of mothers they are depicted as being in the images which advertise the very products they produce'. Advertising and popular cultural images of 'lovely motherhood' were contrasted with photographs and texts describing the production and use of baby care goods. Hans Haacke-style documentation of the size, profits and working conditions at Bond's, Johnson & Johnson and Heinz revealed a large force of low-paid casual labour, no job security or child care provisions, and sexist managerial attitudes. Time-and-motion photography studied nappy changing. It parodied the clichéd connections so often made by management between an innate, feminine capacity for nimble-fingered, repetitive tasks, femininity and motherhood. Like other projects from the

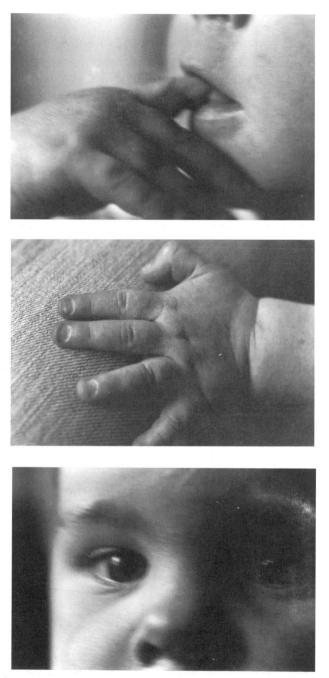

Helen Grace, from the installation *The lovely motherhood show*, (photographic mobile titled *Maternal desire*), 1981. Laminated silver gelatin photograph, 3.5 × 9 cms. Collection of the artist.

period, Grace's serialised documentation of baby care also formed a spoof on the fascination with repetitive systems and diurnal routines in Conceptual Art.

Grace detailed a close relation between maternity hospitals and major baby product manufacturers. She showed that modern motherhood is not only an economic problem. Mother and baby emerge within a grid of medico-administrative coordinates. Obstetrics infantilise the mother as an object of science. A nursery mobile represents conflicting discourses on pregnancy, childbirth and postnatal care. The mother's own desires and anxieties are also suggested, without simply counterposing the idea of social control versus a conception of authentic maternal experience. A reproduction of a Bellini Madonna in Grace's album suggests that while the image of the untouched, untouching and untouchable Virgin remains potent in Western culture, the very nature of the modern mother–child relationship is, from the outset, thoroughly sexual.[7] As Freud observed, the mother is the 'first seducer'. What limit to set upon this tender, sensual relationship? The pregnant body, and later the mother's relation to the child, is subject to contradictory desires and prohibitions.

The mother's personal responses, suspended on fragile mobiles, formed shifting complications or disruptions to dominant economic, social and cultural knowledges. Here quotes from Julia Kristeva and Doris Lessing were interspersed with excerpts from a mother's diary. They spoke of the deeply ambivalent yet 'non-formalised' experience of the maternal body and '... the aphasic pleasure of childbirth'. In a third mobile, the mother's fetishisation of the child was evoked through fragmented glimpses of the child's body. Atmospheric lighting, shallow depth-of-field and soft focus traversed the infant's face, limbs and torso, in a blurred movement akin to touch. This fleeting blur—metaphor for an inarticulable proximity, opaque to the scientific, administrative and ideological orders of knowledge—became a common gesture in later evocations of sexual difference and a pre-oedipal, 'semiotic' register, as described in the work of Kristeva.

The blur was the structuring principle behind Laleen Jayamanne's *The holey family*. This work was exhibited in *Mothers' memories, others' memories* and later edited for reproduction in *LIP 1981/82*.[8] (see also colour section) The original installation formed a metaphorical map of the world, plotted according to the temporal, economic, cultural and psycho-sexual contours of the artist's

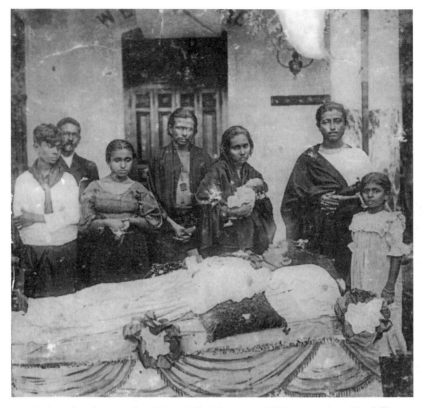

Laleen Jayamanne, detail from *The holey family*, 1979. Reproduced in *LIP*, 1981/82, p.42.

family. This chaotic collage provided multiple points of access and connection, while definitive nominations of the family were suspended. At the time, this apparent formal and conceptual incoherence went against contemporary feminist practices of 'ordering' the family album.[9] Jayamanne's circumnavigatory voyage around the world was punctuated by snatches of commentary, memory, slogans and songs. This messy 'time-and-flow' chart gestured towards a radically non-formalised feminine discourse, extending analyses of the family to questions of women's impossible placement within the symbolic order of language and social exchange.

Halfway around the world, so to speak, Jayamanne escapes from her family by virtue of the dubious passports of class, education and marriage. A postcard 'marriage of convenience for US visa' was appended by the cheeky title: 'Passport to study: passport to freedom: passport to the US of A'. The conditional nature of this conjugal passport to freedom was also noted: 'THE LAW. Can we play with the law of the father?' The governing principles of the symbolic—the domain of language and sociality in Lacan's psychoanalytic schema (to which woman can never successfully accede) — were evoked in relation to women's familial and conjugal obligations, as noted in the caption to a family photograph, dated 1910:

> Feudal, Patriarchal, Extended Family.
> Eldest daughter dies at childbirth
> Second daughter given in marriage
> to widower to keep jewellery in family.

In her shift from one country, culture and familial role to another, Jayamanne's working concept of culture and class broadened to describe patriarchal trade relations. While the illusory passport to the West had its own conditions and limitations, we find that Jayamanne's proposed ticket to freedom lay not in an imaginary 'America' but in a metaphorical and political 'return to the mother'. Jayamanne's personal history was translated in the revised project from 'Third World woman' to 'the "third world" of women'. Mother–daughter relations were recast as a meeting of autonomous female identities, 'Free of the responsibility of being a daughter; Free of the responsibility of being a mother'. In the revised version of *The holey family*, Jayamanne confesses:

> MY MOTHER—I wish you were alive now so that I can begin
> to get to know you. Yet already I feel I know you more than
> I evber (sic) did in all those years we lived as mother and
> daughter, but really as strangers, sometimes hostile sometimes
> friendly, but mostly indifferent. i (sic) speak only for myself, not
> for your inarticulate epileptic pain.
> 28 July 1979 Sydney; 4th anniversary of my mother's death.

Jayamanne invested a generalised, maternal body with the psycholinguistic symptoms of hysteria or aphasia. The revolt of the feminine body was reconceived as a mute, frontline resistance. The loose design of the work itself parallels this 'corporeal' logic, as if symptomatic of the impossible or incomplete formalisation of feminine contents. Jayamanne's gestural, 'performative' principle of feminine excess became a hallmark of subsequent textual transgressions (the blur, the fractured body, fuzzy focus, artificially saturated colour, chaotic or incomplete formalisation). What was at stake here? What was this repressed, alternative economy? As Jayamanne quoted in the coda to *The holey family*, '...it would be the whole of female language which is still in the repressed form'.[10]

Marxist, feminist and psychoanalytic references were brought to bear on Jayamanne's 'family problem'. Her world map was plotted according to the correlates of class, race, culture and sex. These were continually disrupted through reference to a disordered feminine register, which ultimately submerged Jayamanne's more materialist analyses. Her dense collage challenged masculine orders of knowledge by privileging more tactile, fragmented and auto-erotic exchanges between women.

We have already noted how renovations of the family album in the 1970s privileged the mother's experiences and knowledges of the domestic. At the close of the decade, the album became a vehicle for more detailed analyses of motherhood as a psycho-sexual and social construct. Increasingly, the mother was cited as a figure of cultural and corporeal resistance. This image was a far cry from Sue Ford's negative zone of isolation and child-centred domestic labour. Motherhood now provided a key to the workings of the feminine unconscious. This under-theorised psychoanalytic arena, Freud's 'dark continent', was explored as a site of a radical alterity. The pre-oedipal, maternal relation was an unknown quantity in patriarchal systems of signification. It lay completely outside the ballpark.

The social and economic worlds faded from view in later psychoanalytic investigations of maternal desire. In the rush to rid artwork of a stale Marxism and the didactic or experiential aesthetic of 'seventies-style' feminism, the themes of family maintenance and its problems were largely overlooked. The historical specificity of family album work also disappeared. Economic and social history became the 'blind spots' of feminist projects in the 1980s. These political omissions were related to a powerful gallery-driven myopia. When the chic white cube returned in the 1980s, the conceptual and curatorial space for messy family album installations and more didactic socio-political analyses effectively disappeared. The 'clean up' of feminist art pared down the ambitious (though under-developed) interdisciplinary nature of 1970s projects.

Deconstructing the family album

The family album didn't entirely disappear from the critical stage in the 1980s. Jacky Redgate's *photographer unknown. A Portrait*

Chronicle of Photographs, England, 1953–62 (1984) has been exhibited and reproduced in major surveys of contemporary art and photography. Redgate enlarged a series of 'found' or inherited snapshot negatives and exhibited the prints in a conventional museum mode. The anonymity and haunting intimacy of these scratchy images probed the commemorative and narrative power of family photography in its broadest sense. The woman who clasps her arms in a tight knot, what is she doing there, having her photograph taken in a graveyard? Who is the little boy who looks out so frankly? Is he at church, or school? But why are his sleeves rolled up, then? Yet these mute and forlorn figures have a propriety about them that keeps us at a distance. The puzzling, anecdotal contents of these prints, whilst fascinating, are suspended in a more respectful archival reverie on the 'human condition' of photography itself.

Redgate, like Elizabeth Gertsakis and other artists working with family photography from the mid-1980s, brought the family album into the orbit of broader cultural debates around authorship, desire, popular memory and archival retrieval. Unlike earlier albums, emphasis was on the institutional and photographic conditions of looking, reading and remembering. Photography was no longer accepted at face value as a transparent vehicle for filial identity and expression.

Anecdotal questions about identity and kinship structured Elizabeth Gertsakis' 1987 project *Innocent reading for origin*. They give her family album a self-conscious attention to processes of history and popular memory. For Gertsakis, the family album presents a problem of how and what we should remember. An album is a memorial. It is a problem of inheritance. Competing aesthetic, cultural and familial sentiments are brought to each photograph in the act of remembering the years of post-war migration and assimilationist policies. A collision of 'innocent' readings are supplied through the voices of the chronicler, the little girl, the non-English-speaking migrant and the adult who has only partial access to the family story. They complicate the historical clarity of the migrant story ('there and here') and the personal and familial coherence of the ordered album. These 'innocents' repeatedly call our attention to some fugitive detail or peculiarity in certain shots: why does that lady in the white veil look like she is being dragged somewhere? Why is the groom holding wisps of grass? 'That check skirt is a mess', and so on. Gertsakis turns the tables on a decade of feminist albums, as family relations, history and identity refuse to cohere.

Jacky Redgate/*photographer unknown. A Portrait Chronicle of Photographs, England 1953–62, 1984.* 15 silver gelatin photographs, each 762 × 508 mm (frame).

Jacky Redgate/*photographer unknown, West London Cemetery, 1954–62*
(from *A Portrait Chronicle of Photographs, England, 1953–62*) silver gelatin
photograph, 347 × 500 mm (image).

Gertsakis' following project also involved an open-ended family story. Her 1989 series *A glamorous private history* slotted family photographs alongside reproductions of famous paintings and the addictive imagery of popular culture. Each element was given the same value within a diptych or triptych structure. Family photographs supposedly create a quieter space of intimate

'My mother is gazing directly into the camera, fearless, strong, in the present. My father's gaze stares, denying the interrogations of the family photograph.'

Elizabeth Gertsakis, detail from the series *Innocent reading for origin*, 1987.

recognition and mundane order, in contrast to the dizzy magazine spread or exhaulted artistic masterwork. Yet amongst images of Elvis Presley, Berthe Morisot and Avedon-style graphic beauties, her family photographs offered an equally intense play of desire and social investment. The artist suggests that Avedon's beauty can be freely enjoyed as a spectacular, commercial transaction. Manet's women are also beautiful, but they are, after all, 'Manet's women', and so can be appreciated with the respect accorded to aesthetic value. The more private pleasures of family photography can also be sampled, courtesy of the incest taboo and the balance accorded by 'the shared offering of self to and within the family'. As the artist notes, 'In the end it is a matter of taste'. The alternative title, *Some people like to eat alone* provides a witty commentary on this unresolved complex of regulated consumption, history and pleasure.

When shifted from its realist axis, the photographic regulation of family life became a new starting point for work on feminine sexuality as a social and aesthetic problem. The following chapter further examines this line of mutation in feminist photography. Alongside the subject and the social, the female body and sexuality have proved to be major points of contention and intervention.

Eliizabeth Gertsakis, *Framing a brief return*, Triptych, from *A glamorous private history*, 1989. (cibachrome print 22 × 60″)

4   The bare essentials

Just as the social realm became a problematic theatre for feminist photography, the body has also provided unstable points of resistance. Debates around the politics of gender and sexual difference crystallised as the 1970s drew to a close. 'Gender' and 'sexual difference' were commonly conceived as opposite analytical terms, a demarcation associated with differences between radical feminism versus socialist or liberal feminism. Concepts of socialisation and false consciousness were linked to liberal and socialist feminist strategies for women's re-education. Theories of sexual difference have instead emphasised the sexually differentiated body as a determinant factor in masculine and feminine identity. From this position, gender politics criticised for their inadequate theorisation of the body and psycho-social processes of signification. They are also seen to assume a false dichotomy between mind and body, effectively 'disembodying' women and neutralising sexual difference.[1]

While many of the photographs discussed in this book were indeed formulated within simplistic frameworks of sex role stereotyping, they have also marked, examined, celebrated and demonstrated specific *corporeal* attributes and capacities. Arguably, they have not 'disembodied' women. On the contrary, female sexuality has been treated as a problem of knowledge, training and power which is not necessarily reducible to simple conceptions of determinant social relations or consciousness, as the 'difference' theorists describe. Nor can the question of women's re-education, central to feminist photography, be simply dismissed as gender behaviourism. Photographic aids to women's physical and sexual education, for instance, are more usefully described as tools of confession, monitoring and interpreting the body. They cannot easily be explained in advance through some general framework of behaviourism or a 'mythic politics of androgyny'.[2] By suspending *a priori*

71

demarcations and models, the more substantive arguments registered by the sexual difference theorists can be articulated, and influential tendencies within feminist photography can be documented in a critical yet non-sectarian manner.

In fact, it is dubious whether the common opposition between gender and sexual difference provides suitable grounds for deriving a generalised feminist politics across diverse political, social and cultural areas, even if this were desirable. At the very least, no one theory of the body, or its representation, can account for the varied relations between feminist photography and the complex social relations, sensitivities, technologies and practices that are associated with women's bodies, sexuality and identity. There is no general or *a priori* connection to be made between heterogeneous biological, psychic and social relations.

Photographs reproduced here are instruments in the formation, accumulation and dissemination of knowledge about female sexuality. This is not quite the same thing as ideology, for sexual etho-poetics has involved the research, care and training of the body in ways which do not fit schemas of recognition or interpellation. These photographs work at different levels, and not simply within a symbolic field or the domain of signifying structures. For instance, photographs have assisted psychological and para-medical self-examinations. Photography could also be used to heighten sexual pleasure, monitor physical development and sexual health, and regulate the character of female relationships ('coming out' as a lesbian, for instance).

Chapter 5 follows a related, performance-based trajectory of art photography from the mid 1970s to the mid 1980s, a period in which artists sought to problematise feminine corporeal rituals and rites of passage. Chapter 6 also looks at a more recent use of art photography to investigate the organisation of sexual difference in the discourses of popular culture and art history. In each of these areas—whether looking at health photography, the ritualised socialisation of female desire or more recent psychoanalytic investigations into the cultural coding of sexual difference—the female body constituted a point of social instability and ambivalence. The task of feminine aesthetics was to articulate these points of hidden resistance and diffused pleasure.

The call to 'let the body speak (for) itself' was an early feature of women's health imagery, lesbian politics and central core imagery. Paradoxically, work in these areas initially de-emphasised genitally based sexual experience in favour of a diffused auto-eroticism, a romanticised lesbian continuum and the pleasures of speaking about sex. The strategy of liberation through self-examination, consciousness raising and 'coming out' has had un-even political outcomes. Many of its tenets were modified amid a general shift in strategy during the early 1980s.

The camera as speculum: Feminist health imagery

Early feminist health care photography had the contradictory aim of teaching women just to 'be themselves' through highly organised modes of examination and interpretation of intimate experience. These procedures emphasised the ethical dimensions of feminist health culture. They have a history which can be traced through nineteenth century campaigns for family health and hygiene. At issue was not simply control over women's health, away from the punitive legislature with its notorious 'double stan-dard', and away from the perceived incompetent and anti-woman hands of the male doctor. Early feminist campaigns for women's health helped to transform family medicine into the modern, ethi-cal and psychologised arena that we know today.

Those social purity feminists in the forefront of the health campaigns advocated an overriding moral and social, and not merely medical, dimension to all areas of gynaecological-obstetric experience.[3] They argued that women's moral superiority and tem-pering nature fitted them for a guiding role in a nascent com-munity and family health care system. The job of monitoring male as well as female sexual conduct and health came under women's jurisdiction. The feminist promotion of women as sanitary edu-cators was thus an important element in the problematisation of sexuality and sexual health as a matter of individual conscience and moral development. The sponsorship of women as paramedical and ethical guides, within a familial ideology, was important in defend-ing women's economic and political rights. The call for women to enter the health care professions formed part of this campaign.

These promotions framed part of a massive social reinvest-ment in motherhood from the late eighteenth century. Foucault has identified the 'hysterisation of women's bodies' as a major point of this investment, referring to the organisation of women's physical, intellectual and cultural identity around a sexuality that was considered to be potentially dangerous. This involved a threefold process:

> ... the feminine body was analysed—qualified and disqualified—
> as being thoroughly saturated with sexuality; ... it was integrated
> into the sphere of medical practices, by reason of the pathology
> intrinsic to it; ... finally, it was placed in organic communion
> with the social body (whose regulated fecundity it was supposed
> to ensure), the family space (of which it had to be a substantial
> and functional element), and the life of children (which it
> produced and had to guarantee, by virtue of a biologico-moral
> responsibility lasting through the entire period of the children's
> education): the Mother, with her negative image of the 'nervous
> woman', constituted the most visible form of this hysterization.[4]

It is useful to keep this history in mind when evaluating photographic projects. Feminists have made substantial gains within the ethical and psychological dimensions of modern family health. Self-examination, for instance, is now a central mechanism in preventative health care, and photography has played a direct role in promoting women's paramedical skills and understanding of sexuality. Photographs are used in campaigns for free and safe contraception, abortion and health care services. They can also show women how to use contraceptives and perform simple medical procedures such as pap smears or breast examinations. They have even been used to demonstrate the expression of healthy sexual feelings.

Most of these photographs can be found in feminist health handbooks, helping women monitor and maintain health, hygiene and sexual activity as a wholistic, liberatory activity. Influential texts like *Our bodies, ourselves* (first published 1971) reasserted earlier claims regarding women's nurturant qualities and community responsibility: 'our lost identity as healers in the distant past ... and the people's health movement and those women who ran institutions in the last century'.[5] Contrasting images reproduced in *Our bodies, ourselves* illustrated the moral dimension of doctor–patient relationships. A photo captioned, 'The obstetrician-gynaecologist's view of women' emphasises patient passivity and restrictive gadgetry. Under the masculine clinical eye, the encased woman is constituted as a pathological, 'hystericised' subject. This image of the gynaecological abattoir echoes the sentiments of nineteenth century feminist campaigns against the humiliation and 'instrumental rape'

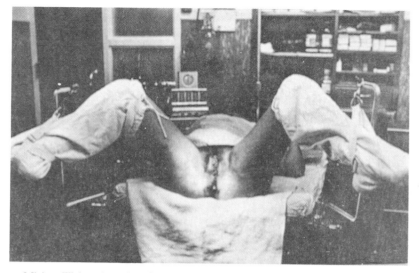

Miriam Weinstein, 'The obstetrician-gynecologist's view of women', Boston Women's Health Collective, reproduced in *Our bodies, ourselves*, 1976, p.353.

Jean Raisler, Untitled photograph, reproduced in *Our bodies, ourselves*, The Boston Women's Health Collective, 1976, p.366.

of female patients.[6] In contrast, 'a women's view of women' discloses an educative circle of warmth and support, under the progressive sub-headings 'Mutual help groups' and 'Women's groups'. The feminist health care regimen trained women to experience their bodies in new ways. Touching oneself, touching others, taking control, talking about it: although feminist health care retained a simplistic moral and political framework of 'women versus doctors', the imagery of feminist health care legitimated a range of sexual experiences which departed from the dominant conventions of heterosexuality and reproductive experience. The affirmation of sexual pleasure against the normative expectations of conjugal relations and public decency constituted an important point of resistance to the hysterisation of the female body. It was, however, mounted from within this same field of social investment. What had provided power—the mother's paramedical responsibilities, along with the perceived excessive or potentially subversive nature of female sexuality—were used to attack it.

Newly defined health and sexual norms demanded a wholistic approach. A case of thrush may suggest careful attention to stress levels. The masochistic crash diet was contrasted with the 'liberatory' exercise routine. Sexual preference was not just a question of pleasurable choices or acts: it was a way of life. 'Women's health' similarly merged with women's liberation, involving questions of identity, lifestyle, responsibility. Assuming a general relation of female sexual experience, photographs in *Our bodies, ourselves* encouraged women to just let themselves 'be'. However, the range of practical procedures and techniques necessary for the regulation of being oneself were narrowly prescribed. These centred around the ability to talk about sex, for 'we increase our skill in expressing our own sexuality to others'. This may explain the plethora of photographs in *Our bodies, ourselves* showing couples how to talk to each other. Talking about sex was not only liberatory. It was a source of pleasure in itself.

Increased value placed on women's interpretative skills reformed, but did not displace, an earlier 'hermeneutics of suspicion' surrounding sexuality.[7] The hystericisation of women's bodies had developed in tandem with the construction of a scientific structure to explain sex. The trained doctor, psychiatrist or psychoanalyst, and not the individual, could understand what was being said or examined. Female reproductive and sexual experience were held to be a stubbornly secret and problematic phenomenon. The female patient was not thought capable of interpreting the secrets of her own sexuality. Its deep truth could only surface in an intelligible form by virtue of the mediation of a specialist. Feminist health care photography reformulated the procedures for producing the symptoms and underlying significance of female sexuality. Despite a change in personnel, the hermeneutics of suspicion remained in photographic evocations of sexual feelings and sensations. Woman, now the arbiter of her own discourse, could freely express the poetic 'symptoms' of feminine sexuality, and interpret their contents.

The visual and verbal expression of intimate experience conceived the female body as the seat of pre-discursive desires. This assumption provided a central framework for an emergent etho-poetics of the female body. Sexuality was central to understanding woman's very being, her relation to nature, language and sociality. These relations have provided fertile ground for feminine aesthetics. In early formulations, a potentially dangerous, hysterical 'excess' associated with woman was replayed through romantic codes of incompletion, heterogeneity and natural metaphors of fluidity or fecundity. In some cases, however, these simply added to an historical, sexual 'saturation' of the female body.

Central core imagery

The naked female body has been commonly used as a metaphor for liberation. In its simplest configuration, clothes were discarded as a gestural rejection of restrictive social and cultural codes. The photographic process of 'getting in touch' with a feminine substratum of biological, psychological and spiritual experience blended empirical observation and art photography. The female body became self-expressive. It was seen to motivate, reflect and demand an aesthetics isomorphic with the female form. Hence the assumption of a feminine 'central core' initially directed the invention of natural metaphors for women's bodies, sexuality and identity. International Women's Year in 1975 was also 'the year of the central core cover', with variations by Vivienne Binns (*Meanjin Quarterly*), Frances Budden (*LIP* centrefold) and Pat Fiske (*Cauldron* and *Refractory Girl*).

Pat Fiske's *Cauldron* cover photograph of women dancing in a ring recalled the legendary power of the witch and woman healer,

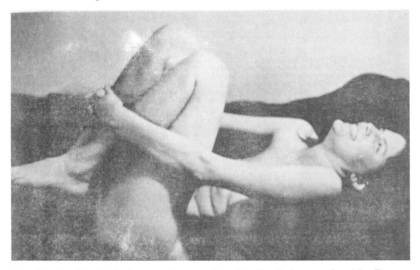

Ann Popkin, Untitled photograph, reproduced in *Our bodies, ourselves*, The Boston Women's Health Collective, 1976, p.39.

Unattributed photograph, reproduced in *Cauldron*, Vol.1, No.3, p.23.

within a code of nature. Inside, unattributed central core photographs also imagined feminine sexuality as a subversive force, nurtured by menstrual blood, orgasmic secretions and the mystery of reproduction. Pat Fiske's 1975 *Refractory Girl* cover made this connection explicit (see colour section). An accompanying 'interior text' quoted American artists Judy Chicago and Miriam Schapiro:

> We are suggesting that women artists have used the central cavity which defines them as women as the framework for an imagery which allows for the complete reversal of the way in which women are seen by the culture. That is to be a woman is to be an object of contempt, and the vagina, stamp of femaleness, is devalued. The woman artist seeing herself as loathed takes that very hallmark of her otherness and by asserting it as the hallmark of her iconography, establishes a vehicle by which to state the truth and beauty of her identity.[8]

Along with nappy-and-tampon projects, the re-evaluation of woman's 'deadly secret' was shockingly anti-aesthetic and anti-social. Central core imagery simply *came up too close*. It hit you in the face, so to speak. Over-proximity between image and spectator negated the viewing distance necessary for aesthetic sublimation, voyeuristic management or fetishistic contemplation. This style of vaginal imagery was not only an assertion of autonomous artistic identity. Vaginal forms confronted lingering formalist obsessions. The introduction of vaginas, nappies, tampons, family snapshots and related feminine 'unmentionables' in art certainly transgressed principles of aesthetic autonomy. In the terms of Greenbergian criticism, central core imagery epitomised a tactile, theatrical and thus 'impure' aesthetic. Few mainstream critics engaged with the physical aspect of central core in alternative art-historical terms, such as action painting, performance or self-portraiture. Feminist critics certainly avoided mainstream historical, stylistic and conceptual frameworks, and instead scanned the history of women's art for other telltale signs: enveloping or veiling forms, pastel colours, soft fabrics and other non-traditional media and other feminine tropes (Lucy Lippard's famous feminine aesthetics 'shopping list'). The aim in historicising feminist aesthetics was to invent an alternative art language, no less. Feminist artists and writers were simply not interested in traditional formal and art-historical frameworks.

They preferred to take an interdisciplinary (and at times problematic) social–historical approach to aesthetics.

In contrast to formalist aesthetic traditions, central core imagery illustrated women's ontological and epistemological difference in response to political demands for autonomy. Some photographs framed female sexuality as a self-enclosed, auto-erotic system, as in an unattributed pornographic shot used to punctuate a 1978 translation of Luce Irigaray's *This sex which is not one*.[9] Blurred and abstracted by their close proximity and rendered indistinct through a wash of soft, mid-grey tones, these vaginal lips testify to a perverse abstraction.

In other cases, the explicit sexual contents and aesthetic transgressions of central core imagery were undermined by traditional invocations of fecundity. Here the vagina was evoked as a sea-anemone, tree root, moss or cave, within pictorialist conventions. Ann Roberts' *Amazon acres* series in *Refractory Girl* (1975), whilst not strictly central core, depicted the first separatist commune in Australia as a feminine Arcady in this way.[10] 'Nature herself' assumed the shape and rhythms of the female body. A persistent strand of eco-feminist and anti-nuclear photography continues to associate a generalised, nurturant femininity with the earth, peace and Aboriginality. Spiral dancing, vaginal hand signs, humming and related motifs peppered photographic exhibitions of the mid-1980s Pine Gap and Cockburn Sound anti-nuclear campaigns. These and later imagery resuscitated nineteenth century feminist discourses on women as biologically destined for social and moral good, along with an equally problematical conflation of woman, nature and land rights.

The naked body as *tabula rasa*

Sydney-based artist Anne Graham was not alone in visualising the search for feminine autonomy as a performative *process*. Her work in Perth from 1983–4 fragmented and accentuated the body through clinical tableaux, documented performance work and serialised images of strenuous physical exercise. *Veneers II* arranged the cultural codes of femininity as layers constantly and anxiously adjusted in public.[11] In *No protective layers '84*, Graham performed this feminine masquerade as a general cultural condition. Photographic panels itemised an historical wardrobe of physical agony:

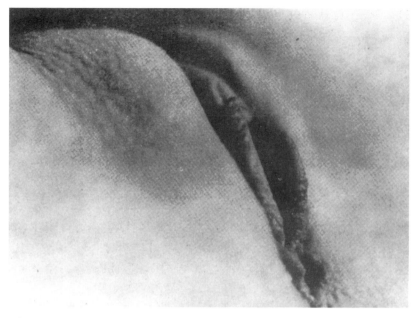

Unattributed photograph, reproduced in Paul Foss and Meaghan Morris (eds), *Language, Sexuality and Subversion*, Feral Publications, Sydney, 1978, p.160.

Ann Roberts, from the series *Amazon acres*, reproduced in *Refractory Girl*, No.8, March 1975, p.21.

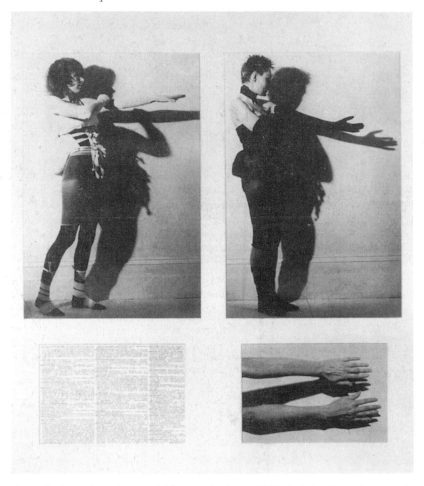

Anne Graham, from the panel *No protective layers*, 1984. Gelatin silver photograph. Collection of the artist.

corsets, gloves, crinolines, bustles, purdah. Graham and fellow performer Pam Lehman modelled these disciplinary items in an associated performance piece. From head to foot, the female body was marked, shaped and photographed with 'protective layers' of clothing. These foreclosed any unmediated physical contact with oneself, other bodies or the external world. In this schema of encirclement and passivity, women's sexual pleasure and self-knowledge were progressively denied. The effects of patriarchal ideology was thus recognised through what it refused: women's sexuality, self-expression, freedom and growth.

This conception of feminine socialisation was organised through the negative actions of social prohibition, censorship, and denial, grouped together as a central mechanism destined to say 'no'.[12] The performance of femininity as repressive layers presupposed a liberatory alternative, encouraging the spectator to metaphorically apply cleanser or 'break the mirror'. This gesture was mooted in a series of photographic screens in which the image of a naked woman progressively leapt from a bowed crouch to contest the framing edge. Here the feminine body tries to mark a break with the social completely. Women's experience, whether in a state of oppression or liberation, remains caught within a fixed framework of denial and difference. Feminine specificity is constituted as an eternal opposition of given values, and within the very codes that Graham sought to resist.

Sydney photographer Leslie Solar gave a related performance of the naked body in 1981.[13] She projected nude self-images on three light cotton sheets suspended from the ceiling (see colour section). The lightest breeze would ripple across the sheets, causing a temporary incoherence in the female form. The soft rippling gave the body a silky skin and a warm luminosity. Whilst these poetic codes belong to Romantic painterly traditions and soft-core pornography, Solar's frank nudity borrowed its truth and power from the medical chart or police mug shot. The latter techniques have historically been used to elicit anatomical, biological or psychological evidence of sexual difference. As Frank Mort has noted of photography's scientific applications:

> ...the history of such discourses... has been a history of the increasing attempt to fix the sexual positionality of individuals through the construction of a number of absolute courts of appeal—legal, medical, psychiatric etcetera. With this process, biological and anatomical constructions of sex and gender have achieved a powerful and sustained hegemony: they are the most difficult to combat in a politics of sexuality.[14]

Why have feminists based poetic affirmations of female nudity upon institutionally oppressive tools of biological and anatomical 'evidence'? Graham and Solar are not the only artists who have poeticised the naked female body in a metaphorical reversal of

Anne Graham, installation *Veneers II*, 1984. Freestanding photographic silk screens, wood frames. Collection of the artist.

inculcated stereotypes. Photographing the 'unadorned fact' of oneself naked was a common gesture of 'wiping the slate clean' in the 1970s and early 1980s. The pre-social state, as represented by the biological and anatomical female body, was privileged as both object and means of self-knowledge. It was seen to be a minimally coded area of human experience. The etho-poetic value given to frank, naked disclosures was largely based on the force of metaphor. As Denise Riley has argued, biology or anatomy is often assumed to be a 'literally underlying substance':

> so that if for instance you put a sliver of brain under a microscope you will see cells of tissues and blood—[which is] is also seen as a base, basic, primary. That is, biology is in some quasi-literal way closer to the bone it is therefore also ontologically prior. Just because it is underlying, it is therefore fundamental.[15]

Feminist campaigns for control over reproduction, health and sexual self-determination, however, have shown that biology *does* figure, but is never lived out in a pure form. Feminism has a stake in rejecting rigid delineations between a homogenised conception of social relations versus biological and psychical phenomena, for

'To remain continually aware that we are embodied need entail neither a fetishism of "the body" nor a dissolution into "the social"', as Riley has argued.[16]

Against the 'corporeal fetishism' of nude resistance and central core imagery, an equally dominant, although perhaps more debilitating tendency emphasised a diffuse, non-genital eroticism within a general romance of female companionship. This centre-piece of radical feminist culture prescribed the erotic parameters of women's physical, sexual and political conduct. The clearest manifestation of this culturalist strategy was the 1970s idea of a 'lesbian continuum'.

From the 'Lesbian continuum' to 'The politics of desire'

The lesbian continuum initially drew attention away from genitally based sexual pleasure. Female sexuality was reconceived as a baro-meter of sisterhood, and lesbianism as a state of being rather than a question of sexual activity.[17] The continuum embraced 'coming out'—speaking out about one's sexual identity—within a general affir-mation of sisterhood. What was its outcome? Did associated photo-graphic strategies consolidate or shift existing sexual definitions?

In the November 1971 issue of *Camp Ink*, four gay men from Brisbane came out by having their photographs printed on the cover. The subsequent issue parodied a police 'most wanted' list when gays and lesbians came out 'to wish readers a Merry Christ-mas'.[18] As a personal–political corollate of the fight for homo-sexual law reform, civil rights and community acceptance, coming out meant transforming self-doubt or self-hatred into self-acceptance and gay pride. A *Vashti* report on the first lesbian-feminist confer-ence (Victoria, 1973) evoked the discursive pleasures involved: 'Women together, women laughing, women in pain, women under the looking glass, women relating, women loving—glad to be women, glad to be gay!'[19] Coming out as a lesbian-feminist in the early 1970s did not, however, simply refer to genital preference, which put 'fucking first and excluded warm and real sisterhood which is non-genital. Gayness is a consciousness—knowing that we love our sisters'. Holiday snapshots from the Sorrento Radica-lesbian Weekend indicated how lesbianism could be reconceived as an emotional field.

An earlier image of lesbianism, as discreet private lives organised around genital sexual preference and monogamy, was seen to be politically regressive. As the Sorrento Radicalesbians argued:

> If we think monogamy and the nuclear family are oppressive
> institutions, it is necessary to understand why they are so hard
> to get rid of in our own relationships. For some of us at the
> conference, the primacy given to genital sexuality provided the
> key to this understanding.

New coordinates for female sexuality were organised along a continuum which took heterosexual penetration and its butch-fem lesbian echo as points of departure. Non-genital auto-eroticism, radical celibacy and a romantic yet asexual comradeship replaced the old image of the heterosexual and lesbian couple. Sexual preference, sexual identity and feminism were conflated, so that 'ultimately the very notion of "lesbian" disappeared in a general affirmation of "woman"'.[20] The ideologically sound image of passionate comradeship led to a plethora of fairly conventional snapshots, such as the one used to illustrate Sevgi Kilic's reminiscences of coming out, reproduced in a 1981 issue of *Vashti*.[21] Sevgi, tidying up her bedroom, comes across an old photograph. 'My heart gave a little skip... Cavide! I said her name out loud as the memory of that hot summer day came back into my mind.' A closely cropped snapshot (the one accidentally found?) visualised coming out in the conventional genre of the holiday romance:

> One day I decided to go for a long walk and sort things out. By
> the time I got home I had decided that I was a lesbian ... It was
> a question of accepting and becoming comfortable with feelings
> that I had always had ... Cavide and I had learned a lot. We are
> both more experienced lesbians and are still searching for our
> identity as women and as lesbians.

Kilic's story and snapshot mirrored the genre of heterosexual romantic fiction, and as such Wilson observed, with some exasperation:

> The theme is the familiar one of self-discovery, of the searching
> for a lifestyle that will embody the heroine's dreams. Lesbianism
> as destiny, lesbianism as alternative lifestyle, lesbianism as
> enactment of sexual liberation: why are these themes so
> unsatisfactory?

Unattributed photographs, reproduced on the front cover of *Camp Ink*, December 1971.

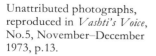

Unattributed photographs, reproduced in *Vashti's Voice*, No.5, November–December 1973, p.13.

That was a Long Time Ago

I want to write an experience about a lesbian relationship. A woman who changed my life. I want to write about moments I regard as gifts — good moments and bad moments.

I was tidying my bedroom when something fell from my hankie-box and fluttered to the floor. Thinking it was a piece of paper, I picked it up to throw it away. Then, realising it was a photograph, I turned it over and as I saw who was on the other side my heart gave a little skip... Cavide! I said her name out loud as the memory of that hot summer day came back into my mind. And suddenly a hundred other memories were there too — of the way we'd met, so very long ago now...

I'd gone to the park to sunbathe, but it was so hot that after a few minutes I'd fallen asleep. I'd probably have slept all afternoon, if a big dog hadn't suddenly decided it was time I woke up and licked my face...

I started to yell at it, then it's owner was by my side apologising to me. And there was something in her smile that set me heart skipping so I couldn't stay angry. 'My name's Cavide', she said as she sat down beside me throwing a ball into the distance for the dog to chase.

We no longer wanted to kid ourselves about our mental and sexual feelings for each other. We wanted to come out of the cupboard and live our beautiful lesbian lives, full of caring and understanding for each other.

Unattributed and untitled photograph (Sevgi Kilic?), reproduced in
Vashti's Voice, No.29, Autumn 1981, p.2.

Sevgi's camera captured the 'decisive moment' of realisation of a difficult truth of personal identity. This was framed as a question of sexuality, and the realisation and proclamation of this truth enabled important lifestyle changes. These involved new modes of individuating oneself and others.[22]

The history of these photographic true confessions can be located within an exhaustive range of discourse and behaviour associated with the confessional, 'the first technique for producing the truth of sex', as Foucault observed. The consciousness-raising group, the lesbian-feminist snapshot, the love story or magazine cover provided instances of self-regulated confession. Cavide, Sevgi and the Sorrento Radicalesbians place the no-longer-troubling truth of their lesbian identity in a complex discursive framework.

These snapshots have a second line of genealogical development, of administrative, scientific, legal and literary classifications which have constructed the category 'homosexual' as a pathological personality type.[23] The lesbian coteries in the late nineteenth and early twentieth centuries—those that have been researched in any detail, that is—were more discreetly upper class and literary than their male counterparts. The growing number of professional

women in the 1920s housed, for the first time, the possible subcultural articulation of lesbian identity. This provided the context
for a number of highly publicised literary scandals, culminating
in the banning of Radclyffe Hall's *The well of loneliness* in 1928. It
was largely through these events that lesbianism became an issue
of social concern, and the medical conception of the lesbian as a
'tormented invert' coloured both literary and popular conceptions.

The theory of inversion drew upon eugenicist doctrines, and
was given an added political imperative in the repression of homo-
sexuals in Nazi-occupied Europe and Stalinist Russia. However,
as Aldrich, Berube and others note, during the war, single sex
military institutions provided relative freedom of association for
homosexual men and women. Those American servicemen and
women who received the 'blue discharges', for instance, formed
the first wave of gay veterans seeking refuge in the larger cities.
These groups patronised the first exclusively gay and lesbian bars.[24]

The Homosexual Law Reform Society formed in Canberra in
1969, and the Melbourne Chapter of the Daughters of Bilitis (later
known as the Australasian Lesbian Movement), came together in
the following year. These organisations retained the (medical)
conception of self-definition through erotic life. These discreet
support groups, with their 'odd mixture of courage and apology'
aimed to help individual adjustment, the encouragement of responsible research and the investigation of penal codes relating to
homosexuality.[25] This 'sensible' public image and closeted social
network was later replaced by the politics of gay pride and lesbian-
feminism. In this shift, lesbian-feminist ideology curiously retained
both the deviant status of the medical model and the asexual
assumptions of its Victorian precursors.

Photographs by Pat Fiske and Ann Roberts romanticise this
history in a 1975 issue of *Cauldron*.[26] Photographs show a 'coven'
of Sydney Women's Liberationists in witches' hats, stirring the
magazine's namesake cauldron. A discreetly erotic Edwardian postcard and a demonstration photograph of sisters in arms complete
the picture. This 'unchanging heart' account of the lesbian continuum celebrates 'the history of women who—as witches, *femmes
seules*, marriage resisters, spinsters, autonomous widows, and/or
lesbians—have managed on varying levels not to collaborate'.[27]
From the hidden garden to the main street, relations between
women were subtlely de-eroticised. The lesbian continuum echoed
discourses on bourgeois female sexuality which predated the

construction of the lesbian as a distinct personality or 'condition' in the early twentieth century. This allowed for a 'pre-lesbian' discourse of asexual though passionate female bonding, an ideal of companionship which replayed dominant assumptions about female asexuality.

This prescriptive sexual ethics had its critics. Many lesbians felt that lesbian-feminism had unnecessarily reiterated anachronistic 'social purity' conceptions of lust, power and sex as being masculine, as against a natural, 'loving and caring' female sexuality. It also avoided issues of class. In 1982, Ardhill and Neumark argued that the consolidation of lesbian-feminist ideology within Women's Liberation had 'occurred in conjunction with working-class dykes having to clean up their acts in order to be accepted as feminists (the "out of the bars and into the CR groups" syndrome)'.[28] While critical focus had been given to masculine behaviour and attitudes, the position of bourgeois femininity and social purity, from which these criticisms were made, had been left unexamined. Lesbians were claiming a central place within Women's Liberation throughout the 1970s, but they met with resistance within the movement to the implications of lesbian sexual activity.

In the early 1980s these complaints crossed paths with the long-simmering pornography debate. Feminist arguments over pornography had moved away from their origins in anti-rape campaigns. Calls were made for the outright censorship of pornography, along with the denunciation of sexist imagery from *Women's Weekly* to *Penthouse*. The fact that many women also enjoyed looking at these pictures remained an unexplored complication, however. Distinctions between sexist and sexual contents in pornography were sometimes blurred, and anyway, feminists needed to account for the complex pleasure and power of objectifying images. Discussions around pornography soon broadened to examine the psycho-social mechanisms of signification. Female sexual fantasy and the issue of 'ideologically unsound' images and pleasures were confronted.

Concurrently, punk subcultural styles had promoted non-stereotyped rationales for wearing sexually provocative clothing. Many younger lesbians and feminists had become alienated from the sartorial and behavioural norms of lesbian-feminism. At the same time, many older lesbians were also finding themselves 'inadvertently inching further and further from the party line when our experiences in bed bore less and less resemblance to the depiction of ourselves out of it'.[29]

Jay Morris, *Theatre of life*, reproduced in *Wicked Women*, Sydney, n.d., p.17 (model: Natalie).

Jay Morris, *Theatre of life*,
reproduced in *Wicked Women*,
Sydney, n.d., p.18 (model:
Natalie).

The 'politics of desire' in the early 1980s gave feminism, gay and lesbian politics common ground. Challenges were mounted against the 'unchanging heart' ethos of gay historiography and the lesbian continuum. The assumption of an essential link between sexuality and personal identity was questioned. The idea that one 'is' a homosexual in some fundamental way was criticised for narrowing sexual possibilities, and lesbianism was consequently reconceived as a framework for pleasurable choices. The sanitised image of female comradeship in feminist art and fiction was replaced by explorations of female desire and the unconscious.

Lesbian sado-masochism formed a controversial element in this expanded debate. 'Putting the sex back into lesbianism' became a particularly contentious issue in the debates surrounding the Australian release of the American s&m anthology, *Coming to power*.[30] Some argued that photographs in the book, like those reproduced in later Australian s&m magazines such as *Wicked Women*, could provide useful insights into feminine sexual fantasy. They provided evidence of a theatrical and consensual structuring of romance and cruelty. Indeed, Ardhill and Neumark argued that looking at s&m photographs was akin to the dynamic of the s&m fantasy itself, in dramatising and eroticising a situation which may appear to be superficially neutral.[31]

Lesbian photography soon departed from poetic realism and coy snapshots. Increasingly, subcultural strategies of 'radical drag' appropriated and complicated masculine and feminine codes. For instance Melbourne photographer Glenda Gerrard's *Curles & Curves* (1980) reformulated 1950s women's magazine icons, art historical erotica and the feminine pleasures and fantasies of shopping and pulp romance (see colour section). Other areas of appropriation have included earlier lesbian imagery, Country and Western, science fiction, motorcycle culture and Mills & Boon. Lesbian drag flirts with the historical discourse of homosexual inversion, while seeking to fragment and replace the debilitating category of the homosexual. The aim is:

> [to] recreate a certain style of existence, a form of existence or art of living, which might be called gay. It is possible that changes in established routines will occur on a much broader scale as gays learn to express their feeling for one another in more various ways and develop new lifestyles not resembling those that have been institutionalised.[32]

Lesbian drag spearheaded a feminist aesthetic trend towards irony, faked femininity and the 'failure' of sexual identity. Surface gloss not central core, fraudulence not authenticity, and the unknown field of female fetishism reversed earlier feminist strategies which had sought to realise the female body as a natural and wholistic field of experience.

This shift acknowledged that points of corporeal resistance, affirmation and identity were necessarily formulated within a field of power relations. The following discussion observes a decade of more strategic and piecemeal explorations of sexual differentiation.

5   Female desire and feminine tutelage

On the art photography circuit from the mid-1970s to the mid-1980s, hammed photo-documentary and directorial techniques cleverly 'mispronounced' the photographic punctuation of feminine lives. This bungled theatre of feminine tutelage revealed the micro-dynamics of feminine subjectivity, in rituals of dress, birthdays, games, boyfriends, engagements, weddings. Here was no simple tale of false consciousness and true paths. Our guide was no longer Judy Chicago's call for female integration, but the deft savagery of a Hannah Hoch. Feminist art adopted what could be called the logic of collage, piecing together a disconcerting feminine subjectivity from alien forms. The spectator was now considered an active participant in textual possibilities of ironic reversal, excess and rupture.

The theatre of feminine tutelage

One example of this cultural assemblage was Melbourne photographer Carolyn Lewens' 1981 to 1983 chronicle of little girls at play.[1] In an expanse of flouncy, ribboned fabric, these girls relentlessly enacted the constraints of feminine cuteness. The alarm of the freeze-frame fabricated early rehearsals for a lifetime of party frocks, hampered movement and delicate behaviour. Signalling a departure from photo-documentary objectivity in favour of the declared participation in a theatrical performance, Lewens' episodic framing suggested continuity and a limited repertoire of characters and plot reruns, in games of 'going out', 'mothers', or 'shopping' —the seamless, classic narrative of female conditioning. Feminine socialisation was reconceived as a pantomime which fragmented sexual identity into a discontinuous series of unstable, spectacular arrangements.

Carolyn Lewens, untitled gelatin silver photographs, reproduced in
LIP, 1981/82, p.29.

Photo-performances like these visualised femininity as a life-time's textual production. Nanette Carter's 1981 *Puberty threat* follows the little girl's progress in our feminine narrative.[2] Menstruation has been associated in our culture with shame and the demand for modesty, traceable through the high store set in our society on the ability to control bodily waste and fluids:

> ... that the flow of blood would have profound psychical
> significance for [the pubertal girl] is clear and that this
> significance would centre around ideas of castration, sexual
> attack and socially reinforced shame is highly probable. The
> female's first act of coitus would probably also bear on this.[3]

Puberty threat illustrated these social anxieties through a mock ethnographic study of an imaginary puberty rite. Carter's celebratory tableau delivered a grim possibility: a little girl offered up to a bleak future in a frilled bassinet. In strict central core formation, the little girl is ringed by a menace of tampons arranged as a supermarket 'vagina dentata'. Aesthetic and social codes of innocence and maternity (the threshold of womanhood) are undercut by corporeal malevolence. The simulated shame of an unspoken sexuality and a perceived lack of bodily control echoed cultural discourses on the female body as an unknowable threat requiring punishment or banishment. Frilled tulle and sprinkled confetti claim Carter's menstrual cycle as a domestic treadmill. In this context, mock hysteria seems an appropriate response to the point where biological and cultural experience join in a web of oppressive cultural significations.

In contrast to earlier calls for positive imagery, the female body in this strand of work dutifully elaborates masochistic exercises for the camera. In each case, however, something goes a little askew. This off-key performance of cloying compliance remained characteristic of work throughout the 1980s. Instead of rejecting feminine stereotypes, the game of over-identification followed the antics of an exhaustive cast of feminine characters, and a sense of claustrophobic closeness pervades each episode.

In the dictionary sense, the pantomime dame has dubious, even pathological origins. According to the *Shorter Oxford*, she is one 'addicted to or having an aptitude for mimicry', who is 'histrionic; hence, hypocritical' and who dissembles 'as by painting'. Later in the decade, artists like Robyn Stacey, Julie Brown-Rrap, Sandy Edwards and Anne Ferran skilfully made use of these

Nanette Carter, *Puberty threat*, 1981. Gelatin silver photograph, 25 × 30 cms.
Collection of the artist.

hysterical 'symptoms' as metaphors of feminine style. Earlier on, however, the operation took place on Dr Frankenstein's slab and not Dr Freud's couch. The feminine tableaux reviewed here form the swift cut-and-paste jobs of the collagist and not the textual layering of resemblance and simulation, 'as by painting'.

Robyn Stacey's untitled punkette (1982) was an early representative of feminine collage (see colour section).[4] Her mix-'n'-match generic Girl was fashioned as a ready-to-wear multiple choice. Articles of femininity were adorned like clothing in an interminable game of substitution. They say that clothes make the man; but what of the ease with which woman slips in and out of her feminine garb? Claiming no reality behind the image, absence and representation supplant illusion and simulation. Stacey reconsidered connections between femininity and the visual as a field of

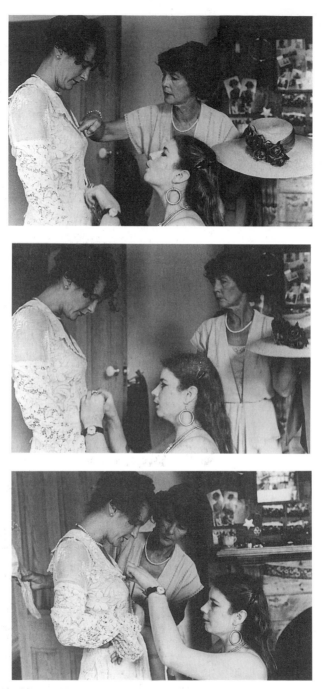

Ruth Maddison, detail from the series *When a girl marries*, 1979. Gelatin silver photographs, 3 of 32 with colour dyes and pencil, 16.5 × 24 cms. Collection: National Gallery of Australia, Canberra.

Marie McMahon, installation, *Experiments in vitreous enamels*, George Paton and Ewing Galleries, 1976.

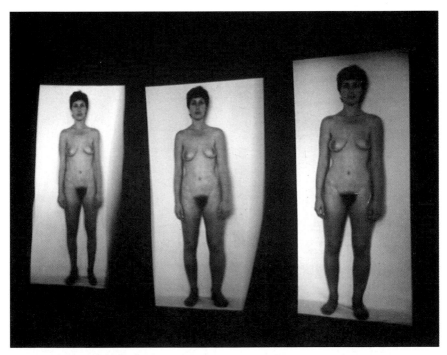

Leslie Solar, untitled installation, Sydney, 1981. Slide projection on cotton sheeting. Collection of the artist.

Robyn Stacey, untitled, 1982. Hand-tinted photographs on hinged panels, 6 × 4',
exhibited in *The Panel Show*, Australian Centre for Photography as part of the
NSW Women and the Arts Festival (curator: Leslie Solar).

Suzi Coyle, from the series *Imaging*, 1986. Cibachrome print, 37.5 × 47.5 cms.
Collection of the artist.

Julie Brown-Rrap, *Philosophies of the boudoir—Justine/Juliette*, from *Thief's Journal*, 1985. One of two panels: photo-emulsion, acrylic and oil on canvas on three-ply, 6 × 4'. Private collection.

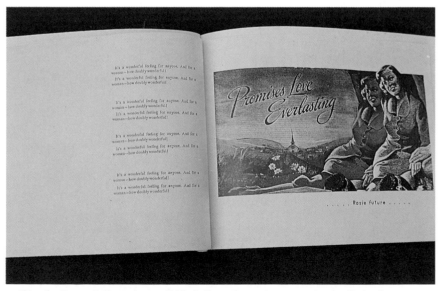

Glenda Gerrard, *Rosie future*, 1980. Collage from the artist's book, *Curles & Curves*. Collection of the artist.

Laleen Jayamanne, installation, *The holey family*, in *Mothers' memories, others' memories*, University of New South Wales, Sydney, 1979.

Tracey Moffatt, *Untitled*, from the *Something more* series, cibachrome print, 1989,
90 × 150 cms.

Jay Younger, *Anxiety as style, 'Nice blue version': 'Noisrev eulb ecin'*
Elyts sa yteixna 1 (between delusions), 1989. Cibachrome, 105 × 119 cms.

Julie Brown-Rrap, *Puberty*, from the installation *Persona and shadow*, 1984. Direct positive colour photograph 193.6 × 104.9 cms. Kodak (Australasia) Pty. Ltd. Fund, 1983, Australian National Gallery.

Janet Burchill and Jennifer McCamley, detail from the installation *Temptation to exist (untitled)*, Australian Centre for Photography, 1986. Three type-C photographs dry-mounted and laminated on aluminium sheeting, 225 × 225 cms.

Janet Burchill and Jennifer McCamley, *Temptation to exist (Tippi)*, 1986. Two type-C photographs dry-mounted and laminated on aluminium sheeting, 50.5 × 76 cms. Private collection.

Refractory Girl

A WOMEN'S STUDIES JOURNAL   NO. 8   MARCH 1975

We are suggesting that women artists have used the central cavity which defines them as women as the framework for an imagery which allows for the complete reversal of the way in which women are seen by the culture. That is to be a woman is to be an object of contempt, and the vagina, stamp of femaleness, is devalued. The woman artist seeing herself as loathed takes that very hallmark of her otherness and by asserting it as the hallmark of her iconography, establishes a vehicle by which to state the truth and beauty of her identity.

WOMEN IN THE VISUAL ARTS

Refractory Girl cover, March 1975. Photo by Pat Fiske; design by Beverley Garlick.

signs, a theatre of representation. The ironic play with powerful aesthetic effects drew feminist artwork further from content analyses and realist prescriptions which were still dogging other areas of cultural politics.

Techniques of print manipulation, hand-colouring, serial work and related strategies of de-naturalisation were used to highlight the sexual saturation of the female body as a textual production. The female body was seen to be literally shaped, inscribed and channelled along a healthy and (re)productive course. Ruth Maddison's *When a girl marries* (1979) transformed a friend's wedding album into one such spectacle of feminine fabrication.[5] The social graces of wedding photography were thrown to the wind as the bride's Big Day turned into a serialised pantomime of pleasure and power. The passage from bride-to-be to wife has never looked so uncomfortable. Wedding day ablutions and the ritual drama of putting on the gown were stylised through the slow, anticipatory pacing of sequential images, lending an expectancy to arbitrary gestures. The reduction of that special event into a conventional narrative progression from a point of stasis (single woman), disequilibrium (bride-to-be), climax (bride) and resolution (wife) suggested an uncomfortably tight 'shooting schedule'. The entrance of the bridegroom (climax of the story) effected the transition from a feminine orbit of preparatory 'dressing-up' to a male-centred visual field. Ironic technical 'failures' and deviations from conventional wedding photography (high contrast film, arbitrary framing, harsh lighting) presented the bride's social and visual objectification as if it were a clumsy television soapie.

Ann Balla's *Bedrooms* (1978) investigated the wedding's consummation and aftermath, revealing a startling development in this heterosexual economy.[6] *Bedrooms* focused on the intensification and displacement of female sexuality within the conjugal relation. Balla's foil was the intrusive 'human interest' of pop sexology. Balla masqueraded as Shere Hite to tabulate the erotic life of her subculture: white, middle-class couples in their late thirties.

In the movement from wedding to the master bedroom, the sexual promise of the bride's body is curiously displaced onto a wealth of conjugal commodities. Balla photographs women's sexual disenfranchisement as a bedroom farce. The wife literally fades from view as the décor is invested with the renewed chain of masculine desire. An hysterical proliferation of feminine stand-ins (presumably purchased by the wife herself) form an index to the

Anne Balla, from the series *Bedrooms*, 1978. Gelatin silver photograph.
Collection of the artist.

Anne Balla, from the series *Bedrooms*, 1978. Gelatin silver photograph.
Collection of the artist.

liberal realm of masculine fantasy that constitutes 'the privacy of one's own home'.

A motif of masculine ignorance seals the complicit exchange of 'powder room' philosophy between imaginary female protagonists. In one print, the husband serves as ventriloquist's dummy, ostensibly reading a children's sex education book, *What is happening to me?* He is infantalised within a tight photographic family circle of mother and sons. The wife's disappearance also lays claim to the cry of 'What is happening to me?', as the puzzle of sexual identity doubles as Betty Friedan's 'problem with no name', in a grim joke of suburban despair.

From bassinet to nuptial bed, a serialised rerun of hysterical pleasures and options suggests the black, 'bitter and twisted' characterisation that has dogged feminist sight gags and sexual jokes. A complex relation between the (blurred, excessive) non-identity of the performer and the decorative echo of her characters adds a sour ingredient to feminine pantomime. She conceals this non-identity in a surfeit of textual trickery.

Stylish play with seductive feminine scenarios has thus provided a rich game with endless permutations. Our pleasures have been elaborated and complicated by alienating twists which mime the failure of the female figure to become a fully realised subject to impossible disjunctions between competing feminine representations. Like verbal puns, these sight gags turned upon a sickening familiarity of gestures, objects and images. Intertextual confusions, doublings, displacements and other joke techniques complicated already parodic feminine forms. Feminist aesthetics now sought to undo the sexual fix which organised femininity as a form of sexual indifference—that is, as complement, lack or opposition to a masculine standard.

The girl in the mirror

In the 1980s the question of sexual difference was given added impetus with the impact of semiotic and psychoanalytic theories. Earlier materialist and structural analyses of the mass media from the 1970s had already gained some ground in the area. Melbourne WAF member Virginia Coventry's *Miss World televised 1974* was one such project, calling into question the assumed naturalism of television and photographic codes.[7] The ritual crowning of Miss World was fragmented and serialised in eight sequential

Virginia Coventry, from the
series *Miss World televised 1974.*
Gelatin silver photograph, 15.2
× 13.2 cms. Private collection.

freeze-frames, progressively closing in on a televisual grotesquerie.
The final, disintegrating close-up unhinged Miss World's smile and
censored her vision. The idea of woman as object (but not subject)
of the media gaze was thus initially registered and destabilised by
foregrounding the material grain of the medium itself.

In the same period, Sydney WAM members Jude Adams and
Sandy Edwards investigated the codes and conventions of fashion
imagery. This work culminated in a 1979 joint exhibition, *Fashion
images*, which essayed the pleasures women themselves felt in looking and being looked at.[8] Mock magazine spread-sheets graphically
constructed the field of vision as one of desire, corollating the
desire of the female spectator with an obsessive plethora of feminine codes. This narcissistic structure, they argued, was regulated
and exploited by commercial interests. At this stage, both Adams
and Edwards lacked the conceptual tools with which to account
for these psychic mechanisms, beyond the simple orchestration of
powerful feminine 'special effects'.

The regressive identificatory structure of fashion photography was perhaps most explicitly elaborated in panels and text by Jude Adams:

> By utilising the tools of (a) psychoanalysis (for an understanding of how we are made feminine in a patriarchal society), and (b) the decoding of advertising images (so we can begin to recognise the unfulfilled, often suppressed desires that advertising capitalises on), we will have a clearer understanding of how femininity is maintained and constructed within a patriarchal society.

Scattered advertising images and handwritten commentary chronicled the socialisation of female desire. Simplified psycho-analytic terms were applied to a set of feminine stereotypes. By juxtaposing family snapshots with fashion imagery, Adams held that there was no personal space that could be claimed outside existing cultural frameworks. Even the most casual or intimate pose that women could assume had already been colonised by a Guy Bourdin or Richard Avedon.

These early analyses of female spectatorship formed an im-portant transition from models of repression and false conscious-ness. Sexual difference was seen to be continually reproduced and renegotiated. The ideology of photographic transparency was itself challenged for connoting a world in which social and sexual relations appeared natural and immutable. In criticising photo-graphic realism, Edwards and Adams challenged the effacement of the material and psychic processes by which sense was constructed.

Film theorists had observed how the realist codes of classical Hollywood cinema (and by historical association, photographic realism) were organised around the laws of Renaissance perspect-ive. These framing devices produced a particular subject position and point of view (in particular the privileged illusion of total command). Analysis of the photographic, cinematic and psychic apparatus thus provided the basis for a materialist textual politics:

> This setting-into-place of the subject is simultaneously secured through the harnessing of sexual drives and their forms of gratification (fetishism, voyeurism, identificatory processes, pleasure in recognition and repetition). The breaking of these circuits, these processes of coherence that help secure the subject to and in ideology, becomes a central task for artists ... [9]

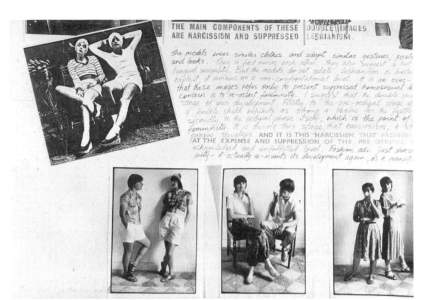

Jude Adams, detail from untitled panel, 1976. Collage of photographs and magazine imagery, with text. Collection of the artist.

Jude Adams, detail from untitled panel, 1976. Collage of photographs and magazine imagery with text. Collection of the artist.

Joy Stevens, *Untitled*, 1982. Gelatin silver photograph and red crayon. Reproduced in *Graduating photography*, Australian Centre for Photography, Sydney, 1982, p.7.

Women's studies courses in the art schools took up issues of representation, desire and sexual difference as a necessary focus for feminist art practice. An untitled montage by Joy Stevens (Sydney College of the Arts, 1982) ripped and defaced a Hollywood glamour portrait to elicit and then break its scopophilic circuitry.[10] Stevens gridded this circuitous visual field as a military manoeuvre, in which the movie star's vision was commandeered by the cameraman. The lower centre frame was similarly dominated by an instructional image reproduced from a camera manual. The camera pointed down the woman's off-screen body under the ambiguous technical commands of 'advance', 'focus' and 'shoot'.

Fellow Sydney College of the Arts graduate Anne Zahalka also examined the production of sexual difference in glamour images.[11] Her large panel, *And the winner is…*(1985) gridded up assorted movie and television stills as a mock 'photo-romance'. Contests of power (the Western showdown, Epic Theatre, gladiator combat) were jostled with contests of beauty (the melodramatic love triangle, the digital rating system of the Miss World Pageant). While these subtitled dialogues and images were interchangeable, their sexual character types and plot remained fixed.

Sandy Edwards, *An alternative ending*, 1981. Panel of two gelatin silver photographs, each 25 × 30 cms. Collection of the artist.

Anne Zahalka, *Seeing double*, 1985. Photo-emulsion on glass. Collection of the artist.

Companion pieces *Framed* and *Seeing double* made direct reference to the work of photographer and writer Victor Burgin.[12] *Framed* gave a simple, literal demonstration of sexual differentiation in the photographer's studio by reproducing techniques from an old Rolliflex manual on glamour portraiture. In *Seeing double*, Zahalka photo-stencilled an advertising image of feminine perfection onto a mirror, so that the spectator literally saw herself 'doubled'. This idealisation, Zahalka argued, epitomised the mass media restaging of a primary (mis)recognition of the self. The mass media template for feminine subject formation structured narcissistic and regressive pseudo-identifications.[13]

Under the impact of feminist film theory, serial work on the fragmentation and manipulation of cinematic narratives and advertising images became common. Sandy Edwards had already been working in this way for a number of years through her association with Jude Adams and Blatant Image. Edwards' work from 1981–83 investigated the narrative structures of 'classical' Hollywood cinema. *Towards something else: Ida Lupino finds strength in solitude* and *An alternative ending* (1981) isolated and reassembled sequential film stills to form improbable character variations and narrative solutions.

Edwards' concern with femininity, visual pleasure and narrative structure culminated in 1983 with the project titled *A narrative with sexual overtones*.[14] Edwards filled an index card container with postcard 'pages' to recount stories on sexual differentiation and the mass media. This compact epic reproduced the imagery of skilled fashion photographers such as Harri Peccinotti, Alice Springs, Helmut Newton and Richard Avedon, along with the melodramatic glamour of the *film noir* heroine. The story was divided into eight chapters which traversed an imaginary female body from head to toe. While the pleasures of looking at images of women require the reassurance of a 'whole' body, Edwards' bionic woman was stitched up as a bundle of fetishised parts.

The relation of female pleasure and fetishism is both complex and largely unexamined in traditional psychoanalytic theory. Edwards' project put forward the view that women's visual pleasure oscillated between a complementary exhibitionism and narcissism, along with a collusive identification with the masculine viewpoint: in other words, the dubious pleasure of female transvestism.

This ambivalent schema was further complicated by the contradictory voices of imaginary narrators. The assault of a misogynist

She gives the matter some cool collected thought   87

And commands him to keep his...   88

HANDS   89

Sandy Edwards, pages from the artist's book, *A narrative with sexual overtones*, 1983. Laminated gelatin silver prints, each 15 × 11 cms. Collection of the artist.

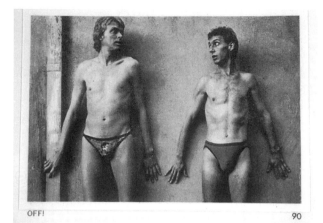

OFF! 90

BANG 91

BANG 92

voice written in italic capitals (for example 'SLUT'; 'SHOW A BIT OF LEG LOVE') was interspersed with the double messages of advertising ('WHY DON'T WE DO THIS MORE OFTEN?') and the voice of parental instruction ('HER MOTHER ALWAYS SAID, "PUT ON A CLEAN PAIR OF UNDIES, DEAR, IN CASE YOU ARE CAUGHT IN AN ACCIDENT"'). An imaginary female voice-over (third person singular and lower-case typeface) formed a preferred identification for the reader. ('She gives the matter some cool collected thought.')

Visual rhymes and puns gave an amusing, catechistic inflection to the story of the body, and the collisions between image and text disrupted anticipated sequencing. While the feminist voice-over gave added pleasure in coherence and control over the text/body, it did not claim a space of resolution and truth external to its articulation. Rather, the use of the third person ('she') fictionalised a compound character (storyteller, protagonist and spectator) in the investigative/voyeuristic structure of the story itself. She provided no direct answers, however, only the evasive, mocking laughter and murderous duplicity of the *film noir* heroine. The secret of media femininity remained an unresolved, masculine problem.

Along with the photographic blur, the metaphoric 'power of woman's laughter' (or sexual pleasure) became a dominant feature of feminist photography through the later 1980s. In both cases, the feminine body was reclaimed as a point of representational excess. This strand of work is elaborated in the following chapters.

One immediate outcome of psychoanalytic models was the construction of images of a frigid and fraudulent femininity, through dressing photography in clothes borrowed from theatrical, cinematic and painterly sources. Photographic transvestism spawned a knife-edged game of 'dare' that became more sophisticated as the decade progressed.

The influence of feminist cinema studies, art history and philosophy increasingly diverted attention from the home to the museum as a site for cultural intervention. Interest in women's work, child care and domestic contradictions waned as 1980s obsessions with history, aesthetics and commodity markets gained mainstream visibility. Pleasure and power were plotted according to philosophical and art-historical tropes rather than contemporary political debate. The 'clean up', or aesthetic sublimation, of the sexual difference question had begun.

6 'Faking it': Feminine fraudulence

The strategy of photographic bluff or masquerade introduced by photographers like Sandy Edwards drew upon psychoanalysis to recover a feminine subjectivity 'out of synch' with the mythic and normative feminine stereotype. The promotion of psychical fragmentation differed from earlier feminist projects which had urged women to find a cultural and political voice through bringing together the disassociated components of their lives in an aesthetic programme of self-realisation. Later analyses of sexual differentiation took the opposite tack, emphasising the instability of gender positioning and the impossibility of 'recovering' an authentic feminine voice. Paradoxically, these difficulties were explored through feminine strategies of hyper-passivity and over-compliance. In this schema, woman could only represent herself as a subject of desire through recourse to hysterical identification with 'masculine' pleasures of voyeurism and exhibitionism.

The dilemma of representation and woman's pleasure had been raised in late 1970s debates concerning pornography, punk and lesbian politics. This was the hybrid context in which Sydney photographer Robyn Stacey developed her retro-pop imagery. Like many others whose work gained a high visibility in gallery and museum shows in the early 1980s, Stacey had little contact with the Women's Art Movements. Her hand-coloured and cibachrome prints and postcards were instead schooled in the post-punk aesthetics of the 'second degree'.[1]

Images from later work, *Kiss kiss bang bang* (1987) and *Redline 7000* (1989) extended this aesthetic to flirt with the binary logic of sexual difference, as constituted in low-brow popular cultural imagery. Stacey's fetishised 'woman-effects' employed all the traditional feminine artifices: enigma, affect, masquerade. If in popular culture woman has existed too much as signifier, then Stacey deliberately

111

Robyn Stacey, *Kiss Kiss Bang Bang*, 1987. Gelatin silver photograph with colour
dyes, 50.8 × 65 cms. Private collection.

exacerbated this sexualisation. From the (prone) position of the
pulp fiction cover-girl, these models turned on their own history
with the ironic cry of 'Sex you have said we are, sex we will be'.[2]
Like others before her, Stacey's imagery argued that it was impossible to represent femininity outside traditional idioms. She instead
inverted the Freudian question: what does woman want? Her
answer to the question of male desire (what does man want?) was
drawn from the pages of Hammett, Chandler and Carter Brown.
The response, of course, was 'total womanhood'.

Writers such as Gayatri Chakrovorty Spivak have cautioned
against the simple application of such strategies, arguing that texts
which mirror masculine discourses on femininity should not be
conceived in isolation from substantive *her*storical research.[3] Yet
Stacey's icons are already history, so to speak. They have a still
perfection that can only be found in the city morgue. High-key

passion has never felt so chilly and composed. Stacey displays her exquisite corpses *in extremis*, turning the pleasures of being looked at into an act of mock aggression. A familiar theme in radical drag, these retro-beauties turn on a sado-masochistic matrix, the taunting display of the vamp and 'don't touch' ice queen. They recalled the subversive gesture of 'striking a pose/posing a threat' that Dick Hebdige celebrated in punk girls:

> ... playing with themselves in public, puncturing, distending, parodying the conventional iconography of fallen womanhood ... In punk, girls played with the forbidden iconographies of menstruation and female desire.[4]

Kiss kiss bang bang and *Redline 7000* avoided Hebdige's subcultural romance with punk girls. For a start, Hebdige did not foresee how easily the youth market could reappropriate both the gestural style of punk and the semiotic insights of feminist texts.[5] Stacey is well-aware of contemporary retro-styling. She historicises the sexual ambivalence and aggressive glamour of the bad girl through appropriating the codes of an anachronistic studio genre. Poised as *rigor mortis*, femininity is laid out on the chilly slab of style. Stacey staged the threat of 'total womanhood' as a campy, necrophilic romp. In the contemporary art, fashion and design world in which these images circulate, the once-dominant, threatening discourse of the *femme fatale* is rerun and enjoyed, without the anxiety. It was as if Stacey and her models did not really believe in the thrill, threat or truth of their own subject(ion)—only the style. Derrida has observed this elegant play with feminine seduction:

> ... woman needs the effect of castration, for without it she would neither know how to seduce nor to stir desire—but evidently she does not believe in it. 'Woman' is this; she does not believe in it, but she plays with it. Plays with: with a new concept or a new structure of belief that points to laughter.[6]

What was this structure of belief that pointed to laughter? Playing the tease, feminist projects from the 1980s masked an intellectual impertinence. This strategy can be traced through Joan Riviere's psychoanalytic thesis of female masquerade as a form of compensation for the (intellectual) woman's 'theft' of masculinity:

Womanliness ... could be assumed and worn as a mask, both to hide possession of masculinity and to avert the reprisals expected if she was found to possess it—much as a thief will turn out his pockets and ask to be searched to prove that he has not the stolen goods.[7]

The idea of feminine masquerade as a form of compensation was reformulated by Lacan, for whom masquerade constituted the very nature of woman's relation to the phallic term. What was compensated was not women's theft of masculinity, Lacan argued, but its very lack, organised in reference to a masculine sign:

> ... it is in order to be the phallus, that is to say, the signifier of desire of the other, that the woman will reject an essential part of her femininity, notably all its attributes, through masquerade. It is for what she is not that she expects to be desired as well as loved.[8]

In being the phallus for the other, woman actively poses in the passive mode, becomes a feminine picture of herself. In the Lacanian view, masquerade and frigidity are twin figures resulting from the status granted to the phallus. They stand as the impossibility or difficulty inherent in sexuality itself, as Jacqueline Rose observed, as 'the disjunction laid over the body by desire, at the point where it is inscribed into the genital relation'.[9]

Stacey's icons of lifeless passion approximated these twin figures of failed femininity. The pose of sex, love and passion pointed to a 'total womanhood' which is frigid and fraudulent, even when totally 'abandoned'. This sexual tease has also been described by Gayatri Spivak, through a strategic misreading of Neitzsche's famous aphorism on women: 'Finally—if one loved them ... what comes of it inevitably? That they give themselves, even when they—give themselves. The female is so artistic.' Spivak translated this as follows:

> Or: women impersonate themselves as having an orgasm even at the time of orgasm. Within the historical understanding of women as incapable of orgasm, Neitzsche is arguing that impersonation is women's only sexual pleasure. At the time of the greatest self-possession-cum-ecstasy, the woman is self-possessed enough to organise a self-(re)presentation without an actual presence (of sexual pleasure) to re-present. This is an originary displacement.[10]

The evacuation of any real passion or presence in Stacey's work recast woman's displacement as an ironic and strategic evasion. The image of an 'actively passive, faked orgasm' was thus claimed to be both symptomatic of, and potentially disruptive to, the notion of representation, for this would presuppose the presence of an original model (in this case, sexual pleasure). If, as Spivak claimed, there was no fixed meaning or truth in the reading of a text, then woman was doubly displaced, for she has been excluded from the truth and the language of the text in the first place. Like Sandy Edwards before her, Stacey took advantage of this doubly displaced position, by faking cinematic texts to highlight their historically specific 'sexual differentials'.

This work departed from earlier feminist inquiries in to 'what are women really like?' Without claiming access to an authoritative or authentic female subjectivity, feminist masquerade enabled women to assume the position of a questioning subject, for femininity was worn in the interrogative sense. Femininity was played as an open question, and so too was photography itself. In the 1980s work became increasingly draped in the borrowed finery of cinema and theatre. The rich *mise-en-scène* of *Something more*, a 1989 collection of imaginary 'film stills' by artist and film-maker Tracey Moffatt, draws its power from big-screen melodrama (see colour section). *Something more* was produced whilst Moffatt was working on the film *Night cries*, a 'rural melodrama' restaged in the shadow of the Hollywood B-grade weepie *Picnic* (Joshua Logan, 1956) and the Australian outback assimilationist tragedy *Jedda* (Charles Chauvel, 1953).[11] Many of the structuring elements in *Something more* carry the oblique trace of these prior texts, whilst *Night cries* implicitly underwrites the photographic series, despite differences in media and plot.

The photographic series' title and loose narrative structure is a traditional one for the genre: a story of longing, desire and misadventure, as the heroine leaves her troubled provincial past in search of something better in the big city. However, she never really gets there; the narrative fails to deliver a satisfactory ending and we can't even work out just who she is. We suspect that the end may be tragic, for an undercurrent of violence and masochism pervades many of the images, and no male lead enters to save the day. True to the title, all manner of imaginary encounters, characters and dramatic twists are left open. Moffatt herself plays the lead role wearing a cheongsam, 'confus(ing) the stereotype of the "half-caste", adding

Anne MacDonald, *The Romance*, 1985, installation shot (detail).

a third element whose presence and significance remains unexplained by the proto-narrative established by the images', as Ingrid Periz observed in her exhibition notes. Inexplicable twists on a formal level lend an added expectancy to unresolved narrative and character effects. High-key cibachrome colour is interspersed with black and white film stock. Occasional close-ups of arrested movement further fragment plot and character. The sophisticated textual and political nuances in *Something more* exemplified a decade of feminist research into the scenography of cinema, photography and theatre.

An earlier and simpler foray into the melodramatic genre, by Hobart photographer Anne MacDonald, avoided the narrative approach to photographic tableaux. Her 1986 installation, *The romance*, had no 'storyline' whatsoever. It dipped into the clammy, low-brow repertoire of Mills & Boon as a source of emblematic images. A swirl of bon-bons, roses, clasped hands, hearts, cakes and exotic fish drifted around the gallery. Amid the debris, a naked couple floated past. In romance, the difficulty of sexual difference and identity disappears in an impossible complementarity. Yet this cloying symmetry also prompted a claustrophobic response in the most hardened gallery-goer. Amid the romance, malevolent flashes of bread knives and fish hooks further ensnared a nauseated audience, as the reassuring pleasures of recognition and proximity reached a hysterical pitch. The feminine love principle was seen to be low-brow, neurotic and dangerous to one's mental health. *The romance* was one of a number of projects in the mid-1980s which dissembled constellations of powerful surface effects at work in both high- and low-brow texts: oil and acrylic, cibachrome and graphite, the clarity of the billboard and the rubbery sheen of the *Vogue* tear-sheet. If pushed just a little, overtly feminine imagery became suffocating, hysterical and dangerously low-brow. The slender margin between art and kitsch had a feminine morphology.

The artist's model run amok

Of course, the difficulty of sexual identity has been a preoccupation of modern art itself. The relation between the feminine and the unconscious has fostered the vision of an unspeakable sexuality, which John Rajchman has joined with an 'amoral love' and 'the Law of language' as primary ingredients in modernist etho-poetics.[12] The genealogy of this sexual/textual/ethical linkage can be traced in early character-types and sexualisations of the body. The motif of an excessive or monstrous femininity, for instance, circulated in nineteenth century discourses on educational opportunities for women, birth control and reproduction, sexually transmitted diseases, hysteria and related nervous disorders. This character-type was later formulated within a psychoanalytically based ethics of language, via Lacan's 'return to Freud'. What was once the concern of medical, religious or juridical regulation resurfaced in a radical ontology of the subject. As Rajchman observes:

> Psychoanalysis is not a medical treatment any more than the unconscious is a medical disorder—a dysfunction or maladaptation. Rather the unconscious is a structural or constitutive fact about ourselves as speaking subjects, and analysis is the work through which one comes to terms with this fact.[13]

In this etho-poetic field, social, political and moral matters were raised as questions of language. Such questions took the place of traditional prudential morality (duty, virtue, the good life). Increasingly, Rajchman suggests, modern art has formed a cultural resistance to the very idea of an objectively good human arrangement. It could articulate those nameless monsters lurking on the

verge of our experience. Restless and undaunted, art has taken us
to the outposts of the representable: 'performing', as Rajchman
proposed, 'something we believe we cannot represent in ordinary
discourse—our own death, our objectless angst, our nameless
desire, our fitful "eroticism"'.[14]

Modern libertinage has been characterised by the defamiliar-
isation and ironic inversion of the norms and values shaping bourgeois culture. Touchstones of familial and social cohesion have
been flaunted, unstuck and declared a repressive sham. Testing the
confines of experience and language became a way of thinking and
comportment. Modern art, as 'design for living' could exemplify
the expulsion of 'fascism' from our speech, hearts, bodies and
pleasures. In this libertarian scheme, the artist, the insane and the
feminine formed a privileged trio, revealing the most uncivilisable
and inarticulable in ourselves: that point where words fail.[15]

It is in this intersection between modernity, art and the psychoanalytic notion of the divided subject that sexuality acquired its
modern role. The obsessive place of sexuality in modern art and
writing no longer revolved around questions of virtue or morality,
but appeared as an insistent, unsettling truth:

> There arises a literature of a 'sexuality' that is not love,
> happiness, or duty but trauma, otherness and unspeakable truth.
> Sexuality becomes the ruination of harmonious, 'centred' love.
> It turns the conjugal or familial forms into structures of Law
> and repression. It reformulates the very idea of childhood and
> memory; it is inscribed in the very being of the subject beyond
> any of his actual sexual acts or relations. Sexuality comes to lie at
> the heart of a writer's relation to his culture.[16]

In the visual arts, woman was a representative figure in this
relation, a telling metaphor for our incomplete self-knowledge.
Arguably, she became the problem of art itself: her interrogation
was a liberating response to fundamental truths of our condition.

Feminists have both used and taken issue with this modernist
apparatus of sexual 'discursification'. The female nude, the brothel
scene, the intimate encounter of the artist's studio: these have
commonly housed the description of existential states, innermost
thoughts and aesthetic self-realisation from Degas to de Kooning.
For feminists, the hysterisation of the female nude was an example
of how the production of truth cannot be inherently neutral or
free, but is thoroughly imbued with relations of power. The

modernist confessional did not necessarily displace oppressive forms of individualisation. On the contrary, it helped to generate a knowledge of the subject, 'not so much of his form', as Foucault noted, 'but of that which divides him, determines him perhaps, but above all causes him to be ignorant of himself'.[17]

It is this resistance to identity at the heart of psychic life that has been of interest to feminism. From the early 1980s, Sydney artist Julie Brown-Rrap has subjected the totalising claims of modern transgression to critical modification. Using her body as a surrogate for modern masterpieces, she put the relation between artist and female model into question. What happens when the exemplary object of modern transgression (the eroticised, objectified female body) turns with vengeance and wit on her own history? The artist's model run amok?

A relational and strategic conception of power replaced earlier visions of repression and liberation. Brown-Rrap and others worked from the premise that points of resistance were not constituted independently of cultural forms, but were invested, even demarcated by them. Her 1984 installation, *Persona and shadow*, targeted the neo-expressionist revival in painting, after a visit to the celebrated *Zeitgeist* exhibition in Berlin, which had represented the work of only one woman artist (see colour section). In this period, the *fin-de-siècle* spirit of the age was being heavily promoted through neo-expressionist eyes. But whose history was teetering on the brink? Who was speaking for whom? Brown-Rrap's fake modern masterpieces disturbed both the expressionist myth of authenticity and the sense of inauthenticity which pervaded the 'wild boys' from Berlin.

Modelling herself in the shadow of Edvard Munch's models, Brown-Rrap faked the feminine precondition of the (neo)expressionist ego. The artist retained odd vestiges, such as a hairstyle, a belt, collar or shoe, in memory of an unnerving femininity, lynch-pin to Munch's suffocating world of illness and death. Temptress, mother, virgin—this was the unholy trinity which fuelled Munch's art and life. Brown-Rrap's posturing gestured beyond Munch as individual artist, however, to quote a broader modernist ethic. Her shallow, painterly ground, heightened palette and corporeal fragmentation simulated the constitutive anxieties of a modern artistic subjectivity, as it emerged and played its part within a feminine orbit.

As Griselda Pollock observed of Manet's Paris, the feminine

body has formed a privileged site over which male artists could
claim their modernity, develop an aesthetic individuality and fight
for leadership of the avant-garde.[18] Brown-Rrap posed as a contentious archive and monument to this battleground, drawing
attention to the feminine precondition of neo-expressionist amnesia.
As model, performer and critic, she blurred the distinctions between action and passivity, subject and object, mastery and submission. The discourse of desire, decrepitude and dissolution of
the self was overtaken by the more abominable, shameless display
of the female model's objectification.

Brown-Rrap later developed this theme in a three-part project,
Thief's journal (1985–6). The reference of the title to Jean Genet
signified a more aggressive and ambivalent relation to art history
than contemporary strategies of appropriation or pastiche, which
presupposed a direct line or access to the past. Brown-Rrap's preference for theft and forgery implied that women's displacement in
art history was not a simple, negotiable problem of form, authenticity or the history of ideas. Her title proclaimed more violent
stakes, wringing from the imagery of Degas, Balthus, Magritte and
Delvaux an acknowledgement of the masculine body 'evacuated
and disavowed by' modern art's totalising discourse on perception,
self-knowledge and pleasure.[19]

Part One of *Thief's Journal*, titled *Looking through the gaps*,
declared the violent nature of Brown-Rrap's theft through use of
the screen, with all its tactical, psychoanalytic, cinematic, domestic
and erotic connotations. Two wall screens, *Justine/Juliette* and *Gradiva/
Gravida*, and a free-standing screen, *Philosophies of the boudoir—
Dangerous relationships* folded back to disclose 'pages' from Balthus,
Delvaux and Magritte, read through Genet and Sade (see colour
section). In a talk at the Australian Centre for Photography in
1986, the artist described her thief's logic in the following terms:

> I'm borrowing works from the past, and I'm re-painting them.
> A bit like a thief who steals something from somewhere and
> whacks another coat of paint on it, so you don't recognise
> it instantly, and then you put it back into the market again.

As *Justine/Juliette*, Brown-Rrap performed 'a "bedroom philosophy" that must play out the tragic and hilarious game of domination and subordination. Between them there are too many false
harmonies of compromise, too much disobedient dependence, too

much sublimated rage.'[20] As Angela Carter observed in *The Sadean woman*, these aristocratic whores were generally more cruel than their libertine partners, using their sexuality as an aggressive instrument to extract vengeance for their own humiliations. Re-clad in modernist garb, they share the threatening style of Stacey's punk girls. In a world without property rights (either sexual or juridical), the Sadean woman's monstrous freedom was seen as a condition of personal privilege, a prostitution of identity for pleasure rather than money. As Sade's phallocrat Saint-Ange exclaimed:

> Here are the truly loveable women, the only true philosophical women! As for me, my dear, who for twelve years has worked hard to deserve [the name whore], I assure you that far from taking offense, ... I enjoy it.[21]

Jane Gallop has championed the radical whoredom of the Sadean woman as operating within an ironic, 'fluid' sexual economy not unlike Luce Irigaray's dream of an 'exchange without commerce' ('between us, neither proprietors nor acquirers, no determinable objects, no prices').[22] Gallop speculated whether Saint-Ange offered a subversive deviation from a phallocentric sexual economy:

> Instead of the rigid resistance of the militant virgin, Saint-Ange/Irigaray points to the disruptiveness of pliancy, prostitution of the self. The whore gives man all he wants without ever being broken, tamed, possessed; the vagina welcomes entry, expands for reception, yet regains its shape.

As in arguments for lesbian s&m, Gallop insisted upon Sade's theatrical (as against juridical) use of terms such as possession and despotism. The staging of cruelty or violation need not be formalised into property rights. Brown-Rrap's compliancy echoed Irigaray and Gallop's answers to Lacan by calling on the paradoxical force of 'feeble resistance'. In Saint-Ange/Gallop's terms:

> 'If your father, who is a libertine, desires you, marvellous, let him use you for his pleasure ... but without enslaving you.' ... Let him take possession of you, let him have orgasm from you, but without subjecting you to his law.

The 'bedroom philosophy' of *Thief's journal* avoided Gallop's romantic and uncritical investment in theatrical whoredom, through its persistent concern with property and theft. Slippages between the idea of possession as property and as sexual enjoyment were central to the structure and impact of the installation. The woman artist/thief/model paraded both a masochistic exhibitionism (Sade's prostitution of identity) and the joy of violating property rights (prostitution as commerce). On the reverse side of the standing screen was pencilled an excerpt from Genet's *Thief's journal*:

> Having broken the lock, as soon as I push the door it thrusts back within me a heap of darkness, or, to be more exact, a very thick vapour which my body is summoned to enter. I enter. For half an hour I shall be operating, if I am alone, in a world which is the reverse of the customary world. My heart beats loudly. My hand never trembles. Fear does not leave me for a single second. I do not think specifically of the proprietor of the place, but all my gestures evoke him insofar as they see him. I am steeped in an idea of property while I loot property. I recreate the absent proprietor. He is a fluid element which I breathe, which enters me, which inflates my lungs. The beginnings of the operation goes off without too much fear, which starts mounting the moment I have finally decided to leave. The decision is born when the apartment contains no more secret corners, when I have taken the proprietor's place.

Like Genet's thief, the woman artist sought access to the position of aesthetic subject through masquerade, prostitution and burglary. In this manner, Brown-Rrap attempted to answer the dilemma posed by masquerade itself: how to be at once subject and object of desire.

The second 'volume' of *Thief's journal*, titled *Reading between the lines*, addressed this problem as a strategic, hysterical identification with the male voyeur. This option was introduced through the title *La toilette*, used by Genet as slang for making up, or the trappings of femininity. Brown-Rrap took three imaginary days from the thief's journal, days spent 'looting' Degas' *oeuvre* and reading between the lines of the proprietary text. Paramount was Genet/Degas' mixed fascination and disgust for the feminine *toilette*:

> In Pedro's room, I looked at the skirts with melancholy. He gave me a few addresses of women's outfitters, where I would find dresses to fit me.
> 'You'll have a *toilette*, Juan.'

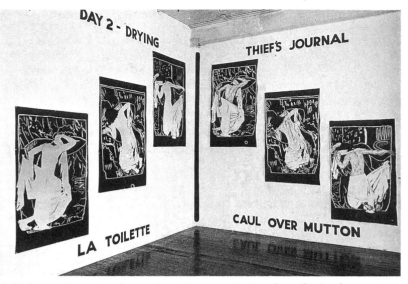

Julie Brown-Rrap, installation shot, *Day two—Drying—La toilette/caul over mutton*,
from *Thief's journal*, 1985. Three archival photographs on paper, each
157 × 92 cms; three works photographic emulsion, acrylic and oil on canvas,
each 152 × 92 cms. Courtesy Mori Gallery, Sydney.

I was sickened by this butcher's word. (I was thinking that
the *toilette* was also the greasy tissue enveloping the guts of
animal's bellies). It was then that Stilitano, perhaps hurt by the
idea of his friend in fancy-dress refused.
    'There's no need for it,' he said. 'You'll manage well
enough to make pick ups.'
    Alas, the boss of the Criolla demanded that I appear as a
young lady.
    As a young lady![23]

Brown-Rrap's strategic misreading of literary and art-historical
texts traced the language of pornographic slang as it entered its
modern phase, around the banal, domestic spaces of woman's
toilette. The eroticisation of the male artist's own *toilette* (the artist's
studio as locus of modern virility), was given the once over
through the central role of an unacknowledged player, the artist's
model. By (un)masking masculine discourse in female shape,
Brown-Rrap represented the blind spot of the modern etho-poetic
subject.
    Freud's puzzled observation, 'Throughout history people

Maria Kozic, *Maria Kozic is bitch*, from the Add Magic billboard project, 1990, in situ, Sydney (photo: courtesy the Australian Centre for Photography, Sydney).

have knocked their heads against the riddle of the nature of femininity', formed a centrepiece in *Break and enter* (1986), an informal 'coda' to *Thief's journal*.[24] As in earlier work by Brown-Rrap and other artists working on 'the nature of femininity', we are given no easy answer to Freud's riddle, for this would simply reinstate business as usual: representations of woman modelled in the monocular, symmetrical economy of phallocentric etho-poetics. Instead, the artist claims that 'it is within the unsolved riddle that the confrontation with otherness is possible'.[25] The aim of artists as diverse in practice as Sandy Edwards, Elizabeth Gertsakis and Julie Brown-Rrap was to mime the riddle itself, flaunting femininity's stubbornly held secret.

'The secret' was all surface: glossy, seductive, fetishistic. These immodest strategems made art's scopophilic pleasures chillingly ironic. A flirtation with theatrical whoredom replaced older, nameless terrors with a more feminine, abject gesture. Yet, unlike Sade's libertine or Genet's homosexual thief, the radical whore promised no liberatory bearing, nor access to the 'truth' of femininity. Such questions, themselves implicit in the modern romantic tradition, have offered women very little.

Brazen cutouts and billboards from 1990 by Melbourne artist Maria Kozic have taken feminist masquerade to parodic proportions. These utilised the sexual violence and glamorous anachronism of Pop Art and pulp fiction. A typical location: a lonely city underground railway platform. Drowsy late-night commuters were startled by a flashy billboard, *Maria Kozic is bitch*, part of a series prompting public consternation with its cheek and inappropriate installation in the suburban hinterland. Complaints by the conservative organisation, Call to Australia, led to the removal of one offending billboard by officers of the Sydney vice squad.[26]

Kozic's pseudo-promotional self-portrait, executed months before Neo-pop guru Jeff Koons swung his publicity machine into action at the 1990 Venice Biennale, pays tribute to the venerable and vengeful man killer. If the 1970s inaugurated the Year of the Woman and positive imagery, to all intents and purposes the 1980s signalled the decade of the Bitch. Kozic farewelled the 1980s with a nostalgic nod to earlier, pre-feminist precedents. Like Stacey, her typography, lighting, costume and pose are strictly 1960s. All those glamorous Russian spies who loved Bond and Deighton shared Saint-Ange's phallic flexibility on the St Moritz ski slopes and on bear-skin rugs. Kozic's Pop Art Love Godess wears her fetishised history like so many knotches in the hand drill she is carrying.

Feminist art had discarded its anti-aesthetic and antisocial stance in favour of a sly virtuosity. The aesthetics of masquerade attended to surface effect, not central core, fabricating frigid glamour, not liberated essence. It aimed to look good, and played off international styles, museum collections and the fetishism of commodities. Central here was the seduction of highly finished 'objects of desire'. Who was desiring what? In the traditional sense, fetishism is a mechanism of disavowal, a means for the little boy to see that his mother does not possess the phallus, and yet avoids the consequences of that knowledge—the suggestion of his own castration. The fetish is thus always a memorial to loss. It carries with it the possibility of reversal, the returned look, and hence anxiety is central to the fetishic power of the images we are discussing here. Yet this strategy of feminist fetishism only toyed with the primacy of the masculine signifier.

Feminine 'special effects' (seduction, threat, desire) both utilised and undermined the principal tenets of Freudian and Lacanian psychoanalysis, in the name of a feminine 'laughter' or pleasure that lay 'beyond the phallus'. Where was this space? Whilst Kozic wielded her hand drill at one end of the feminist art spectrum, the maternal body took liberties at the other end, signalling the potential locus of an autonomous feminine rationality. The following chapter elaborates the possibilities and the limitations of 'radical maternity'.

7 'The revolutionary power of women's laughter'?

What would an independent representation of female sexuality entail? This aesthetic autonomy has been sought in what Irigaray termed 'the gestural code of women's bodies': that which resisted, subsisted or otherwise lay beyond feminine masquerade.[1] In this view, masquerade is a necessary transitional measure, a point from which prescribed, phallocentric modes of feminine pleasure could be indicated and the possibility of an 'impertinent', questioning subject mooted. The projects discussed in the last chapter posed their questions within traditional representations of hysteria and prostitution. This chapter looks at the historical complement of these twin 'feminine failures', and so, along with the Virgin and the Whore we find the Mother—or rather, strategies of textual transgression that have been based around this metaphoric figure.

A decade after Sue Ford's photographic zone of child-centred isolation, motherhood was privileged as a key to the feminine unconscious, sexual pleasure and cultural resistance. The psychiatric and sociological image of the neurotic housewife (as latter-day 'nervous woman') was replaced by more poetic flirtations with a 'psychotic' femininity (as blind spot of psychoanalysis and limit-case of language and sociality). How could writers and artists represent this sublime register? Many projects took recourse to a photographic 'blur', to confound the representational legacy of photography in a welter of abstract, grainy prints. The aim was to deny the visual 'sexual fix' in a pseudo-tactile indeterminancy.

In more sophisticated examples, the blurred gesture interrupted selected cultural texts. It forced a fissure in the representation, it was something glimpsed in between point A and point B. It was the visual equivalent of a giggle, a flash, an undercurrent which slipped between the significatory units from which we construct meaning. The 'blur' was a photographic parallel to the polysemic modernist text.[2] This strategy reformulated earlier connections between language, sexuality and subjectivity. The poetic realism of the 1970s had associated a feminine morphology with certain forms, textures and materials, as in central core imagery. The anatomical essentialism of the central core was later rejected in favour of psychoanalytic and semiotic configurations of maternal desire. More sophisticated, but less shocking: this important shift in feminist strategy paradoxically 'cleaned up' its anti-aesthetic erotics. An initial element in this clean-up involved renewed attention to the photographic apparatus.

The pleasure of the text

At the end of the 1970s, when Sandy Edwards and Jude Adams were investigating the regulation of fashion imagery, Julie Brown (later Brown-Rrap) addressed the same issue as a studio skirmish. *Disclosures (Surrogate I): A photographic construct* (1981–82) mapped an opposition between representational closure (the fashion plate) and the pleasures of a more open-ended text.[3] Brown was among the first in non-Women's Art Movement circles to take up texts by Barthes, Lacan and the British *Screen* project. Of particular relevance was the notion of determinant connections between textual production and sexual difference: connections that had not always seemed so self-evident, as Williamson notes. This schema, while formalised by Lacan, was bound to an earlier, residual Romantic theme of the incomplete self. It activated a tension 'between thought and feeling, mental consciousness and pulsional experience, and indeed, between the masculine closure of representation and feminine possibility of excess'.[4]

The spectator became a pivotal link in this configuration. He or she was drawn into the process of meaning, more often than not as a voyeur-transvestite, ripe for textual reprogramming. Readers are not born, but made, and so too the spectator learnt to activate this tension between masculine closure and feminine heterogeneity. The aim was to identify feminine principles of textual excess or disruption as a metaphoric 'stutter' that one adopts when speaking in a foreign tongue. Spectators learnt to recognise the ambiguous, minoritarian status of the feminine voice.

Brown, whose background lay in conceptual and performance art, took the spectator into a strenuous, disciplinary 'workshop' on

Julie Brown (later Brown-Rrap), installation shot, *Disclosures (surrogate 1): A photographic construct*, 1981/82 (detail). Central St. Gallery, Sydney, April–May 1982.

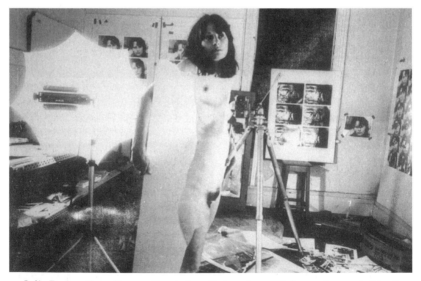

Julie Brown (later Brown-Rrap), installation shot, *Disclosures (surrogate 1): A photographic construct*, 1981/82 (detail). Central St. Gallery, Sydney, April–May 1982.

studio photography. A corridor of photographic panels hung freely from the ceiling of a narrow room. On one side, vertical panels disclosed the naked artist (or her life-size, cut-out surrogate) wearing a camera slung around her neck. These were paired off with panels photographed by the artist-surrogate's camera. These wild shots scanned the studio and centrally placed camera and tripod. Each pair of images were taken simultaneously through the activation of self-timers. The spectator was sandwiched between the two cameras, 'bisected by and subjected to their interrogating gaze', as one reviewer described his response.[5]

These studio views slowly accumulated a jumble of objects and images, building up a memory of the work as it developed. Fetish items worn by the artist or her surrogate (mirrors, plastic sheeting, pantihose, knickers) heightened the sense of pleasurable anxiety that pervaded the installation. Five multiple-image panels were mounted on the end wall of the gallery. A sequence of seven prints progressively tore away a full-length black and white image of the surrogate, to reveal a colour image of the 'real model' underneath. In an inverse movement, the gallery of panels suspended from the ceiling concluded with the surrogate, now wearing the knickers, pantihose and camera, taking a picture of the naked artist lying amongst the studio debris.

By the end of the viewing pathway, the spectator had lost control over the image of woman through the fractured visual field: an excess of images, props, postures and pairings and the disjunctions set up between colour and black and white, model and surrogate, looking and being looked at. The performative female body proposed the spectator's undoing: pleasures of recognition, identification and control were suspended and replaced by more dangerous pleasures; in Barthes' terms, the loss of preconceived identity. Such a 'readerly' photographic text '... discomforts ... unsettles the reader's historical, cultural, psychological assumptions, the consistency of his tastes, values, memories, brings to a crisis his relation with language'.[6]

Dislodging the process of photographic voyeurism, *Disclosures* signalled links between the idea of feminine excess and the infinite possibilities of textual play. This performance rehearsed new structures of vision, thought and deportment. As a reviewer wrote in appreciation, 'this is the photography we had dreamed of, the total photography we had carried in our hearts ... the photography we wanted to make, or more secretly no doubt ... wanted to live'.[7]

Julie Brown-Rrap, *Manet/Jeu de Pomme*, from the installation *Secret strategies—Ideal spaces*, 1987. B&W archival photograph, 150 × 100 cms. Private collection.

Brown-Rrap's *Propositions: Secret strategies—ideal spaces* (1987) and later photographic and mixed media installation *Theory of games* (1989) focused this strategy on institutional and aesthetic issues. Principles of feminine indeterminancy or alterity were featured as undeclared props in the scenography of art history. In the first series, woman's status as public property in the Louvre, L'Orangerie and the Moreau Museum was treated as the scene of aesthetic confinement and violent repossession. The artist's indiscriminate forgeries levelled out divergent histories and subject matter. The archival sedimentation of the art museum flattens and unifies specific social, sexual and political representations under the patronym of the Masterpiece. Brown-Rrap forged her washer-women, courtesans and odalisques as she found them: as interchangeable museum exhibits. Moreover, all connoisseurial protocols were flaunted in the process of recirculation, for the authorial sources of these images were rarely or wrongly attributed. Each figure was instead catalogued through reference to the museum from which it was stolen.

Brown-Rrap's poses were accentuated or blurred to the point of indecision. In some scenes the model literally fell out of place and tumbled from the frame. Inversely, the painted backdrops dripped and spilt like blood over the model's limbs. This imaginary museum walk caught the female model in the gap between poses. The corporeal gesture of indecision was not reducible to the simple opposition of master and model, transcendence and matter, signifier and signified. It instead sought to recover what Jacques Derrida has broadly termed 'writing'; as a (repressed) common root or precondition of writing and speech. Derrida linked this notion of 'archi-writing' to a chain of other terms (supplement, reserve, articulation, *différance*):

> ... *différance* refers to the (active *and* passive) movement that consists in deferring by means of delay, delegation, reprieve, referral, detour, postponement, reserving. In this sense, *différance* is not preceded by the originary and indivisible unity of a present possibility that I could reserve, like an expenditure that I would put off calculatedly or for reasons of economy. What defers presence, on the contrary, is the very basis on which presence is announced or desired in what represents it, its sign, its trace ...[8]

This feminine 'trace', Brown-Rrap argued, is a necessary precondition for the metaphysical status of art. The meshing of sexual difference with the Derridean concept of *différance* was one outcome of Luce Irigaray's influence on academic feminism from the mid-1980s. The photographic gesture towards an alternative feminine 'syntax' could not, however, be simply read within a conventional aesthetic framework, for as Irigaray claimed:

> ... there would no longer be either subject or object, 'oneness' would no longer be privileged, there would no longer be proper meanings, proper names, 'proper' attributes ... Instead, that 'syntax' would involve nearness, proximity, but in such an extreme form that it would preclude any distinction of identities, any establishment of ownership, thus any form of appropriation.[9]

The metaphoric blur, signifier of feminine excess, tried to evoke the evasive power of what Irigaray termed 'women's laughter': 'in what they "dare"—do or say—when they are among themselves', and in the language women used in psychoanalysis.

Photographing the imaginary

Photography's scientific, pornographic and documentary legacy proved particularly resistant to this plural, non-appropriating mode of signification and visual pleasure. It was equally difficult to avoid slipping back into a biologism or poetic naturalism. Both these problems surfaced in the work of Suzi Coyle, a Newcastle-born photographer exhibiting in Sydney in the mid-1980s. Her joint exhibition with Anne Zahalka at the Union St. Gallery, *Outside the poem ... Inside the dream ... A story unfolds ...* (1985) sought to evoke the sensation of dislocation, as precipitated through sexuality—in particular, through women's different trajectory through the oedipal and castration complexes. It was a tall order. Hand-manipulated Polaroids were informally grouped as psychic 'episodes' on the gallery wall. The informality of the installation, harking back to earlier, domestic projects, suggested a sensate realm of pre-oedipal experience.[10] The intimate scale, unnatural colour and shallow depth of field of Coyle's Polaroid prints rejected the 'flat mirror' of photographic realism in favour of Irigaray's image of the concave 'speculum'. Titles such as *Through the mirror* suggested an 'elsewhere' of feminine pleasure which can be found only through passing back through 'the mirror that subtends all speculation', as Irigaray observed in 'Power of discourse'.[11] Coyle's hieroglyphic surface markings and resistant fields of opaque colour suggested the feminine unconscious as a maze to be traversed, without clear entry points, signposts or exits.

In *Intimations of elsewhere*, an ecstatic motif of a woman arched in a high dive jostled against surface tracings of female faces, lips and breasts. The scratched surface allowed new textures and forms to emerge from below. The reworked surface of the print aimed at a semiotic irruption in and of the symbolic, as a kind of *pleasure*, in which the desire of the subject comes up against language and disarticulates it. Poetic tropes and emblematic figures aligned the feminine form with the decentred speaking subject.

The problem Coyle came up against was the recovery of the feminine within simple oppositions of mind/body or nature/culture. It is all well and good to signal the feminine as locus of this libidinal process, yet woman also needs to constitute herself as a speaking subject, for her entry into the symbolic is the condition of her survival. A third and related problem faced in reifying a feminine, pre-symbolic register was that it is easily collapsed back

Suzi Coyle, detail from *Intimations of elsewhere*, 1985. Nine polaroid photographs, each 9 × 10 cms.

onto the female body. In rendering the phallus redundant, the celebration of the female body also rendered the unconscious redundant. Mitchell and Rose have cautioned that this privilege granted to the biological female body effectively re-establishes a pre-Freudian, fixed division between normality and neurosis—a dangerous political strategy for feminism, they argue, for 'once you're normal you become female properly. You get back to stable gender identities'.[12]

Other projects from the mid-1980s by Suzi Coyle, Medi Wangen and Maureen Burns wove their way through this field with mixed success. Wangen's 1985 installation, for example, appealed to an alternative, corporeal expression which did not necessarily create new attributes for the feminine body, but merely inverted traditional oppositions. The feminine body acquired features previously accorded to the 'mind', or intentionality. Burns'

Mise-en-abyme employed a *bricoleur's* approach, creating composite images from sources as diverse as *National Geographic*, postcards and cake tins on the copy-stand. Her sources, like Wangen's, were also mythic. A recurrent, washed-out image of an Egyptian mummy rubbed over with hieroglyphic markings suggested a realm of language and culture inaccessible to Western civilisation. For Burns, *Mise-en-abyme*, literally 'to be in a state of suspension', was a metaphor for contemporary feminist and deconstructive work on language and culture.

Suzi Coyle's 1985 installation, *Imaging*, was more specific in its suggestion of the imaginary, as that space inhabited by the fantasised unity between mother and child, self and other. Like Burns, Coyle superimposed images in a field of saturated colour across an undifferentiated terrain (see colour section). This reverie of self-containment and plenitude was interrupted, however, by the curious alienation and distancing of the figures. As Anne Ferran commented on the series, 'In the constant reappearance of the two figures there's a play with approach and distance that hints as much at an uneasy or even impossible relation between them as it does at their fusion or reconciliation'.[13]

This time Coyle's problems were of a different order. Her investigation of the no-man's-land between the visual and the sensate grouped discontinuous notions of difference (sexual differ-ence, *différance*) within a range of poetic tropes (saturated ciba-chrome, soft focus, superimposition, somnambulant female figures in a romantic, 'Heidelberg School' bush setting). Ferran again:

> It can be a dangerous game, this play with images of women and landscape...As always when the feminine and the pleasurable come together, there is more than one order of interpretation ready and waiting to enclose the images, to assign them a place and meaning. It could be glossy colour photography but it could just as well be Australian landscape painting, with its own dreams of identity and difference.

Coyle's difficulty lay in correlating a necessarily limited range of photographic codes with determined structures of recognition. In another context, *Imaging* could easily slip into the genres of glossy commercial photography, landscape or feature films. A similar pro-blem befell Sydney photographer Suellen Symons, whose exquisite, life-size panels of flaxen-haired, identical twin models, *Paris and Lara* (1987), were steeped in the glamour of studio virtuosity. Her study in feminine narcissism, like Coyle's imaginary landscape, proffered an all-too-perfect picture. Unlike Anne MacDonald's claustrophobic love-absorbtion, not even an adjacent text on these girls' lives managed to disturb the spectator's identification with what was, in effect, conventionally beautiful imagery.

More recent cibachromes from Brisbane artist Jay Younger also played upon the feminine 'habit' of over-identification with the image. Her images also basked in the romantic tradition: memory fragments that slithered across screen-size, saturated surfaces. This hermetic and reflective field was underscored in the installation's mirror-title, *Anxiety as style*, '*Nice blue version*': '*Noisrev eulb ecin' elyts sa yteixna 1 (Between delusions)* (1989) (see colour section). A young woman travels through a dream landscape, a series of encounters, an intuitive search for new metaphors of the self. Is there such a thing as a truly excessive text? Younger's filmic evocation of the feminine unconscious carries vestiges of a traditional image of woman as an elusive Other.

Relying upon the power of feminine mystique for both aesthetic and conceptual impact, the artists discussed here have played a dangerous game. Setting up mirror structures of fascination to trap the unwary, feminists flaunted the feminine as a slippery, weak link in the history of Truth and Beauty. Yet poetic codes, in themselves, do not necessarily rupture phallocentric mechanisms of subjectification. The persistent problems associated with this strategy of feminist art photography suggested that broader connections made between art, language and sexuality need critical reconsideration. As Williamson argued towards the end of the decade:

> That the idea of difference in the signifier should be associated with possibilities of sexual difference, whose recognition marks the division endlessly played out within the subject's own being ... has not always seemed a self-evident connection to make between linguistics and knowledges of sexuality.[14]

Once we relinquish the assumption of some essential link between language and subjectivity, psychoanalysis loses its interpretative hegemony and becomes a more flexible tool. Narrative structures, blurred and grainy prints or photo-documentary techniques can no longer be automatically linked to preconceived mechanisms of recognition. Cultural, historical and institutional frameworks at work in the constitution of difference—whether sexual, cultural, racial—cannot be reduced to particular modes of address. By taking up overly-simplified psycho-linguistic connections, artwork tended to generalise an historical Eurocentric and Romantic 'sexual aesthetics'.

From here to maternity

The rejection of a general theory of language and sexual difference fostered a more strategic use of psychoanalysis in the second half of the decade. Photographers investigated objects of knowledge (sexual difference, visual pleasure, structures of fantasy and desire) common to cultural discourses on maternity. Unlike the domestic labour projects from the 1970s, which maintained close links with contemporary political campaigns around the social wage, later projects on motherhood enjoyed a high public profile within the institutional sites of contemporary art: museums, galleries and academic debates about language, art history and postmodernism.

The maternal body, site of cultural taboos and inarticulable pleasures, has been for centuries an object of medical, religious, scientific, administrative and aesthetic anxiety. The iconography of motherhood has provided a broad field across which feminist art projects mapped the stakes of desire. Work by Anne Ferran (1985) and Pat Brassington (1986) used these cultural anxieties as points of departure. Anne Ferran's 1985 series *Carnal knowledge* drew upon both the ambiguous spectacle of maternal desire and the pleasures women experience in producing and looking at images of women. Larger-than-life faces of sleeping girls (including Ferran's daughter) were superimposed on the imagined texture of weathered gravestones. A dream of young flesh meshed states of death and sleep, enveloped in a fog of mid-grey tones. They formed a sexual tease, and hence the title, which conjured a host of shocking pleasures relating to adolescent sexuality (a problem of discovery, innocence, legal constraints). Yet *Carnal knowledge* offered no fixed entity or viewpoint; Ferran instead interrogated aesthetic and psychoanalytic discourses within which the 'truth' of a fascinating yet troubling female sexuality has been constituted. As an accompanying passage in the series recounted:

> Ovid tells the story of Jupiter, mellowed by deep draughts of
> nectar, teasing Juno: 'Of course, you women get far more
> pleasure out of love than men do.'

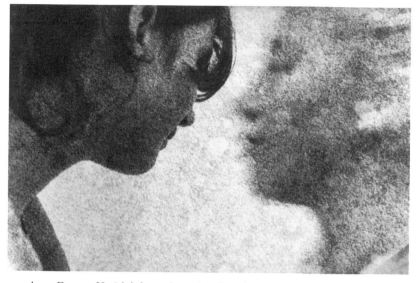

Anne Ferran, *Untitled*, from the series *Carnal Knowledge*, 1984. Gelatin silver photograph, 39.5 × 58.5 cms. Collection of the artist.

Juno denies that this is true and the opinion of Tiresias is sought in settling the matter, since he has experienced love both as a man and a woman. He confirms what Jupiter has said, whereupon Juno becomes very indignant and condemns the judge to eternal blindness—which Jupiter, unable to reverse, modifies by granting Tiresias the power to know the future.

This story has also been noted by the French writer Hélène Cixous. She focuses on the figure of Tiresias to pose the rhetorical question, 'What is woman for man?'.[15] Ferran instead looked to Juno's speech for subtle ambiguities, puzzling at Juno's indignant response to Tiresias' judgment. In turn, she claimed:

> I too want to suggest something of the unspeakable of feminine desire, to allege that Oedipus is not the end of the story, however useful such an ending may be in ensuring that subjects are put in their places and the order of the familial preserved.

Kristeva's reinterpretation of the phallic mother was posited here as a welcome shift in focus away from a culture constructed around the oedipal figure. As Ferran's inscribed story continues,

The space which has to be traversed—that of language, desire, the body and knowledge—is that same risky terrain where Tiresias, the seer, came to the state of knowledge through blindness.

This relation with the maternal was impelled by a non-symbolic, non-paternal causality; as Kristeva argued, a metaphorical journey to the limits of primal regression experienced in childbirth:

> By giving birth, the woman enters into contact with her mother; she becomes, she is her own mother; they are the same continuity differentiating itself. She thus actualises the homosexual facet of motherhood, through which a woman is simultaneously closer to her instinctual memory, more open to her own psychosis, and consequently, more negatory of the social, symbolic bond.[16]

Criticisms of the centrality Lacan accorded to the phallus as transcendental signifier prompted this 'move to the mother' as a metaphor for woman-centred exchanges and the primary object of bisexual drives. This bonding within the imaginary was seen to house the potential for a feminine, 'bio-social' *jouissance*. The maternal relation, according to Kristeva, 'is a whirl of words, a complete absence of meaning and seeing; it is feeling, displacement, rhythm, sound, flashes, and fantasised clinging to the maternal body as a screen against the plunge'.[17] Ferran's images and text referenced these theoretical positions as important cultural markers, without claiming to somehow step outside culture. The erotic relations she established were already saturated with cultural codings of photographic reproduction, classical beauty, youth and femininity.

These funerary monuments also indicated a singularly maternal history: the compensatory activity of the mother. In the 1970s, Mary Kelly's *Post-partum document* and Helen Grace's *Lovely motherhood show* had introduced the notion of the maternal fetish. As Kelly has noted, the mother may retain objects and memorabilia such as locks of hair, first shoes or school reports. She may dress up or continue to feed the child no matter how old the child gets. The fear of castration, in terms of a loss of loved ones or objects, was also relevant to Ferran's work:

In order to delay, disavow, that separation she has already in a way acknowledged, the woman tends to fetishise the child ... A trace, a gift, a fragment of narrative; all these can be seen as transitional objects, not in Winnecott's sense, as surrogates, but in Lacan's terms, as emblems of desire.[18]

Anne Ferran's 1986 work, *Scenes on the death of nature*, extended the fetishistic aspect of the maternal relation, via an incisive visual essay on neo-classical aesthetics.[19] She carefully composed the bodies of her daughter and daughter's friends along a life-size frieze. While in many respects *Carnal knowledge* shadowed the nineteenth century photographer Julia Margaret Cameron, an austere clarity, uniform illumination and formal ordering of bodies and images in *Scenes* followed the strict rules of neo-classical aesthetics. As the artist noted in a 1987 talk in Hobart,

> ... everything in the pictures is visible, knowable. There's nothing of the sublime in them, the sublime being that which shows itself in unfathomable darkness—or in blinding light, that which dazzles the eye. It is this as much as the formal coherence of the work that allows me to say that it is on the side of the symbolic (as opposed to the side of the imaginary) ... it is on the side of order, knowledge, rationality, consciousness, intellect ... it's a question of not giving way entirely to feeling, to the irrational, the chaotic—which is where women are usually placed, voluntarily or involuntarily.

Ferran's models posed according to contemporary strategies of frigid, feminine compliance. In this case, passivity was tailored to the art-historical demands. Ferran's frozen tableaux registered the rules of restraint and containment central to standards of ideal, Classical beauty. Such harmony required a compositional balance between horizontal and vertical forms, attention to the golden mean, the repression of uncontrolled gesture or facial expression and the eradication of fugitive movement, details or extraneous objects that might suggest allegorical or narrative contents.

The submission of young female models to these strict compositional rules and Classical codes posed questions of taste, tradition, judgment and desire in a thoroughly public form reminiscent of nineteenth century funeral monuments. The orchestration of powerful aesthetic effects through historically specific formal codes replaced the Romantic notion of individual sensibility or vision in

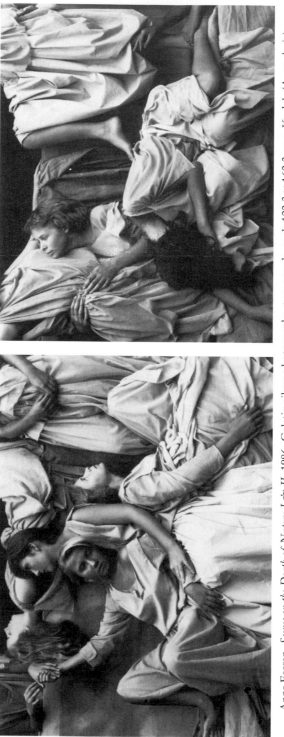

Anne Ferran, *Scenes on the Death of Nature I & II*, 1986. Gelatin silver photographs, two panels, each 122.3 × 162.3 cms. Kodak (Australasia) Pty. Ltd. Fund, 1987, Australian National Gallery.

favour of period connotations, cultural conventions and the questioning of the aesthetic canon. Ferran thus faked the emergence of aesthetics as an intellectual and corporeal 'discipline'.

The cultural ambivalence surrounding the maternal domain has also been central to work by Hobart photographer Pat Brassington. *Eight easy pieces* (1986) took up Kristeva's concept of abjection to visualise rites of passage in the constitution of the ego. The installation took the form of a loose jigsaw puzzle, and plays on the title, beyond the immediate reference to Vonnegut's swaggering *Five easy pieces* (and the film of the same name), suggested violent forms of dis-ease (excising or exorcism) and derogatory propositions on women (as a 'piece'; as being 'easy'). Brassington addressed the aesthetic sublimation of indeterminate phenomena: the undead, the deformed, the mind-invaders, the 'monstrous feminine'. Reproduced images of phobic material, phallic forms and mutilated faces from the darker recesses of art history, science fiction and horror movies marked a set of aesthetic and experiential 'limits'. Her 'Hammer Horror' replay questioned the generic demand in these texts for the aliens amongst us to be discovered and annihilated before they can take over the human mind or body. With their elimination, a threatened loss of distinction between human and non-human, chaos and order is removed.

In our culture, abject phenomena are a source of disquiet or revulsion often associated with taboos surrounding corporeal phenomena like skin and body tissue, menstruation, childbirth, death, faeces, bodily fluids. In her catalogue notes, Brassington suggested that certain images and image combinations may prompt a like response: 'These images are pitched just off the verge of normality into those dense patches where, mediated by our phantasms, our fears peer back at us.' Her golems and phobias staged a confrontation between the healthy body politic and its diseased underbelly. These darker recesses of social life are in fact the latter's necessary support, for as Kristeva argues, 'the refuse (*plechet*), like the corpse, *indicates* to me what I keep permanently at a distance in order to live'.[20]

Brassington similarly visualised abjection as a strangeness within our social identity. In psychoanalytic terms, abjection is a fundamental lack, developmentally prior to any possibility of organised representation, and thus prior to the unconscious. This archaic experience is associated with a crude, permeable division at the very limit of originary repression. It is therefore not the work of

Pat Brassington, *The lamb*, 1986. Twelve gelatin silver photographs on mural paper, 140 × 180 cms. Collection of the artist.

Pat Brassington, *Cumulus Analysis*, 1987–1988, photographic installation 274.5 × 457.5 cms. Purchased 1989. Art Gallery of New South Wales.

repression or negation, but a more uncertain movement, as in borderline experiences and limit behaviours. Abjection can be registered as a corporeal mark, symptom or involuntary movement (repugnance, nausea). This frontier, this 'repulsive gift' perpetually threatens the subject from within.

Brassington conceived this 'gift' of the self as the source of a diabolical ('sublime') *jouissance* that Kristeva nominates as masochist, nomadic, 'situationist'. The imagery in *Eight easy pieces* trod a fine line between condemnation and effusion, violence and docility. Brassington implicitly associated this oscillation with a threatened relapse into dependency on a stifling maternal power. More specifically, the artist tried to locate here that aspect of the mother that becomes abject as the female subject enters the oedipal and castration complexes. The tenuous, negative relation between the maternal and the symbolic, and the necessary repression of desire for the mother subtended these images of female masochism and castration.

The lamb visualised the self offered up as a 'precious non-object' to the Other's repugnance. Brassington saw this violent precondition for entry into the Symbolic as necessary for woman's social and psychic survival. Femininity comes at a high price, and the motif of castration and defilement in *The judges* further declared Brassington's ambivalence. Here, however, castration was visualised in terms of a bloody decapitation. The image of woman's lack was thus reformulated as a violent 'loss of speech'. To become a woman was to become an automaton, an hysteric, a mute. Here Brassington echoed the sentiments of Hélène Cixous' article 'Castration or decapitation?'. '... if masculinity is culturally ordered by the castration complex, it might be said that the backlash, the return, on women of this castration anxiety is its displacement as decapitation, executon, of women, as loss of her head.'[21]

The headless body is a bloody reminder of that residual, intimate base of memory. Women's unresolved relation to castration and reproductive function was visualised in an ambivalent relation to this corrupting, spasmodic force. Abjection thus became a metaphoric, creative irruption, linked to the mother's body and to pleasure. In Cixous' words, 'Woman ... takes up the challenge of loss in order to go on living: she lives it, gives it life, is capable of unsparing loss ... This makes her writing a body that overflows, disgorges, vomiting as opposed to masculine incorporation.'

But wait a minute. Could one photographic installation really deal with *all that*? Is it fair to hold up an art project to its theoretical coordinates and say, 'but this piece is unconvincing on these terms'? As work by Suzi Coyle and others from this period showed, it is not so easy to create photographic texts to embody this 'situationist' *jouissance* (or anarchic suicide, as Josette Feral describes it).[22] Photography's representational baggage, and Brassington's choice of old horror stills, could not rid themselves of the musty decay of art history and the cinematic archive. The walking dead, perhaps; but dread? Not exactly. Her work from 1990 orchestrated a sense of sublime unease more convincingly, as her imagery was not so easily identified with old-time gothic ghoul.

The hysteric

In many ways the lesson had been learnt: concepts could not simply be 'illustrated' from the realms of psychoanalysis, philosophy or literary criticism. Photography has its own history, which stubbornly refuses to cooperate with the meta-discursive status of philosophy or psychoanalysis. Indeed, Jacky Redgate's work from the late 1980s concentrated again on the history and material properties of photography itself. Anne Ferran also sought out specific historical intersections between photography and other discursive events. Her 1989 presentation of nineteenth century asylum photographs is a case in point. Imagine a total theatre of representation, with its examinations, interrogations and experiments:

> [a] theater of ritual crises, carefully staged with the help of ether or amyl nitrate, its interplay of dialogues, palpations, laying on of hands, postures which the doctors elicited or obliterated with a gesture or a word, its hierarchy of personnel who kept watch, organised, provoked, monitored, and reported, and who accumulated an immense pyramid of observations and dossiers.[23]

The Salpetriere Hospital in Paris was such a place. It provided the cast and crew for consultations and lectures performed by Freud's one-time teacher, Charcot, who would take his hysterical patients through their paces in front of a crowd of curious onlookers. Charcot also compiled an impressive photographic casebook on hysteria and related nervous disorders. A century later, Anne Ferran dipped into the Salpetriere archives for a series which brought together the discourses of medical photography, modernism and hysteria under the title, *I am the rehearsal master.*

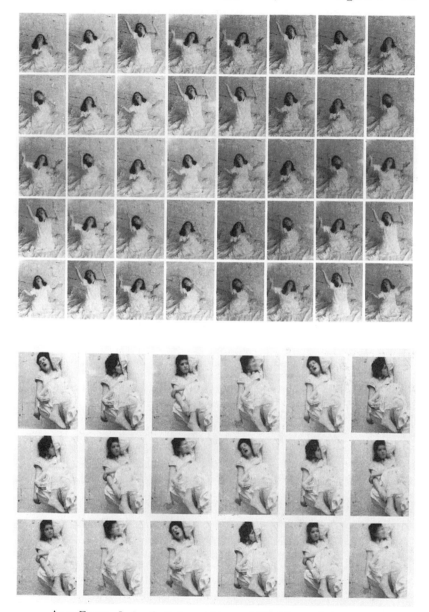

Anne Ferran, *I Am the Rehearsal Master*, 1989. Silver gelatin prints.

Whilst the series has an exquisite high-grain finish, reminiscent of archival prints, Ferran eschewed the poetic codes of art photography in favour of the medium's more mundane talent for documentation. Ferran directed young models to perform states of ecstacy, physical convulsions and other psychosomatic symptoms documented by Charcot's camera. Indeed, Ferran's rehearsal pays as much attention to representation as to hysteria itself, or rather, the latter is used as a metaphor for certain representational *difficulties*. For the hysterical symptom—the nervous cough, facial tic, paralysis of the limbs—has no actual physiological base; it is pure representation. Or rather, it stands for the *failure* of representation, for there is an incoherence, a formlessness to each of Ferran's hysterical gestures. The chaotic, feminine 'creativity' of Ferran's psychosomatic hysterical symptoms unravels both the historical certainties of photographic documentation and the utopian regulation of the modernist grid. The feminine becomes a metaphor for representation itself, and yet it is also the element which falls short of, or short circuits, representational structures: Ferran takes scientific photography into the heartland of modernist principles of textual deformation. A latter-day case of *amour fou*? The hysteric sits in pride of place, alongside the mother and the whore, as an unacknowledged lynch pin of modernist transgression.

Who's afraid of red, yellow, blue?

Janet Burchill's and Jennifer McCamley's 1986 installation *Temptation to exist* tried to systematise the sensation of abjection, overproximity and indeterminancy at another formal level (see colour section). Burchill and McCamley eschewed strategies of textual deformation, reflexivity and critical distance. A deflective surface gel, sado-masochistic imagery, primary colour filters and an unrelieved tension between vertical and horizontal axes orchestrated a suffocating proximity. Their citation of cinematic ice queens such as Catherine Deneuve (*Repulsion*) or Tippi Hedren (*The birds*) did not claim to unravel scopophilic or voyeuristic structures for audience re-education. Instead, they tried to solidify the bizarre, psychotic and obsessive associations of these film-still nightmares. The artists make no claim for a 'liberating' play of the signifier or narrative disruption.

Working against the grain of other projects from this decade, McCamley and Burchill's collaborative work from 1981/2 exploited the transgressive value of the feminine within avant-garde texts, but not within a problematic of subject formation. They took issue with the way cine-semiotics and psychoanalysis had been adopted in the visual arts, by refusing to examine the problem of sexuality as a problem of language.

Through a radical reading of Irigaray's work, Burchill and McCamley attributed a fictional status to psychoanalysis in their projects for *The male show* (1982/3), *The exchange of women* (1982/3), *Soft geometry* (1983) and *Temptation to exist (Tippi)* (1986). These photography and mixed media projects used the feminine as an aesthetic effect. Notions of fantasy and fetishism were exploited as powerful yet puzzling elements in modernist poetics. For instance, tensions between attraction and repulsion, desire and refusal were essayed through spatial relations, architecture, images and objects. These were assumed to be always and already gridded for certain aesthetic possibilities. What could happen here? How could one *formalise* paranoia or fetishism, without recourse to the obvious imagery of dread and desire? What happens when you reverse common linguistic assumptions about the endless productivity or proliferation of meanings, and instead concern yourself with matter, endgames, self-contained units: the aesthetics of asphixiation rather than semiotic excess?

On another level, McCamley and Burchill's use of photography as one element among many (rope, wooden frames, bodies, floors, surfaces) prefigured a widespread move away from the strictly image-based analyses that had dominated 1980s photomedia. By the end of the decade, many artists reconsidered questions of representation, pleasure and vision in historical and interdisciplinary terms, across a range of media. Prominent artists like Brown-Rrap, Ferran, Redgate and Gertsakis submerged questions of 'the photographic' in highly finished installations referring to broader institutional, technological and art-historical sources.

By the early 1990s, McCamley and Burchill had discarded the photographic image completely in their collaborative and solo projects. This move towards photo-object and installation work paralleled international trends; however, it is not reducible to them. On the whole, these Australian artists were swifter in their repudiation of psychoanalysis and the 'politics of the image' than their American and British counterparts. This could, of course, be partly attributed to an inadequate understanding and less-than-thorough deployment of theoretical models. Certainly the enthusiastic and at times uncritical adoption of psycho-linguistic models in the 1980s had its share of reductive aesthetic outcomes.

By the end of the decade the tight embrace between semiotics, psychoanalysis and art had been loosened. It should be noted, however, that the contribution of psychoanalysis to questions of representation and sexuality has been as fruitful as it has been problematic. From earlier work which drew together the concepts of representation, ideology and female socialisation, photographers increasingly prioritised the invention of critical *and* pleasurable possibilities for the woman as subject of desire, with mixed success. Experiential models for feminine art and conduct were replaced by genealogies of 'sexual aesthetics' (neo-classicism, modernism, postwar popular culture). Women assumed the role of subject and object of desire through recourse to a 'question-effect', an effect produced through use of Stanislavsky's 'Method' performance of female characters (mother, model, whore, hysteric).

Narrowing feminist aesthetics to questions of femininity, sexuality and language has raised questions of strategy for some feminists. These are certainly important, but they are not the only problems for feminism. Although femininity is a political problem, 'it is not coextensive with women, (and) it is certainly not coextensive with all areas of women's subordination', as Parveen Adams notes.[24] Less successful projects tried to harness linguistic, aesthetic and sexual codes to a radical ontology of Woman. Whilst the 1970s had indicated the dangers of biological or anatomical essentialism, the 1980s faced a similar problem in relation to language. Indeterminate, a-social, pre-oedipal: this poetic morphology echoed the romanticised, natural forms, but not the institutional challenges, of central core imagery. It is important not to overestimate the radical implications of linguistic and aesthetic indeterminancy, without accounting for broader ideological, historical and institutional frameworks. For one thing, aesthetic prescriptions for feminine subversion can easily generalise the experience of white, Western, middle-class women.

Part of the problem lay in taking psychoanalytic, literary or philosophical discourses on board in their interpretative and meta-discursive form. Yet textual strategies are not the only space for deconstructing truth, sexual identity or social regulation, and so we need to avoid claims for an alternative feminine rationality or alterity based on these culturalist precepts. Art projects are best evaluated within their own market and institutional locus, and they cannot claim to provide an etho-poetic blueprint for all other areas of feminist politics. After twenty years of prescriptive feminist aesthetics, the 'lesson of psychoanalysis' has been to stop mortgaging feminist politics to such overarching cultural frameworks. Projects by Brown-Rrap, Ferran and others indicated in turn that the 'sexual fix' and processes of individuation cannot simply be countered by textual deformation. Brown-Rrap's work in particular showed that the presupposition of an essential relation between subjectivity, language and the body has a history which is coterminous with the psycho-social dimension of modernist ethics, an ethics which revolves around an 'hystericised' feminine characterology.

8 Current speculations, future bearings

I have tried to discuss the shifting field of feminist photography in a way that might be useful for solving problems and conducting practices. This has involved documenting projects by women that would otherwise be overlooked; and I have maintained a methodological concern with the political use of photographic documents. The twin undertaking of historical documentation and strategic argument for present practices meant discarding conventional art-historical categories of authorship, stylistic development and 'artwork-within-its-social-context'. Photographs are not simple reflections of these broader determinants. There are many possible relations that can be identified between photographic statements and particular social and economic bearings or art institutions, but these cannot be usefully stated in advance through some overriding figure like the photographer, the spirit of a decade or even 'patriarchal relations'.

I prefer to think of feminist photography as a discursive field. Photographs are best documented in association with related statements (other photographs, political campaigns, contemporary art debates), institutional developments (women's studies, Australia Council programmes, the art market) and pedagogical techniques (curatorial practices, skill sharing, consciousness raising). The consideration of feminist photography as an ethical practice also enables us to link photography with other areas of feminist cultural politics, and to elaborate the key thematic points of my argument: associations made between feminist photography and personal liberation, the assumption of women's separation from the public sphere and the attribution of a repressed, subversive feminine sexuality. Feminist etho-poetics seemed to demand a specific subject, a complex relation to the social and a libertarian investment in the body.

The 'subject'

Feminist etho-poetics was initially formulated on the basis of certain non-didactic and non-coercive exercises of self-scrutiny, criticism and transformation. Women learnt to raise and monitor their consciousness as part of their artistic training and professional practice. In other words, photographers learnt how to become the subject of feminist aesthetics.

The feminist artist had a particular job: to visualise and exemplify the path to liberation. The camera was used in consciousness-raising projects to investigate women's creative nature, social experience and sexual identity, and to bring together the fragmented and devalued aspects of women's lives in a programme of self-realisation.

This voluntarist programme, of personal scrutiny and liberation through art, challenged the narrow, formal parameters of contemporary art practices. Feminist etho-poetic strategies stood in direct contrast to the still-prevalent formalist obsessions of mainstream artists and art institutions of the early 1970s. Equally challenging was the demand for the equal representation of women artists and their work within the public and private sectors of the art industry. The call for equal representation was complemented by a critical concern with representations of women.

On the negative side, the inordinate attention given in the 1970s to the politics of personal liberation helped to shape the subject of feminist photography according to a prescriptive and overtly moralistic code of behavioural norms and aesthetic co-ordinates. These included a supportive yet uncritical notion of sisterhood, pedagogic responsibility and an essentialist aesthetics. In more extreme cases, the notion of 'the personal is political' generalised the autobiographical experience of white, middle-class women, in often conservative valuations of women's family and community maintenance, social responsibility and civilising agency.

'The social'

In the same period, photographic analyses of the conditional power, oppressive discipline and invisibility of women's work inside and outside the home formed major points of resistance. Women's voluntary and paid labour was seen to be related in ways which challenged simple demarcations between public and private. Projects dealing with familial, welfarist, industrial and community relations constructed a network of interdependencies that could not be accounted for through terms like familial ideology, economic requirements or the State. These projects instead formed crucial interventions within a hybrid field of social relations.

In their simplest form, feminist photographs examined gender socialisation and sex-role stereotyping at home and in the work force. These nevertheless formed important initial points of conflict. They paved the way for more detailed analyses in the late 1970s which targeted specific photographic, industrial or welfarist discourses and disciplinary practices. These have historically constituted woman as the pivotal point of social intervention and normative influence.

Not all photographic strategies adopted a critical stance in relation to the social. Concurrent affirmations of women's presence in the community or in the work place celebrated women's access to the public realm, in and of itself. These liberal schemas of emancipation could not, however, deal critically with the contingent and restrictive nature of women's public powers and responsibilities. Similarly, radical feminist revaluations of women's traditional arts and cultural contribution, and liberal feminist interventions within so-called 'malfunctioning' communities reiterated women's historical relation to family and community service. Techniques of consciousness raising and self-transformation, first developed by small groups of white, predominantly middle-class women artists, were applied to other socio-economic groups, with uneven outcomes.

In the late 1970s a growing concern with the truth value and power relations involved in photo-documentary strategies effectively weakened the critical purchase of realist positive imagery and simple affirmations of women's public presence. Photographic realism itself became subject to investigation as an ideological tool. These critiques threw the welfarist concept of community photography into doubt, and the historical assumption of women's power for social and cultural 'good' came under fire. Feminist projects increasingly attended to their own institutional and ideological conditions of production and circulation. A deconstructive relation to the photo-documentary subject meant that humanist investments in the social were avoided as projects came to grips with the powerful instrumentality of the medium.

The sexual

Work on female sexuality also formed important though problematical points of social and cultural resistance. The body, like 'the social', proved a particular problem for liberal, socialist, lesbian and radical feminists alike. The most successful projects to date have focused on specific instances of inequitable sexual differentiation, within the discursive operations of the home, the work place, the mass media and high culture. Unlike sociologically based analyses of sex-role stereotyping, these projects assumed the sexually differentiated body to be an important variable in feminine subjectivity. Feminists photographed the micro-dynamics of female sexuality to see how the female body has been shaped, marked, adorned, disciplined and saturated with a sexuality that has historically been identified as potentially dangerous.

Across these social and cultural constructions, it has been argued that no one theory of the body can fully account for the diverse political, legal, medical or photographic inventions of female sexuality. In the context of feminist photographic practices, the academic division between a re-educative gender politics and theories of sexual difference tended to blur. Photographic assistance given to feminist physical and sexual education, or the analysis of images of women, cannot be adequately explained through any one sociological, psychoanalytic or ideological framework. That said, we may observe how, by the late 1970s, the issue of female desire was opened up in diverse analyses of pornography, popular culture and lesbian politics. In these selected instances, residual social purity arguments and simple appeals to false consciousness came under constructive scrutiny.

Psychoanalysis became a useful tool in these contexts. A prior ethics of wholistic self-realisation gave way to an image of polymorphous pleasure and radical refusal. The clear focus of photo-documentary was replaced by the blurred form and ambiguous experience of female desire. Deconstructive strategies emphasising difference, instability and fraudulence replaced earlier searches for a unified and authentic sexual experience.

Speculum or glass slipper?

During the 1980s feminist photography gained high institutional prestige behind the contemporary art banner of 'neo-conceptualism' and 'Continental theory'. While so many of us were busy promoting these gallery triumphs, they also highlighted the conditional nature of feminism's acceptance within the mainstream of contemporary art. This is an art-historical problem, involving the inscription of feminist art within a progressive history of ideas in which formal and conceptual shifts assume a privileged developmental and innovatory status.

In its crudest form, the category: '1970s feminism' was hitched in the popular imagination to an outmoded, experiential politics. Feminism in the 1970s meant Lippard and Chicago and all those motherhood exhibitions which were eclipsed by more glamorous '1980s' investigations into sexual difference and aesthetics. And, as I suggested at the start of this book, '1980s' feminist photography has itself been laid to rest. Curatorial, pedagogic and market pressures can easily trivialise substantive research from both decades through simplistic narratives of aesthetic and conceptual innovation. What shifted from the 1970s to the 1980s was not the invention of a specific feminine aesthetic, for this has always been a central concern. Nor can we say that 1970s work was 'political', whilst projects that enjoyed a high profile in art museums, galleries, publications and art curricula through the 1980s necessarily evacuated the political dimension. This work simply addressed women's relation to representational systems, art history and its institutional supports from *within* these structures. Nor is it so easy to say that this '1980s' tendency had run its course by the end of the decade. The problem of representation and sexuality is still with us, and perhaps, now more than ever, feminists need to take stock of the humanist, psychoanalytic and modernist paradigms in which they have intervened for twenty years.

A second and related item of institutional myopia has accompanied mainstream acceptance. In the 1980s, pedagogic and market value accrued to a narrow strand of work sporting a poststructuralist conceptual base and dealing in issues of sexuality and aesthetics. Projects on the social construction of femininity, in contrast, faded into the background. Jane Gallop's metaphor of radical whoredom could indeed describe both the possibilities and limitations of this work within the contemporary art industry. What have feminists offered as counterpoint to the representation of the artist as virile creator, insane genius or utopian thinker? Stacey, Brown-Rrap, Brassington, Ferran and others disingenuously proffered the figures of hysteria, frigidity, theft, stuttering and mimicry as the only forms of articulation available to women within this modern authorial problematic. Feminists artfully deconstructed a historically circumscribed, feminine 'creativity'— and the art world lapped it up. A decade earlier, the same art audiences had gagged on unsublimated versions of the woman-as-artist story (a tale of tampax, vaginas, washing-machines, nappies, family photos). Is feminist access to the art market conditional on its displaying aesthetic and sexually pleasing qualities, providing the sensual and intellectual stimulation demanded by the discourse of high culture? It is still perhaps a little early to judge, but 'market indicators' seem to swing to the affirmative.

Aesthetic strategies in themselves cannot shift the scenography of high art. Under what conditions could '1980s' work on aesthetics and sexuality affect the ordering of the archive, with its political structures of art-historical access, retrieval and valuation? Have our art institutions in fact 'hystericised' the work of women artists, negating difference? In response, artists rewired the dynamics of artist's model, prostitute, mother and hysteric. Today, instead of reiterating this nineteenth century taxonomy or opting for an alternative feminine canon, we should reconsider the strengths of feminist photography after twenty years as it departs from the received and inadequate discourses of the social and the sexual through an inventive, shifting etho-poetics of a new femininity.

Endnotes

Introduction: Feminism and art history

1 Anne-Marie Willis, *Picturing Australia: A history of photography*, Angus and Robertson, Sydney, 1988; see also Barbara Hall and Jenny Mather, *Australian women photographers 1840–1960*, Greenhouse Publications, Melbourne, 1986; Virginia Coventry (ed), *The critical distance: Work with photography/politics/writing*, Hale & Iremonger, Sydney, 1986; Helen Ennis, *A decade of Australian photography—1972–1982*, exhibition catalogue, Australian National Gallery, October 1983–January 1984; and *Australian Photography: The 1980s*, Australian National Gallery, 1988.

2 Keith Tribe, 'History and the Production of Memories', *Screen*, Vol. 18, No. 4, Winter 1977/78, p.12.

3 Julie Ewington, 'Past the Post: Postmodernism and Postfeminism', *150 women artists*, Victoria Women's 150th, 1985, n.p.

4 Hubert L. Dreyfus and Paul Rabinow, *Michel Foucault: Beyond structuralism and hermeneutics* (second edition), University of Chicago Press, 1983, p.109; and Michel Foucault, 'What is an author?' in *Language, counter-memory, practice* (D. Bouchard (ed), trans. D. Bouchard and Sherry Simon), Ithaca, N.Y., Cornell University Press, 1977, pp.137–8.

5 John Rajchman, 'Ethics After Foucault', *Social Text*, Nos. 13/14, Winter/Spring 1986, p.180.

Chapter 1: The feminist artist

1 Ian Burn, 'The 1960s: Crisis And Aftermath', *Art & Text*, No. 1, Autumn 1981, p.54.

2 See Michel Foucault, *The use of pleasure: The history of sexuality volume two* (trans. Robert Hurley), Pantheon, New York, 1985; and *The care of the self: The history of sexuality volume three* (trans. Robert Hurley), Pantheon, New York, 1986.

3 A selection of arguments to this effect within Australian 1970s and 1980s feminist cultural debates include Meaghan Morris, 'The Pirate's Fiancée',

in Meaghan Morris and Paul Patton (eds), *Michel Foucault: Power, truth, strategy*, Feral Publications, Sydney, 1979, pp.148–168; Mia Campioni and Elizabeth Grosz, 'Love's Labours Lost: Marxism and Feminism', in Judith Allen and Paul Patton (eds), *Beyond Marxism? Interventions after Marx*, Intervention Publications, Sydney, 1983, pp.113–141; Rosi Braidotti, 'The Ethics of Sexual Difference: The Case of Foucault and Irigaray', *Australian Feminist Studies*, No. 3, Summer 1986, pp.1–14; and 'Ethics Revisited: Women in/and philosophy' in Carol Pateman and Elizabeth Grosz (eds), *Feminist challenges: social and political theory*, George Allen and Unwin, Sydney, 1986, pp.40–60.

4   Barbara Hall, 'Woman as creator', lecture delivered at the Wayside Chapel on behalf of Sydney WAM, February 1975. Published in *Refractory Girl*, No. 8, March 1975, pp.69–70. See also the results of the first Sydney WAM questionnaires (June 1973–June 1974), in the *Sydney Women's Art Movement Newsletter*, No. 2, n.p. The galleries canvassed were Holdsworth, Bonython, Watters, Power, Hogarth, Komon, Clune, Gallery A, Divola, Macquarie and the Art Gallery of New South Wales.

5   Accounts of the group include 'The Women's Art Movement', *Refractory Girl*, No. 8, March 1975, p.71; Jenny Barber, 'Sydney WAM', *LIP* Nos. 2/3, 1977, pp.93–4; Vivienne Binns, 'Group Dynamics', *The Women's Show Conference Papers*, South Australian Women's Art Movement, Adelaide, 1977, pp.67–69; Laura McLeod, 'Sydney Women's Art Movement', Honours Thesis submitted Sydney University Fine Arts Department, 1980. Women closely associated with Sydney WAM (1974–1976) and the Women's Art Group (1976–81) included Jude Adams, Jenny Barber, Vivienne Binns, Frances Budden, Virginia Coventry, Louise Dalton, Pat Fiske, Beverley Garlick, Joan Grounds, Barbara Hall, Paula Lake, Jan MacKay, Marie McMahon, Barbara O'Brian, Toni Robertson, Louise Samuels.

6   Notable exeptions are Beverly Garlick and Virginia Coventry, who were both associated with the Sydney Women's Liberation newspaper *Mejane* from 1971–74. Other Sydney WAM members active in Women's Liberation included Jude Adams, Toni Robertson, Pat Fiske and Barbara O'Brian. Some sporadic feminist art activities had preceded Sydney WAM. The Art Workers For Liberation (1971) was an offshoot of the Glebe group of Sydney Women's Liberation, meeting weekly at Gale Kelly's studio from 27 April 1971. Approximately nineteen women were associated with this group. See also Kate Jennings, 'Organisation And The Female Artists For Women's Liberation', paper delivered at the Sydney Women's liberation Conference on the 'Aims, Organisation and Campaigns of Women's Liberation', 23–25 January 1971, Boilermakers' Hall, Sydney, cited in Sue Wills, 'The politics of liberation: Sydney Sexual Liberation Movements 1969–73', PhD submitted University of Sydney, 1981, pp.46, 49; and Sue Bellamy, 'Women cannot create: They can only consolidate', *Mejane*, No. 4, September 1971, p.12.

7   Barbara Hall, 'Review of the last decade', *Seminar Papers: The Growth of Feminist Art: From manifesto to polemics*, New South Wales Women and the Arts Festival Conference, Sydney, 2–4 October 1982, p.22.

8   ibid., p.23.

9   ibid., p.21.

10   Ian Burn, op. cit. 1981, p.50.

11   *Sydney Women's Art Movement Newsletter*, No. 2, September 1974, p.1.

12   In 1974, Sydney WAM compiled a questionnaire for women students at the National Gallery School to survey 'initial expectations of art and the art school as a woman, and as a student and teacher, colleague and self-image, and projections of life "outside" when they leave East Sydney (Tech)'. *Sydney Women's Art Movement Newsletter*, No. 2, 1974. This questionnaire was devised after the exhibition *50 Years of the National Art School* had shown the work of only two women artists. See also Jeanette Fenalon, 'Women in art schools: Careers for women', *LIP* 2/3, 1977, pp.88–92. See also Annie Minchin, 'Women in art: A fool's paradise', *The Women's Show Conference Papers*, op. cit. 1977, pp.50–53; Anna Havana-Walsh, 'The Women's Art Register Extension Project', ibid., p.64; Vivienne Binns, 'Sexism in Selecting Staff for Art Colleges', ibid., pp.49–50; The Visual Arts Board of the Australia Council, *Tertiary Visual Arts Education In Australia*, Australia Council, 1979; Alison Fraser, 'Tertiary visual arts education—Study and report', *LIP* 1980, pp.90–93; Jude Adams, 'Sexism in art education', *Women's Art Movement 1978–1979*, Adelaide, S.A. WAM, 1980, pp.4–6; Vicki Varvaressos, 'Working conditions affecting Australian women artists', *LIP* 1984, pp.104–5; Johanna Willis, 'Women, education and economics: The thin edge of the wedge', *LIP* 1981/2, pp.66–68.

13   Bonita Ely, 'Sexism and art education', *The Women's Show Conference Papers*, 1977, p.48. Ely and Anna Havana surveyed Victorian secondary and tertiary art education as it affected women, with the help of a 1977 grant from the School's Commission. See also Bonita Ely, 'Sexism in education', Paper delivered at the Alternative Art education Conference, PIT, 30 June 1977, subsequently published in Ann Stephen and Charles Merewether (eds), *The great divide* (no publishers imprint), Melbourne, 1977, p.102.

14   Early examples of voluntary, and/or short-term women's studies courses include Jude Adams' historical survey courses on women and art at Alexander Mackie CAE in 1975; her eighteen-week course at the WEA in 1976; Ann Stephen's Women and Art elective at Preston Institute of Technology in 1976–1978, where Stephen was a part-time tutor; Suzanne Archer's research-based course at Alexander Mackie CAE in 1978, where Archer was a visiting lecturer; Barbara Campbell's Women and Art Theory elective for second year students at Canberra School of Art in 1977, where Campbell was a lecturer; Vivienne Binns' workshops at the University of NSW as artist-in-residence, 1979 (part of the *Mothers'*

memories, others' memories project); and Helen Grace's Women's Studies elective at Sydney College of the Arts 1981 to 1987 where Grace worked as a part-time lecturer.

15 See in a broader context Ian Hunter, 'On reflection theory: Including remarks on John Docker's *In a critical condition', Australian Journal of Cultural Studies*, Vol. 3, No. 1, May 1985, pp.3–28.

16 Griselda Pollock, 'Art, art school, culture: Individualism after the death of the artist', *Block*, No. 11, 1985/6, p.8.

17 Lucy Lippard came to Australia as the 1975 John Power Memorial Lecturer. See Ann Stephen, 'At the edge of a feminist criticism: An interview with Lucy Lippard', *Meanjin Quarterly*, No. 4, 1975, pp.380–386; Lesley Dumbrell, op. cit. 1976; Barbara Hall, op. cit. 1982; Jude Adams, 'Review of Lucy Lippard's *From the center*', *LIP* 2/3, 1977, p.54; 'Interview with Lucy Lippard', *Art & Language*, Art & Language Press, Sydney, 1975, pp.141–142.

18 Lucy R. Lippard, *Art & Language*, p.141.

19 Janine Burke, op. cit. 1977, p.62. Burke's claims were amplified in *LIP* editorials. This interdisciplinary arts magazine was established in 1976 through the efforts of a broad group of women involved in the visual arts (WAR), theatre (the Women's Theatre Group) and film (the Women's Film Festival). *LIP* provided a supportive forum for examining 'art and politics from a feminist perspective'.

20 Lucy R. Lippard, 'Changing Since Changing', *From the center: Feminist essays on women's art*, Dutton, New York, 1976, p.2.

21 Janine Burke, op. cit. 1978/79, p.5.

22 See in this context Toril Moi, *Sexual/textual politics: Feminist literary theory*, Methuen, London, 1985, p.43.

23 Barbara Hall, 'Women and post-object art', in Noel Sheridan (ed), *Post-object art in Australia and New Zealand*, Exhibition Catalogue, Experimental Art Foundation, Adelaide, 1976.

24 As cited by Linda Nochlin, *The politics of vision: Essays on nineteenth century art and society*, Harper & Row, 1989, p.2.

25 Susan Sheridan, 'From margins to mainstream: Situating Women's Studies', *Australian Feminist Studies*, No. 2, Autumn 1986, p.4.

Chapter 2: Family, community, shop floor: Reconstructing the social

1 Jacques Donzelot, *The policing of families* (trans. Robert Hurley), Pantheon Books, NY, 1979.

2 As Gilles Deleuze also observed, 'The question is not at all whether there is a mystification of the social, nor what ideology it expresses. Donzelot asks how the social takes form, reacting on other sectors,

introducing new relationships between the public and the private; the juridical, the administrative, and the customary; wealth and poverty; the city and the country; medicine, the school, and the family.' Gilles Deleuze, Foreword to Jacques Donzelot, ibid., 1979, p.x.

3   Jacques Donzelot, 'Preface to the English edition', ibid., p.xxvii.

4   Gilles Deleuze, ibid., p.xvii.

5   Christopher Lasch, *Haven in a heartless world: The family besieged*, New York, 1977.

6   Patricia Edgar and Hilary McPhee, *Media she*, Heinemann, Melbourne, 1974. *Media she* was prompted in part from the 1973 media study undertaken by the Women's Committee of the United Nations Association of Australia (Victorian Division). See *Media she*, p.1.

7   ibid., p.2.

8   Meaghan Morris, 'Feminist Criticism', *Cinema papers*, November–December 1975, pp.208–209.

9   See Sue Ford, *One sixtieth of a second*, Experimental Art Foundation, 1987.

10   Ailsa Maxwell, *Domestic deviations*, reproduced in Kurt Brereton (ed), *Photo-discourse*, Sydney College of the Arts, 1981, pp.56–57. A revised series was reproduced under the title *Romance*, in *Artists' Pages, South Australia Women's Art Movement*, Adelaide, 1983.

11   The idea of 'partners in leisure' was central to the post-war ethos of home life. For a contemporary discussion on the increased time spent in the home in the post-war period, see Ann Game and Rosemary Pringle, 'The Making of the Modern Australian Family', *Intervention*, No. 12, April 1979, pp.72–73.

12   Maxienne Foote, *Monday to Monday*, reproduced in *LIP* '80, pp.67–73; revised under the title *From Monday to Monday*, 1980 in Kurt Brereton (ed), op. cit. 1981, pp.114–115.

13   Centre for Urban Research and Action (CURA), *But I wouldn't want my wife to work there ... A study of migrant women in Melbourne industry*, Research Report for International Women's Year, Melbourne, 1975.

14   Jacques Donzelot, 'Pleasure in Work', *I&C*, No. 9, Winter 1981/82, pp.2–28.

15   The kit was produced for the Victorian Education Department, and instigated by the combined Victorian teachers unions (the VSTA, TTAV and the VTU) as part of their 'sexism in education campaign'. Research for the kit was by Jude Munro and Sylvie Shaw. See *LIP* 1980, pp.8–11.

16   Deborah Mills, Art and Working Life Project Officer for the Australia Council, interviewed by Ann Stephen in 'Putting Art To Work: Representing Women', *Scarlet Woman*, No. 23, 1987, p.24.

17   *And so ... we joined the union* was co-funded by the Visual Arts Board and Community Arts Board of the Australia Council, the Myer Foundation, 'Women 150th', with the Victorian Trades Hall Council Information and

Resource Centre as support organisation. The exhibition was co-ordinated by Fiona Moore from the Trades Hall Council, and was first installed at Storey Hall in the Royal Melbourne Institute of Technology in October–November 1985 as part of Industrial Rights Week. It has since been used in union training programmes, and individual work prints remain as a resource for the participating unions.

18   Freda Freiberg, 'Review of *And so ... we joined the union*', *Photofile*, Vol. 4, No. 1, Autumn 1986, p.25.

19   Carol Jerrems and Virginia Fraser, *A book about Australian women*, Outback Press, Melbourne, 1974.

20   John Stuart Mill, *The subjection of women*, AHM Publishing, Illinois, 1980, p.16, cited in Janna Thompson, 'Women and Political Rationality' in C. Pateman and E. Grosz (eds), op. cit. 1986, p.99.

21   Merle Thornton, 'Sex equality is not enough', ibid., p.91. Paradoxically, neo-conservatives endow the modern family with an aura of liberal individualism, in opposition to state services. See Judith Williamson's 'Family, education and photography', *Ten-8*, No. 14, 1984, pp.19–22.

22   See Barbara Hall and Jenni Mather, op. cit. 1986.

23   See Val Williams, *Women photographers: The other observers 1900 to the present*, Virago, London, 1986, pp.45–46.

24   Sue Ford, *A picture book for women*, was first exhibited Art Gallery of New South Wales in October 1982 as part of the Women and Arts Festival. *A sixtieth of a second* was published by the Experimental Art Foundation, Adelaide in 1987.

25   Vivienne Binns, 'Extracts from a discussion between Vivienne Binns and Helen Grace, with comments by other contributors from the project' (edited by Peter Thorn), *Art Network*, Vol. 1, No. 1, November 1979, p.20.

26   Ponch Hawkes, *Our mums and us*, reproduced in *LIP* 2/3, 1977, p.21. Six out of Hawkes' series of twelve prints were reproduced in this issue of *LIP* (pp.21–26). According to the artist's recollection, the series was exhibited in the following year at Brummell's Photography Gallery in Melbourne. The work was purchased by the Phillip Morris Collection in 1978.

27   See for example the heated interchange between Julie Ewington and Adelaide critic Peter Ward over the 'messy', all-women installation at the Experimental Art Foundation during The Women's Show. *The Women's Show documentation*, Adelaide Women's Art Movement, 1977, n.p.

28   The hand-coloured series *Christmas with Bob's Family, Mermaid Beach, Queensland, 1977* (1978) was exhibited along with *Parents of my generation* (1979) at the George Paton and Ewing Galleries, November 1979. See Tony Perry, 'Nostalgia Close to Overdose', *The Age*, 30/11/1979.

29   Micky Allan, *Photography, drawing, poetry: A live-in show*, Watters Gallery, Sydney, and George Paton and Ewing Galleries, Melbourne, 1979.

30   *Mothers' memories, others' memories* was mounted at the University of New South Wales (where Binns was artist-in-residence) in 1979. The final exhibition, in 1981, was at Blacktown Marketown, Sydney.

31   Grace Cochrane, *Remarking time*, Australian Centre for Photography, August–September 1984 (in conjunction with Anne Graham's *Veneers II* and Sandy Edwards' *Narrative with sexual overtones*).

32   Thanks to Julie Ewington for suggesting this point.

33   Gilles Deleuze, 'Foreword' to Jacques Donzelot, op. cit. 1979, p.xii.

34   Ros Bower, 'Community arts—What is it?', Paper delivered at the Community Arts Field Officers' Seminar, Wollongong, December 1975, published *Caper 10*, Community Arts Board, May 1981, p.7.

35   Ros Bower, 'The community arts officer: What is it all about?', Paper delivered at the National Community Arts Conference, Melbourne, July 1980, published *Caper 10*, Community Arts Board, May 1981, p.3.

36   Robyn Heks, *Community arts officer review, report to the Community Arts Board*, February 1985, p.xix; and Gay Hawkins, *Constructing Community Arts*, Allen & Unwin, 1993.

37   The *Prahran Neighbourhood House photography project* was funded under the Victorian 'Women 150th' arts programme, which was in turn based on ideas developed during the 1982 New South Wales Women and the Arts Festival. The *Prahran Project* was exhibited in the Prahran Markets Court-yard 5–8 March, and at the Women's Carnival, Carlton Gardens, 9 March, at the Prahran Youth Festival, 30 March, at the Princes Gardens, Prahran, 31 March. The exhibition format has since been refurbished for more extensive touring around similar neighbourhood centres in Victoria.

38   Andrea Hull, 'Women in the Community Arts', *The Women's Show Conference Papers*, Adelaide, 1977, p.63.

39   Jan Birmingham, 'Report on Women and Craft/Art Workshop at Norma Parker 21 October 1982', in *Women and Craft/Arts Committee Report on ideas-based workshops*, Women and Arts Festival, Sydney, October 1982, n.p.

40   See Michel Foucault, *Discipline and punish: The birth of the prison* (trans. Allan Sheridan), Vintage Books, NY, 1977; Barry Richards, 'Psychology, Prisons and Ideology: The Prison Psychological Service', *Ideology & Consciousness*, No. 2, Autumn 1977, pp.9–28; and Jacques Donzelot, op. cit. 1979, p.110.

41   *Mejane* had successfully publicised the legal double standards and conditions at girls' reform institutions in 1972–73. A series of articles, personal letters, clippings, photographs and reports compiled over twenty years by a sixty-seven-year-old woman, Bessie Guthrie, starting with 'You can't run all the time' in *Mejane*, No. 8, August 1972, pp. 8–13, with photographs by Virginia Coventry. These campaigns, along with incidents at Parramatta (December 1973) and Bidura (March 1974), lead to the closing (in its then form) of the Hay Home and the Parramatta Girls' Training School in 1974.

42   See George Zdenkowski and David Brown, *The prison struggle: Changing Australia's penal system*, Penguin, 1982, pp.76–77.
43   Interview with project tutor Joyce Agee, Sydney, 17 November 1987.

Chapter 3: Deconstructing the social

1   Women's Employment Rights Campaign, *Women and unemployment*, Panacea Press, Sydney, 1979.
2   Photographs facing p.64 in Ann Game and Rosemary Pringle, *Gender at work*, George Allen and Unwin, Sydney, 1983.
3   Michel Foucault, *The Birth of the Clinic* (trans. AM Sheridan), Tavistock, London, 1973, p.58.
4   *Re-presenting work* was a project funded under the Art and Working Life programme of the Australia Council, and was sponsored by Lidcombe Workers' Health Centre. It was produced by Helen Grace and Julie Donaldson, with panel design by Ruth Waller, and research assistance by John Jensen. Assistance was provided by the following unions: the Australian Bank Employees Union, The Australian Institute of Marine and Power Engineers, the Amalgamated Metals, Foundry and Shipwrights Union, the Federated Miscellaneous Workers Union, the Printing and Kindred Industries Union, the Water and Sewerage Employees Union and the combined shop committees at Chullora Workshops and Otis elevators. *Re-presenting work* was first exhibited Lidcombe Workers Health Centre, 1983.
5   Julie Ewington, *Domestic contradictions*, exhibition catalogue, Power Gallery of Contemporary Art, Sydney, August 1987, p.45.
6   Grace's concentration on the industrial, medical, administrative and ideological conditions of motherhood were points of departure from Mary Kelly's contemporary work on *The post-partum document* (1973–1981). The bibliography for *The lovely motherhood show* included references to *The post-partum document*, however. In interview, Grace explained that she had read about Kelly's work, but had not seen it. Interview with Helen Grace, Sydney, 13 February 1986.
7   Reference is also made here to Julia Kristeva's influential article, 'Motherhood According to Giovanni Bellini', from *Desire in language: A Semiotic Approach to Literature and Art*, Columbia University Press, NY, 1980.
8   Lahleen Jayamanne, *The holey family*, exhibited in *Mothers' memories, others' memories*, University of New South Wales, 1979, revised for publication in *LIP* 1981/82, pp.42–46.
9   See group discussion in Vivienne Binns, *op.cit.* 1980, pp.38–47.
10   Lahleen Jayamanne derived this concept from Luce Irigaray. See 'Women On The Market' and 'Commodities Amongst Themselves' in *This sex which is not one* (trans. Catherine Porter), Cornell University, Ithaca, 1985, pp.170–198; 192–197.

Chapter 4: The bare essentials

1   See, for instance, Judith Allen, 'Marxism and the Man Question: Some Implications of the Patriarchy Debate'; Mia Campioni and Elizabeth Gross, 'Love's Labours Lost: Marxism and Feminism'; and Moira Gatens, 'A Critique of the Sex/Gender Distinction', all in Allen and Patton (eds), *Beyond Marxism? Interventions after Marx*, Intervention Publications, Sydney, 1983.
2   Moira Gatens, op. cit. 1983, p.149.
3   See for instance Jacques Donzelot, op. cit. 1979; Judith R. Walkowitz, *Prostitution and Victorian Society: Women, Class and the State*, Cambridge University Press, New York, 1980; Peter Botsman, 'The Sexual and the Social: Policing Venereal Disease, Medicine and Morals', PhD thesis, University of New South Wales, 1986; chapters on Josephine Butler in Margaret Forster, *Significant sisters: The grassroots of active feminism 1839–1939*, Penguin, Great Britain, 1986, pp.169–204; and relevant documents on the Australian situation in Kay Daniels and Mary Murnane, *Uphill all the way: A documentary history of women in Australia*, University of Queensland Press, 1980, pp.130–157.
4   Michel Foucault, op. cit. 1980, p.104.
5   *Our Bodies, Ourselves*, The Boston Women's Health Collective, 1976, pp.339–340.
6   Nineteenth century feminists had, for instance, denounced the use of the speculum, in the name of women, as a degrading and unnatural form of 'instrumental rape'. This charge was laid during campaigns against the compulsory internal examination of any woman suspected of being a prostitute, under the Contagious Diseases Acts in England. See Judith Walkowitz, op. cit. 1980; and Peter Botsman, op. cit. 1986.
7   For further discussion on the 'hermeneutics of suspicion' see Hubert I. Dreyfus and Paul Rabinow, *Michel Foucault: Beyond structuralism and Hermeneutics* (second edition), University of Chicago Press, 1983, pp.178–179.
8   Front cover, *Refractory Girl*, No. 8, March 1975. The cover text was quoted from Judy Chicago and Miriam Schapiro, 'Female imagery', *Womanspace Journal*, Vol. 1, No. 3, pp.11–14, as cited by Judy Chicago, op. cit. 1975, pp.143–144.
9   Luce Irigaray, 'This sex which is not one' (trans. Meaghan Morris) in Meaghan Morris and Paul Foss (eds), *Language, Sexuality, Subversion*, A Feral Publication, Sydney, 1979, pp.161–171.
10 Anne Roberts, *Amazon Acres* series, *Refractory Girl*, No. 8, March 1975, facing p.61.
11 Anne Graham, *Veneers II*, Australian Centre for Photography, September 1985.
12 See Michel Foucault on 'The Repressive Hypothesis', op. cit. 1980, pp.15–50.

13 Lesley Solar, untitled private installation in the artist's studio, 1981.
14 Frank Mort, 'In the Domain of the Sexual', *Screen Education*, No. 36, Autumn 1980, p.81.
15 Denise Riley, 'Developmental Psychology, Biology and Marxism', *Ideology & Consciousness*, No. 4, 1978, pp.84–85.
16 ibid., p.88. See also Paul Q. Hirst and Penny Woolley, *Social relations and human attributes*, Tavistock, London, 1981, pp.1–92.
17 See Adrienne Rich's influential text, 'Compulsory heterosexuality and lesbian existence', reprinted in Snitow, Stansell and Thompson (eds), *Desire: The politics of sexuality*, Virago, London, 1984, pp.212–241.
18 *Camp Ink*, Vol. 2, No. 1, November 1971; and Vol. 2, No. 2/3, December 1971/January 1972.
19 See 'Karen', 'Radicalesbian weekend at Sorrento', *Vashti's Voice*, No. 5, November–December 1973, pp.13–14.
20 Elizabeth Wilson, 'I'll climb a stairway to heaven: Lesbianism in the seventies', in Cartledge and Ryan (eds), *Sex and love: New thoughts on old contradictions*, The Women's Press, London, 1983, pp.184–5. In this context, see also Joan Nestle, 'Butch-fem relationships: Sexual courage in the 1950s', *Heresies*, No. 12, 'Sex issue', Vol. 3, No. 4, 1981, pp.21–24.
21 Svegi Kilic, 'That was a long time ago', *Vashti*, No. 29, Autumn 1981, p.2.
22 See Jeff Minson, 'The assertion of homosexuality', *m/f*, Nos. 5&6, 1981, p.21.
23 See Jefferey Weeks, *Sex, politics and society: The regulation of sexuality since 1800*, Longman, London, 1981, p.116; also Carol Smith-Rosenberg, 'The Female World of Love and Ritual: Relations Between Women in Nineteenth Century America', *Signs: Journal of Women in Culture and Society*, Vol. 1, No. 1, Autumn 1975; and Faderman, *Surpassing the love of men*, Virago, London, 1982; Kenneth Plummer (ed), *The making of the modern homosexual*, Hutchinson, London, 1981.
24 See Robert Aldrich, 'From Sodomy to Sub-Culture: A Survey of Male Gay History', *Gay Information*, No. 13, Autumn 1983, p.10, Allan Berube, 'Lesbian and Gay G.I.'s in World War II: Marching to a Different Drum', *The Advocate*, No. 238, October 15, 1981, pp.20–24, John D'Emilio, 'Capitalism and Gay Identity' in Snitow, Stansell and Thompson (eds), op. cit. 1984, pp.140–154.
25 See Sue Wills' account of this precursor to Gay Lib and Camp, op. cit. 1981, pp.63–4. Australasian Lesbian Movement membership was restricted to lesbians and bisexuals over twenty-one years, and married women had to have 'the written consent of their husbands to join'. (*ALM Information Sheet*, Melbourne, late 1970.) ALM members spoke to Lions groups, television and magazines, and the group was involved in charity work.
26 Inside front cover, *Cauldron*, Vol. 1, No. 1, September 1974. These photographs are reproduced as separate, full-page images elsewhere in the issue.

27   Adrienne Rich, op. cit. 1984, p.215.
28   Susan Ardhill and Norie Neumark, 'Putting Sex Back Into Lesbianism', *Gay Information*, No. 11, Spring 1982, p.5.
29   See Sharon McDonald, 'My Body or My Politics', *The Advocate*, No. 357, December 9, 1982, pp.33–5.
30   Members of Samois (eds), *Coming to power: Writings and graphics on lesbian s/m*, Samois, California, 1982; see also Pat Califa, 'Feminism and Sadomasochism', pp.30–34, *Heresies*, No. 12: 'Sex issue', Vol. 3, No. 4, 1981; Paula Webster, 'Pornography and pleasure', pp.48–51; and Amber Hollingbough and Cherrie Moraga, 'What we're rollin' around in bed with', pp.58–62; see also Janice Schrim, 's/m for feminists' and Paula Ettelbrick, 'The point is the pain', in *Gay Community News* (Boston), Vol. 8, No. 41, May 9, 1981, pp.8–9, 13, cited *Gay Information*, No. 8, Summer 1981, p.47; Deirdre English, Amber Hollingbough, Gayle Rubin, 'Talking sex: A conversation on sexuality and feminism', *Feminist Review*, No. 11, Summer 1982, pp.40–52; and Gayle Rubin, 'The Leather Menace', *The Body Politic*, No. 82, 1981, pp.33–35.
31   Ardhill and Neumark, op. cit. 1982, p.11.
32   Michel Foucault, 'Sexual Choice, Sexual Acts: An Interview With Michel Foucault', James O'Higgins, *Homosexuality: Sacrilege, vision, politics* (*Salamagundi* 58/59), Fall 1982–Winter 1983, pp.10–24 (also cited *Gay Information*, No. 13, Autumn 1983, p.52).

Chapter 5: Female desire and feminine tutelage

1   This body of work from 1981–1983 included prints in Lewens' graduating folio, exhibited in *Graduating photography*, Australian Centre For Photography, 1982; '*6 or 16?*', reproduced in Jean-Marc Le Pechoux and Peter Beilby (eds), *The Australian photography yearbook 1983*, Four Seasons, Melbourne, 1983, p.96; *The Diana series*, exhibited in *Matters of personal choice*, a group show of Melbourne photographers, Australian Centre for Photography, Sydney, June 1984 (curator: Carolyn Lewens); *The swing series* and another extensive untitled series (collection of the artist). Three prints from the latter were reproduced in *LIP* 1982/83, pp.28–29.
2   This print was selected from the artist's Preston Institute of Technology graduating folio. The work was produced following Carter's participation in Ann Stephen's women's studies course. Interview with Nanette Carter, Melbourne, March 1985.
3   Moira Gatens, op. cit. 1983, p.149.
4   Robyn Stacey, *Untitled*, 1982. This work was produced and exhibited in *The panel show* at the Australian Centre for Photography (curator: Lesley Solar), as part of the 1982 NSW Women & Arts Festival.
5   Ruth Maddison's series was first produced as the wedding album for film critic and *LIP* editorial collective member Suzanne Spunner. It was

exhibited at the Australian Centre for Photography in 1980, and was purchased for the National Gallery of Victoria collection. It has also been reproduced in Virginia Coventry (ed), *The critical distance*, op. cit. 1986. This book gave the series a broad exposure within a tightly contextualised political frame, endowing the work with a critical status akin to Lewens' photographs in *LIP* 1982/3. Here Maddison was placed alongside other photographers 'whose work with photography comes less from formal training in that area and more from their questioning of the medium, other art forms and photography's meaning in society'. See Judy Annear, *Frame of reference*, exhibition catalogue, George Paton and Ewing Galleries (touring Australian Centre for Photography 1982), as cited Virginia Coventry, op. cit. 1986, p.12.

6   Anne Balla's *Bedrooms* series was exhibited as part of her graduating folio at the Photography Studies College, Melbourne, 1978.

7   *Miss World televised 1974* was first shown in an informal group exhibition in the Carlton Gardens as part of the 1975 International Women's Day celebrations, along with photographs by Sue Ford and Ponch Hawkes. It was later exhibited in *Post-object art* exhibition, The Experimental Art Foundation, 1977. Mention should also be made in this context of a similar project from 1976/77, Sandy Edwards' *Miss Universe*.

8   See Jude Adams and Sandy Edwards, *Fashion images*, first exhibited at the South Australian WAM, 1978. Documented by Jude Adams in the *Women's Art Movement, Adelaide, S.A. 1978/79*, pp.26–7. Work included in *Fashion images* had been previously exhibited in Sydney WAM-organised shows, as discussed earlier in this book, for instance, Sydney University (1976), Hogarth Gallery (1976), ICA Central St Gallery (1977).

9   Lisa Tickner, 'Sexuality and/in Representation: Five British Artists', in *Difference: On representation and sexuality*, exhibition catalogue, New Museum of Contemporary Art, New York, 1985, p.23, citing Victor Burgin, in Tony Godfrey, 'Sex, text, politics: An interview with Victor Burgin', *Block*, No. 7, 1982, pp.2–26.

10   Joy Stevens, *Untitled*, 1982, exhibited in *Graduating photography*, Australian Centre for Photography, 1982. The work was produced in the context of the women's studies Elective taught by Helen Grace and later, Ailsa Maxwell. Interview with Helen Grace, Sydney, 2 February 1986.

11   This work was exhibited in conjunction with work by Suzi Coyle (see Chapter Seven) at Union St. Gallery, Sydney, 8–15 May 1985.

12   Work titled *Framed* and *Seeing double* had formed part of Burgin's *US77* series. Zahalka also quoted Burgin in her exhibition catalogue: 'Forms of representation such as photography don't simply express a biologically pre-given "femininity" or "masculinity"; sexual difference, in the totality of its effects, doesn't precede the social practices which 'represent it', doesn't function outside such practices, but is constructed within them, through them.'

13   See Jacques Lacan, 'The Mirror Stage as Formative of the Function of the I', *Ecrits: A selection* (trans. Alan Sheridan), Tavistock, London, 1977, pp.1–8.

14   Edwards' *A narrative with sexual overtones* was first exhibited in *The critical distance*, Artspace Visual Arts Centre, Sydney, August 1983. Other participants were Micky Allan, Virginia Coventry, Helen Grace, Ruth Maddison, Gillian Gibb, Toni Robertson, Peter Lysiossis, Michael Gallagher, Oliver Strewe. Work from the exhibition was later published in Virginia Coventry (ed), op. cit., 1986. Edwards' *Narrative* was later exhibited at the Australian Centre for Photography August–September 1984.

Chapter 6: 'Faking it': Feminine fraudulence

1   See Paul Taylor's popularisation of Barthes' slogan of the 'second degree' in 'New Wave' and the 'Second Degree', in Paul Taylor (ed), *Art & Text*, No. 1, 1981.

2   See Meaghan Morris, 'The Pirate's Fiancee', in Meaghan Morris and Paul Patton (eds), *Michel Foucault: Power, truth, strategy*, Feral Publications, Sydney, 1979, p.164. *Kiss kiss bang bang* was exhibited at the Mori Gallery, Sydney, August 1987; and *Redline 7000* was also shown at the Mori Gallery in 1989.

3   See Gayatri Chakrovorty Spivak, 'Displacement and the Discourse of Woman', in Mark Krupnick (ed), *Displacement: Derrida and after*, Indiana University Press, Bloomington, 1983, p.186.

4   Dick Hebdige, 'Posing ... threats, striking ... poses: Youth, surveillance and display', *Substance*, Nos. 37/38, 1983, p.85.

5   See in this context Jonathon Morris's appropriation of Barbara Kruger in his *Stilletto* fashion spread, *Your fictions become my romance* (1985); cited Geoffrey Batchen, 'Preferential Treatment', *Afterimage*, Vol. 14, No. 2, September 1986, pp.4–5.

6   Jacques Derrida, 'The Question of Style', in D.B. Alison (ed), *The new Neitzsche*, MIT Press, Cambridge, Mass., 1985, p.181.

7   Joan Riviere, 'Womanliness as a Masquerade', in Henrick M. Ruitenbeck (ed), *Psychoanalysis and female sexuality*, New Haven: College and University Press, 1966, p.213; also quoted in Mary Ann Doane, 'Film and the Masquerade: Theorising the Female Spectator', *Screen*, Vol. 23, Nos. 3–4, September–October 1982, p.81.

8   Jacques Lacan, 'The Meaning of the Phallus' in Mitchell and Rose (eds), op. cit. 1983, p.84.

9   Jacqueline Rose, op. cit. 1983, p.44.

10   Gayatri Spivak, op. cit. 1983, p.170.

11   *Something more* was produced during the artist's residency at the Albury Regional Art Centre in 1989. See also *Night cries—A rural tragedy*,

Director: T Moffatt, Producer: P McDonald, 35mm, 17mins, 1989. See also Ingrid Periz, 'Night Cries: Distance, Communicability and Reference', *West*, No. 2, 1990, pp.6–7.

12 See John Rajchman, 'Lacan and the Ethics of Modernity', *Representations*, No. 5, Summer 1985, p.55. The full quotation is as follows: 'The status of the unconscious is "etho-poetic" if we allow that ethics be extracted from saying-what-is-good. Lacan advanced an ethical theory of the divided speaking subject, based not on a knowledge of our well-being but on the intolerable truth of our discontent. His was a vision of a culture of amoral love, of unspeakable sexuality, and of the Law of language. It may be a vision of *ce qui nous a tenu*, of a culture that has had a hold on us for over a century: a hold from which our thought has perhaps not yet emerged.'

13 ibid., p.42. See also Dugald Williamson, 'Language and sexual difference', *Screen*, Vol. 28, No. 1, Winter 1987, p.24.

14 John Rajchman, 'Foucault or the ends of modernism', *October* 24, Spring 1983, pp.37–62; and 'Ethics after Foucault', *Social Text* 13/14, Winter/Spring 1986, p.44.

15 The 'art of living' is how Michel Foucault described Gilles Deleuze and Felix Guattari's *Anti-Oedipus: Capitalism and schizophrenia*, Viking Press, N.Y., 1977. See Foucault's 'Preface', p.xiii. The unique bonding between the feminine, the poet and the insane has several variations. See for instance Deleuze and Guattari's transgressive triad of 'orphans (no mommy-daddy-me), atheists (no beliefs) and nomads (no habits, no territories)', ibid., p.xxi.

16 John Rajchman, op. cit. 1983, p.57.

17 Foucault, op. cit. 1980, p.70.

18 Griselda Pollock, 'Modernity and the Spaces of Femininity', *Vision & difference: Femininity, feminism and the histories of art*, Routledge, 1988, pp.50–90.

19 The quoted term is from Elizabeth Grosz, 'Feminism, Representation and Politics', *On the beach*, No. 9, 1985, pp.14–19.

20 George Alexander, *Perspecta '85*, Exhibition Catalogue, Art Gallery of New South Wales, 1985, p.9.

21 The Marquis de Sade, 'La Philosophie dans le Boudoir' in *Oeuvres complètes, XXV*, Pouvert, 1970, p.45; cited Jane Gallop, 'Impertinent Questions: Irigaray, Sade, Lacan', *Substance*, No. 26, 1980, p.65.

22 Luce Irigaray, 'When Our Lips Speak Together' in *This sex which is not one* (trans. Catharine Porter), Cornell University Press, Ithaca, N.Y., 1985, p.213, cited Gallop, op. cit. 1980, p.65. Gallop's translation is a little different to Porter's, which is as follows: 'Between us, there are no proprietors, no purchasers, no determinable objects, no prices'.

23 As Genet's translator notes, 'The term *la toilette* also refers to certain kinds of wrappings or casings, for example, a tailor's or dressmaker's wrapper for garments, as well as to the caul over mutton'. Jean Genet,

op. cit. 1971, p.54. *Caul over mutton* also forms part of Brown-Rrap's title for this work.

24   These heads (which Freud also quoted to introduce his famous 'Lecture on Femininity'), illustrated a poem by Heine:

> Heads in hieroglyphic bonnets
> Heads in turbans and black birettas,
> Heads in wigs and a thousand other
> Wretched, sweating heads of humans

25   Julie Brown-Rrap, *6th Biennale of Sydney, the death or resurrection of originality*, exhibition catalogue, Art Gallery of New South Wales, 1986, p.92.

26   The *Add magic* Billboard project was organised in 1990 by the Centre for Australian Photography (curator: Denise Robinson). Robyn Stacey and Pat Brassington were among the participating artists.

Chapter 7: 'The revolutionary power of women's laughter'?

1   Luce Irigaray, 'Questions', in *That sex which is not one*, Cornell University Press, Ithaca, NY, 1985, p.134.

2   See Julia Kristeva, *Desire in language: A semiotic approach to literature and art* (Ed. Leon S. Roudiez, Trans. Thomas Gora, Alice Jardine and Leon S. Roudiez), Columbia University Press, N.Y., 1980; also Roland Barthes, *The pleasure of the text* (Trans. Richard Miller), Hill and Wang, N.Y., 1975.

3   Julie Brown, *Disclosures (Surrogate I): A photographic construct*, Central St. Gallery, April–May 1982.

4   Dugald Williamson, 'Language and Sexual Difference', *Screen*, Vol. 28, No. 1, Winter 1987, p.19.

5   See John Delacour, 'Julie Brown's Disclosures—In Context, Out of the Biennale', *Art Network*, No. 7, Spring 1982, pp.32–34.

6   Roland Barthes, op. cit. 1975, p.14. See also in this context Stephen Heath, 'Narrative Space', *Screen*, Vol. 17, No. 3, Autumn 1976, pp.68–112.

7   John Delacour, op. cit. 1982, p.35. The quote is in turn adapted from J. L. Godard, on the subject of radical cinema.

8   Jacques Derrida, 'Positions', in *Positions* (trans. Alan Bass), University of Chicago Press, 1982, p.8.

9   Luce Irigaray, op. cit. 1985, p.134.

10   Unfortunately this work was lost in a touring 1986–7 Artspace exhibition.

11   Luce Irigaray, op. cit. 1985.

12   Juliet Mitchell and Jacqueline Rose, 'Feminine Sexuality: Interview—1982', *m/f*, No. 8, 1983, p.15. Mitchell and Rose observe how the

celebration of a generalised pre-symbolic register, reified as 'feminine' and collapsed back onto the natural or biological body echoes the positions taken up against Freud in the 1920s and 1930s by Jones, Horney and others.

13 Anne Ferran, 'Imaging', *Photofile*, Vol. 4, No. 2, Spring 1986, p.22.

14 Dugald Williamson, op. cit. 1986, p.24.

15 Hélène Cixous, 'Castration Or Decapitation?', *Signs : Journal of Women In Culture And Society*, Vol. 7, No. 1, Autumn 1981, pp.41–55.

16 Julia Kristeva, 'Motherhood According To Giovanni Bellini', op. cit. 1980, p.239.

17 ibid.

18 Mary Kelly, op. cit. 1984, p.9.

19 *Scenes on the death of nature* was first exhibited at the Performance Space. Details from this installation were later reproduced on the front cover of Luce Irigaray, *Divine women* (trans. Stephen Muecke) and Elizabeth Grosz, *Irigaray and the divine*, both published by Local Consumption Publications, Sydney, 1986.

20 Julia Kristeva, 'Approaching Abjection', in the *Oxford Literary Review*, Vol. 5, Nos. 1/2, 1983, p.132. See also *Powers of horror: An essay in abjection* (trans. Leon S. Roudiez), Columbia University Press, N.Y., 1984. Brassington also drew upon Barbara Creed's use of 'abjection' in the analysis of horror movies. See Barbara Creed, 'Horror and the Monstrous-Feminine—An Imaginary Projection', *Screen*, Vol. 27, No. 1, January/February1986, pp.44–70.

21 Hélène Cixous, op. cit. 1981, p.43.

22 See Josette Feral, 'Antigone or the irony of her tribe' (trans. Alice Jardine and Tom Gora), *Diacritics*, September 1978, p.10.

23 Michel Foucault, op. cit. 1980, pp.55–56.

24 Parveen Adams and Elizabeth Cowie, op. cit. 1986, p.8.

Select bibliography

Journals

Art Network, Vol. 1, No. 1, November 1979–Nos. 19/20, June–September 1986

Black Beauty: Dada Punk Wiminz Artz Anarchist Surreal Magazine (one issue, n.d.)

Cauldron, Vol. 1, No. 1, September 1974–Vol.1, No. 3, 1975

Girl's Own, No. 1, March–April, 1981–No. 11, May–June, 1983

LIP, No. 1, 1976–No. 8, 1984

Mabel, No. 2, March 1976–No. 7, May, 1977

Mejane, No. 1, April 1971–Vol. 2, No. 2, April 1974

Photofile, No. 1, Autumn 1983–

Refractory Girl, No. 1, December 1972–

Rouge, No. 2, August 1979–No. 10, December–January 1980–1981

Scarlet Woman, No. 1, April 1975–

Sydney Women's Art Movement Newsletter, No.1, 1974–No. 4, 1976

Vashti's Voice (later *Vashti*), No. 1, 1971–No. 30, Spring 1981

Articles, Theses, Books

Adams, Bruce, 'Broadside at politics of display', *Sydney Morning Herald*, 20 February 1987, p.10

—— 'Jacky Redgate rules in cool display', *Sydney Morning Herald*, 10 April 1987, p.12

Adams, Jude, 'Women artists as vanguard', *Honi Soit*, 1975

—— 'Review of Lucy Lippard's *From the center*', *LIP*, Nos. 2/3, 1977, p.54

—— (with Jenny Barber) 'Sisterhood—For whom?', *LIP*, Nos. 1978/79, p.54

—— 'Sexism in art education', *Women's Art Movement 1978–1979*, South Australian Women's Art Movement, Adelaide, 1980, pp.4–6

—— (with Sandy Edwards), 'Fashion images', *Women's Art Movement 1978–1979*, South Australian Women's Art Movement, Adelaide, 1980, pp.26–27

—— 'Motherhood' to the suburbs and the country', *Artlink*, Vol. 1, No. 2, May 1981, p.4

Adams, Parveen, 'Representation and sexuality', *m/f*, No. 1, 1978, pp.65–82

—— (with Jeff Minson), 'The "Subject" of feminism', *m/f*, No. 2, 1978, pp.43–61

—— 'A note on sexual division and sexual differences', *m/f*, No. 3, 1979, pp.51–58

—— 'Family affairs', *m/f*, No. 7, 1982, pp.3–14

—— 'Mothering', *m/f*, No. 8, 1983, pp.41–52

—— (with Elizabeth Cowie), 'Interview—1984', *m/f*, No. 11/12, 1986, pp.5–16

—— 'Versions of the body', *m/f*, Nos. 11/12, 1986, pp.27–34

Adler, Louise, 'Pleasure and power...Or how to have one without the other?', *Media Interventions*, Interventions Publications, Sydney, 1981, pp.97–104

Agee, Joyce, 'Photographic programmes in New South Wales prisons', *Photofile*, Summer 1984, p.11

Aldrich, Robert, 'From sodomy to sub-culture', *Gay Information*, No. 13, Autumn 1983, pp.7–14

Alexander, George, 'Persona and shadow', *On The Beach*, No. 6, Spring 1984, pp.46–48

—— 'One bird, one cage, one flight, one song in those far woods', *Studio Collection*, January 1985, p.31

—— Catalogue entry, *Australian Perspecta '85*, Exhibition Catalogue, Art Gallery Of New South Wales, p.9

—— Catalogue Entry, *Pleasure of the gaze*, Exhibition Catalogue, Art Gallery Of Western Australia, 1985, p.14

—— (with Allen Alain), 'Boomerang', *Art Australien, +*, No. 46, February 1987

Alexander Mackie College of Advanced Education, *Sydney Biennale: White elephant or red herring?, comments from the art community*, Sydney 1979

Allen, Judith, 'Marxism and the man question: Some implications of the patriarchy debate', in Allen and Patton (eds), *Beyond Marxism? Interventions after Marx*, Intervention Publications, Sydney, 1983, pp.91–112

Allen, Sheila (with Carol Wolkowitz), 'The control of women's labour: The case of homeworking', *Feminist Review*, No. 22, February 1986, pp.25–51

Altman, Dennis, 'Re-defining sexuality', *Arena*, No. 29, 1972, pp.50–55

Annear, Judy, *Art in the age of mechanical reproduction*, Exhibition Catalogue, George Paton And Ewing Galleries, Melbourne, 1982

Aras, J. (ed), *Postmodernism and politics*, Minnesota University Press, 1986

Ardhill, Susan (with Norie Neumark), 'Putting sex back into lesbianism', *Gay Information*, No. 11, Spring 1982, pp.4–11

Art & Language, 'Interview with Lucy Lippard', *Art & Language*, Art & Language Press, Sydney, 1975, pp.141–142

Arts In Society, Special Volume on Women in the Arts, Vol. 11, No. 1, Spring/Summer 1974

Artworkers' Union of NSW, *Affirmative action for women in the visual arts*, August 1985

—— *In the frame: Affirmative action for women in the visual arts*, Slidetalk, Sydney, January 1988

Australian Centre for Photography, *Graduating photography*, Exhibition Catalogue, Australian Centre for Photography, Sydney, 1982

Australian Commonwealth Government, *The Martin report on higher education*, Government Printer, Canberra, 1964

—— *Green paper on affirmative action for women*, Government Printer, Canberra, 1984

Australia Council, *Tertiary visual arts education in Australia*, Sydney, 1979

—— *Report on the individual artist in Australia today*, Sydney, 1983

—— *Women in the arts*, Sydney, 1983

—— *Women in the arts: A strategy for action*, Sydney, 1985

—— *Community arts officers review: Report to the Community Arts Board*, 1985

—— *Community arts officers in Australia*, Sydney, 1986

Australian National Advisory Committee For UNESCO, *The Professional training of the artist*, Canberra, 1970

Australian National Gallery, *The Phillip Morris Collection: Australian photographers*, Australian National Gallery, Canberra, 1979

—— *Photography No. 1: International Photography 1920–1980*, Exhibition Catalogue, November 1982–January 1983

—— *A decade of Australian photography 1972–1982, Exhibition Catalogue*, October 1983–January 1984

—— *Recent Australian photography from the Kodak Fund*, Exhibition Catalogue, October 1985–February 1986

Australian Women's Broadcasting Co-Operative For 'Coming Out' 1977, 'Mother I can see a light', Three-Part Programme On The Growth Of The Australian Women's Movement, Australian Broadcasting Commission (2FC), 'Coming Out '77', 7 May 1977

Baddock, C. and Cass, Bettina (eds), *Women, social welfare and the state in Australia*, George Allen and Unwin, Sydney, 1983

Barber, Jenny, 'Sydney Women's Art Movement', *LIP*, Nos. 2/3, 1977, pp.93–94

Barrett, Michele, *Women's oppression today*, New Left Books, London, 1980

—— (with Mary McIntosh), *The anti-social family*, Verso, London, 1982

Batchen, Geoffrey, *Borderlines: Recent Sydney photography*, Exhibition Catalogue, Albury Regional Art Centre And New England Regional Art Museum, 1987

Barthes, Roland, *The pleasure of the text*, Hill and Wang, New York, 1975

—— *Image-music-text*, Essays Selected and Translated By Stephen Heath, Fontana/Collins, Glasgow, 1977

—— *Camera lucida: Reflections on photography*, Hill and Wang, New York, 1981

Beames, Nicolas, 'A fine line', *Praxis M*, No. 11, Summer 1986, p.36

Beechy, Victoria, 'What's so special about women's employment? A review of some recent studies of women's paid work', *Feminist Review*, No. 15, 1983, pp.23–46

Belamy, Sue, 'Women in factories', Paper delivered at the First Women's Liberation Conference, 23–5 January, 1971, later published as 'Factory Work', in *Women At Work*, Words For Women, Sydney, 1972, pp.21–28

—— 'Women cannot paint: They can only consolidate', *Mejane*, No. 4, September 1971, p.12

Bellour, Raymond, 'Review of Michel Foucault, *Les usages des plaisirs* and *Le souci de soi*', *m/f*, No. 11/12, 1986, pp.113–120

Bennett, Fran (with Beatrix Campbell and Rosalind Coward), 'Feminists—The degenerates of the social?', *Politics And Power*, No. 3, Routledge and Kegan Paul, London, 1981, pp.83–92

Berube, Allen, 'Lesbian and gay GIs in World War II: Marching to a different drum', *The Advocate*, No. 328, 15 October 1981, pp.20–24

Binns, Vivienne, 'Sexism in selecting staff for art colleges', *The Women's Show Conference Papers*, South Australian Women's Art Movement, Adelaide, 1977, pp.49–50

—— 'Group dynamics', *The Women's Show Conference Papers*, South Australian Women's Art Movement, Adelaide, 1977, pp.67–69

—— (with Helen Grace), 'Extracts from a discussion between Vivienne Binns and Helen Grace', *Art Network*, Vol. 1, No. 1, November 1979, pp.20–21

—— 'Mothers' memories, others' memories', *LIP* 1980, pp.38–46

Birmingham, Jan, *Women And Craft/Arts Committee report on ideas-based workshops*, New South Wales Women And Arts Festival, Sydney, 1982

—— (coordinator), *Connections and separations*, Department of Corrective Services and the Board of Adult Education, 1982

—— (with Tanya Crothers), *Labels and other images: Visual arts project with the women of Mulawa*, *Caper*, No. 21, Community Arts Board, Australia Council, 1984

Bland, Lucy, 'The domain of the sexual: A response', *Screen Education*, No. 39, Summer 1981, pp.56–68

Botsman, Peter, 'The sexual and the social: Policing venereal disease, medicine and morals', PhD Thesis, History Department, University of New South Wales, 1987

Bowen, Julie, 'Women artists: Objects d'art?', *Hecate*, Vol. III, No. 2, July 1977, pp.81–84

Bower, Ros, 'Community arts—What is it?', *Caper*, No. 10, Community Arts Board, Australia Council, Sydney, 1981

—— 'The community arts officer: What is it all about?', *Caper*, No. 10, Community Arts Board, Australia Council, Sydney, 1981

Braden, Su, *Committing photography*, Pluto Press, London, 1983

Braidotti, Rosi, 'The ethics of sexual difference: The case of Foucault and Irigaray', Paper delivered at the Masculine/Feminine and Representation Conference, University Of Sydney, 2 August 1986, published in a revised form in *Australian Feminist Studies*, No. 3, Summer 1986, pp.1–14

Brennan, Theresa (with Mia Campioni and Elizabeth Jacka), 'One step forward, two steps back', *Working Papers In Sex, Science and Culture*, Vol. 1, No. 1, January 1976, pp.15–45

Brereton, Kurt (ed), *Photo-discourse*, Sydney College of the Arts, 1981

—— 'Julie Brown', *Photofile*, Vol. 2, No. 2, Winter 1984, p.8

Britton, Stephanie, 'Motherhood—Be in it', *Artlink*, Vol. 1, No. 3, August 1981, pp.5–7

Bromfield, David, 'Ghouls in the gallery', *Praxis M*, No. 12, Autumn 1986, pp.18–20

Brooks, Rosetta, 'Double-page spread—Fashion and advertising photography', *Camerawork*, No. 17, January/February 1980, pp.1–3

Broom, Dorothy, 'The occupational health of homeworkers', *Australian Feminist Studies*, No. 2, Autumn 1986, pp.15–34

Brophy, Philip, 'Horrality', *Art & Text*, No. 11, Spring 1983, pp.85–95

Brouss-Delanoe, Marie-Helene, 'Two psychoanalysts and a pacifier', *m/f*, No. 8, 1983, pp.30–31

Brown, Beverley, 'Natural and social division of labour—Engels and the domestic labour debate', *m/f*, No. 1, 1978, pp.25–48

—— (with Parveen Adams), 'The feminine body and feminist politics', *m/f*, No. 3, 1979, pp.35–50

—— 'A feminist interest in pornography—Some modest proposals', *m/f*, 5/6, 1981, pp.5–18

—— 'Displacing the difference—Review of *Nature, culture and gender*', *m/f*, No. 8, 1983, pp.79–90

Brown, Pamela, '1982 Adelaide Festival—Micky Allan's family room', *Artlink*, Vol. 2, No. 1, March/April 1982, p.3

Brown-Rrap, Catalogue Entry, *On Site*, Exhibition Catalogue, Tasmanian School Of Art Gallery, Hobart, 1984, n.p.

—— Julie, 'Artist's Talk', Australian Centre For Photography, Sydney, June 1985

—— 'Julie Brown-Rrap', *Express*, Vol. 1, No. 3, March 1986, pp.2–3

—— 'Artist's statement', *Transition*, No. 17, June 1986, n.p.

—— Catalogue Entry, *The death and resurrection of originality, Sixth Biennale of Sydney*, Exhibition Catalogue, Art Gallery Of New South Wales, 1986

—— Julie, 'Questions from the inside', Catalogue Essay, *The Thief's journal*, Mori Gallery, Australian Centre For Photography, Artspace, Sydney, September 1986

Brunson, Charlotte, 'A subject for the seventies', *Screen*, Vol. 23, Nos. 3–4, September/October 1982, pp.20–30

Bryson, Lois (with Martin Mowbray), '"Community": The spray-on solution', in *Australian Journal of Social Issues*, April 1981, pp.254–261

Buci-Gluckman, Christine, 'Catastrophic—Utopia: The feminine as allegory of the modern', *Representations*, No. 14, Spring 1986, pp.220–229

Bullen, Jane, 'Patriarchy, psychoanalysis and historical materialism', *Working papers in sex, science and culture*, Vol. 1, No. 1, January 1976, pp.46–54

Burchell, Graham, 'Putting the child in its place', *I&C*, No. 8, Spring 1981, pp.73–96

Burger, Peter, *Theory of the avant-garde* (trans. Michael Shaw), University of Minnesota Press, Minneapolis, 1984

Burke, Janine, *Australian Women painters: One hundred years 1840–1940*, Exhibition Catalogue, George Paton And Ewing Galleries, Melbourne, 1975

—— 'Experiments In Vitreous Enamels', *LIP*, No. 1, 1976, pp.26–27

—— 'Feminist Art Criticism', *The Women's Show Conference Papers*, South Australian Women's Art Movement, Adelaide, 1977, pp.61–62

—— 'Sense and sensibility: Women's art and feminist criticism', *LIP '78/79*, pp.3–5

—— 'A survey of women's art theory courses and feminine sensibility', *LIP '78/79*, pp.60–64

—— 'Artists working collectively', *Art & Text*, No. 1, 1981, pp.33–42

—— *Australian women artists: One hundred years 1840–1940*, Greenhouse, Melbourne, 1980

Burn, Ian, 'Workers' intervention and creativity', *Art Network*, No. 2, Spring 1980, p.10

—— 'The sixties: crisis and aftermath', *Art & Text*, No. 1, 1981, pp.49–65

—— *Working art: A survey of the Australian Labour Movement in the 1980s*, Exhibition Catalogue, Art Gallery Of New South Wales, August–October 1985

Burns, Ailsa (with Gill Bottomley and Penny Jools), *The family in the modern world*, George Allen and Unwin, Sydney, 1984

Burns, Tom (ed), *Industrial Man*, Penguin, London, 1969

Caddick, Alison, 'Feminism and the body', *Arena*, No. 74, 1986, pp.60–88

Caine, Barbara, 'From "A fair field and no favour" to "Equal Opportunity": Or a new look at campaigns to improve the employment opportunity of women', *Refractory Girl*, No. 30, September 1987, pp.36–40

Caldwell, Lesley, 'Review of Denise Riley's *War in the nursery: Theories of the child and the mother*', *m/f*, Nos. 11/12, 1986, pp.89–94

Califa, Pat, 'Feminism and sadomasochism', *Heresies*, No. 12: Sex Issue, Vol. 3, No. 4, 1981, pp.30–34

Campbell, Beatrix, 'Feminist sexual politics: Now you see it, now you don't', *Feminist Review*, No. 5, 1980, pp.1–18

—— (with Anna Coote), *Sweet freedom: The struggle for women's liberation*, Picador, London, 1982

Campbell, Leonie, 'Women's liberation', *Arena*, No. 27, 1971, pp.31–36

—— 'Process of liberation', *Arena*, No. 28, 1972, pp.9–11

Campioni, Mia, 'Psychoanalysis and Marxist feminism', *Working Papers in Sex, Science and Culture*, Vol. 1, No. 2, November 1976, pp.33–60

—— (with Elizabeth Gross), 'Love's labour's lost: Marxism and feminism', in Patton and Allen (eds), *Beyond Marxism? Interventions after Marx*, Intervention Publications, Sydney, 1983, pp.113–142

Carroll, Ian, 'The new radicals', *Arena*, No. 21, 1970, pp.65–71

Carter, Angela *The Sadean woman*, Virago, London, 1979

Carter, Mick, 'S/he, it; From unisex to androgyny', *Art Network*, No. 10, Winter 1983, pp.28–33

—— 'The strip laid bare, unevenly', *Art & Text*, No. 10, Winter 1983, pp.48–60

Cartledge, Sue and Ryan, Joanna (eds), *Sex and love: New thoughts on old contradictions*, The Women's Press, London, 1983

Cato, Jack, *The story of the camera in Australia*, Institute of Australian Photography, Sydney 1979, (3rd edn)

Centre For Urban Research And Action, *But I wouldn't want my wife to work there: A study of migrant women in Melbourne industry*, Research Report For International Women's Year, Melbourne, 1975

Charman, Karen, *The little blue book for girls: Health and sexuality resources guide for young women*, Sibylla Press, Melbourne, 1983

Chicago, Judy, *Through the flower: My struggle as a woman artist*, Doubleday, New York, 1975

Chinnery, Catherine, *Occasional visits*, Redress Press, Sydney, 1986

—— *Pentimento*, Exhibition Catalogue, Australian Centre For Photography, Sydney, June–July 1986

Chodorow, Nancy, *The reproduction of mothering*, University Of California Press, Berkeley, 1978

Cixous, Hélène, 'Castration or decapitation?', *Signs: Journal Of Women In Culture And Society*, Vol. 7, No. 1, Autumn 1981, pp.41–55

Clarke, Wendy, 'The dyke, the feminist and the devil', *Feminist Review*, No. 11, 1982, pp.30–39

Cohen, Joyce Tenneson (ed), *In/sights: Self-portraits by women*, David R. Godine, Boston, 1978

Comer, Lee, 'The motherhood myth', *Australian Left Review*, No. 34, March 1972, pp.28–34

Community Action, *Community Action No. 58, Special Issue: Photography*, Community Action, London, July–August 1982

Conley, Verena, 'Kristeva's China', *Diacritics*, Winter 1975, pp.25–28

Connors, Lindsay, 'Success sours some women's liberationists', the *National Times*, April 30–May 5th, 1973

Copje, Joan, 'Seduction, sedition and the dictionary—Review of *Feminism and psychoanalysis: The daughter's seduction*', *m/f*, No. 8, 1983, pp.67–78

Coultas, Val, 'Feminists must face the future', *Feminist Review*, No. 7, 1981, pp.35–48

Coventry, Virginia (ed), *The critical distance: Work with photography/politics/ writing*, Greenhouse Publications, Melbourne, 1986

Coward, Rosalind, 'Sexual liberation and the family', *m/f*, No. 1, 1978, pp.7–24

—— 'Are women's novels feminist novels?', *Feminist Review*, No. 5, 1980, pp.53–64

—— 'Sexual violence and sexuality', *Feminist Review*, No. 11, 1982, pp.9–22

—— *Female Desire: Women's sexuality today*, Paladin, London, 1984

Cowie, Elizabeth, 'Woman As Sign', *m/f*, No. 1, 1978, pp.49–64

—— 'Introduction to post-partum document', *m/f*, Nos. 5/6, 1981, pp.115–123

Cox, Eva, 'Reclaiming the household budget', *Refractory Girl*, No. 29, May 1986, pp.15–17

Coyle, Suzi (with Anne Zahalka), *Outside the poem ... inside the dream ... a story unfolds*, Exhibition Catalogue, Union St. Gallery, Sydney, 1985

—— 'Intimations of elsewhere', Unpublished Postgraduate Diploma studio documentation and seminar paper, submitted Sydney College of the Arts, 1985

Creed, Barbara, 'Horror and the monstrous—feminine—An imaginary projection', *Screen*, January/February 1986, pp.44–70

Curthoys, Ann, 'Historiography and women's liberation', *Arena*, No. 22, 1970, pp.35–46

—— (with Lyndall Ryan), 'Up from radicalism ... problems of organisation in Sydney Women's Liberation', Unpublished paper presented at the First Women's Liberation Conference, Sydney, 23–25 January 1971

—— Eade, Susan and Sperritt, Peter (eds), *Women at work*, Australian Society For The Study Of Labour History In Australia, Canberra, 1975

—— 'The family and feminism', *Hecate*, Vol. XI, No. 1, 1985, pp.110–117

D'Aprano, Zelda, *Zelda: The becoming of a woman*, no publisher's imprint, Melbourne, 1975

Daniels, Kay, and Murnane, Mary (eds), *Uphill all the way: A documentary history of women in Australia*, University of Queensland Press, 1980

—— 'Women's history', in Osborne and Mandle (eds), *New history: Studying Australia today*, Allen and Unwin, Sydney, 1982, pp.32–50

—— 'Review of *Surpassing the love of men*', *Gay Liberation*, No. 13, Autumn 1983, pp.23–25

Davidson, Robyn, 'Beyond backyards and backsides', *Praxis M*, No. 2, July 1983, pp.28–33

Davis, Ken (with Paul Van Reynk), 'A continent of mannerisms: The politics of radical drag', *Gay Information*, Nos. 9/10, Autumn/Winter 1982, pp.40–45

Davis, Tricia (with Phillipa Goodall), 'Personally and politically: Feminist art practice', *Feminist Review*, No. 1, 1979, pp.21–36

'Deb' (et al.), 'Dyketactics: Working with gay men', *Gay Information*, No. 8, Summer 1981, pp.12–15

De Groen, Geoffrey, *Conversations with Australian artists*, Melbourne, 1978

Delacour, John, 'Julie Brown's disclosures', *Art Network*, No. 7, Spring 1982, pp.32–35

Dengate, Roseann, 'The quest for a feminist art methodology', MA (Prelim) Thesis, Fine Arts Department, University of Sydney, 1985

Derrida, Jacques, *Of grammatology* (trans. Gayatri Chakrovorty Spivak), Johns Hopkins, Baltimore, 1974

—— (with Christie McDonald), 'Choreographies', *Diacritics*, 1981, pp.66–76

—— *Positions* (trans. Alan Bass), University Of Chicago Press, 1982

—— 'The question of style', in Allison, D.B. (ed), *The new Nietzsche*, MIT Press, Cambridge, Mass., 1985

Dixon, Jill (with Chris Johnson, Sue Leigh and Nicky Turnbull), 'Feminist perspectives and practice', in Mayo, Marjorie et al. (eds), *Women and community*, Routledge & Kegan Paul, London, 1977, pp.59–71

Dixon, Miriam, *The real Matilda: Women and identity in Australia 1788–1975*, Penguin, Melbourne, 1976

Doane, Mary-Ann, 'Woman's stake: Filming the female body', *October*, No. 17, Summer 1981, pp.23–36

—— 'Film and the masquerade: Theorising the female spectator', *Screen*, Vol. 23, Nos. 3–4, September/October 1982, pp.74–88

Dolliver, Cliff (with Ian Atherton), 'Interview with Julie Brown-Rrap', *Paper Burns*, No. 3, Summer 1985, pp.8–14

Donald, Anne, 'Lunch on a Tuesday', *Lesbian News*, No. 8, January/February 1985, p.11

Donzelot, Jacques, *The policing of families* (trans. Robert Hurley), Pantheon Books, New York, 1979

—— 'The poverty of political culture', *Ideology and consciousness*, No. 5, Spring 1979, pp.73–86

—— 'Pleasure in work', *I&C*, No. 9, Winter 1981/82, pp.2–28

Dowse, Dale, 'Towards a feminist aesthetic', Paper delivered at the National Women's Liberation Theory Conference, Mt. Beauty, 27–29/1/1973

Doy, Gen, 'Women, history and photographic imagery', *Camerawork*, No. 19, July 1980, pp.11–13

Dreyfus, Hubert L. (with Paul Rabinow), *Michel Foucault: Beyond structuralism and hermeneutics* (2nd edn), University of Chicago Press, 1983

Dumbrell, Lesley, 'The Victorian women's slide register', *LIP*, No. 1, 1976, pp.11–12

Duncan, Carol, 'Virility and domination in early twentieth century vanguard painting', *Artforum*, Vol. XII, No. 4, pp.30–39

—— 'Art history and the family', Unpublished paper delivered at the Power Foundation, University of Sydney, 1986

Dykes' Decadence Calendar, 1985

Edgar, Patricia (with Hilary McPhee), *Media she*, Heinemann, Melbourne, 1974

Edwards, Meredith, 'Economics of home activities', Unpublished paper delivered at the SAANZ Conference, July 1979

Ehrenreich, Barbara (with Deirdre English), *For her own good*, Pluto Press, London, 1979

Ehrensaft, Diane, '*When women and men mother*', *Politics and power*, No. 3, Routledge and Kegan Paul, 1981, pp.21–48

Ehrlich White, Barbara, 'A 1974 perspective: Why women's studies in art and art history?', *Art Journal*, Vol. XXXIV, No. 4, Summer 1976, pp.340–344

Eisenstein, Zillah R. (ed), *Capitalist patriarchy and the case for socialist feminism*, New York and London, 1979

Eisenstein, Hester, *Contemporary feminist thought*, George Allen and Unwin, Sydney/London, 1984

Ellis, John, 'Photography/pornography, art/pornography', *Screen*, Vol. 21, No. 1, Spring 1980, pp.81–108

Ellis, Julie, 'Women's liberation', *All That's Left*, Vol. 1, No. 4, December 1971, pp.41–47

Ely, Bonita, 'Sexism in art education', *The Women's Show conference papers*, South Australian Women's Art Movement, Adelaide, 1977, p.48

—— 'Women's art register extension project', *LIP '78/79*, pp.64–66

Encel, Sol (with N. Mackenzie and M. Tebbutt), *Women and society: An Australian study*, Cheshire, Melbourne, 1974

English, Deirdre (with Amber Hollingbaugh and Gayle Rubin), 'Talking sex: A conversation on sexuality and feminism', *Feminist Review*, No. 11, 1982, pp.40–52

Ennis, Helen, 'Carol Jerrems and the politics of consent', Paper delivered at the Australian Art Association Conference, Canberra, July 1984

—— '1970s photographic practice', *Photofile*, Vol. 4, No. 1, Autumn 1986, pp.12–14

—— 'The 1970s and now', *Afterimage*, Vol. 14, No. 2, September 1986, pp.7–8

—— 'Women's photography in the 1970s', unpublished paper delivered at the Australian Centre For Photography, September 1986

—— *Australian photography: The 1980s*, Australian National Gallery, 1988

Ewens, Rod, 'Uneasy voyages of the mind', the *Mercury*, 19 July 1986

Ewington, Julie, Untitled paper; 'It should have been a feminist show'; and 'The women's show conference', in *The Women's Show Conference Papers*, South Australian Women's Art Movement, Adelaide, 1977, pp.79, 45 respectively

—— 'Fragmentation and feminism', *Art & Text*, No. 7, Spring 1982, pp.61–73

—— 'Problematising political art: The case of feminist artists in Australia in the '70s', *Third Women And Labour Conference Papers*, 1982, Vol. 2, pp.319–320

—— *Heartland*, Exhibition Catalogue, Wollongong Regional Gallery, May 1985

—— 'Past the post: Feminism and postmodernism', Catalogue Essay, *150 Women Artists*, Women 150th, Melbourne, September 1985, n.p.

—— *Domestic contradictions*, Exhibition Catalogue, Power Foundation Gallery, Sydney, June–July 1987

—— 'Review of "Living in the '70s"', *Photofile*, Vol. 5, No. 3, Summer 1987–88, pp.27–29

—— 'Postmodern excellence', *Praxis M*, No. 18, pp.8–12

Feinstein, Sharon, 'Our bodies, ourselves', *Gay News*, No. 245, 22 July– 4 August 1982, pp.52–53

Felman, Shoshana, 'The critical phallacy', *Diacritics*, Winter 1975, pp.20–24

Felski, Rita, 'German feminist aesthetics: Review of *Feminist Aesthetics*', *Australian Feminist Studies*, No. 3, Summer 1986, pp.143–152

Fenelon, Jeanette, 'Women in art schools: Careers for women', *LIP*, Nos. 2/3, 1977, p.88

Feral, Josette, 'Antigone or the irony of her tribe' (trans. Alice Jardine and Tom Gora), *Diacritics*, September 1978, pp.2–14

Ferguson, Anne (with Jacqueline Rita and Katherine Pyre Addelson), 'On "Compulsory heterosexuality and lesbian existence": Defining the issues', *Signs*, Vol. 7, No. 1, Autumn 1981, pp.158–199

Ferran, Anne, 'Imaging', *Photofile*, Vol. 4, No. 2, Spring 1986, pp.22–23

—— Artist's Talk, University of Tasmania (School of Art), Hobart, 1986

—— Artist's Statement, Australian National Gallery, Canberra, 1987

Fildes, Sarah, 'The inevitability of theory', *Feminist Review*, No. 14, 1983, pp.62–70

Firestone, Shulamith, *The dialectics of sex: The case for the feminist revolution*, Bantam Books, New York, 1971

Fletcher, Diana, 'Marginalism or intervention?... A methodological study of feminist needlework histories', IV Year Honours Essay, Fine Arts Department, University of Sydney, 1985

Flitterman, Sandy, 'Woman, desire and the look: Feminism and the enunciative apparatus in the cinema', *Cine-Tracts*, Vol. 2, No. 1, Fall 1978, pp.63–69

Foote, Maxienne, 'From Monday to Monday', *LIP*, 1980, pp.67–73

Ford, Sue, *A photo-book of women*, Exhibition Catalogue, Art Gallery Of New South Wales, October 1982

—— *One sixtieth of a second*, Experimental Art Foundation, Adelaide, 1987

Forrester, John, 'Freud, Dora and the untold pleasures of psychoanalysis', *Desire*, ICA Documents, London, 1984, pp.4–8

Forster, Margaret, *Significant sisters: The grassroots of active Feminism 1839– 1939*, Penguin, Great Britain, 1986

Foucault, Michel, *The order of things: An archaeology of the human sciences*, Tavistock, London, 1970

—— *The birth of the clinic: An archaeology of medical perception*, Tavistock, London, 1973

—— 'Film And Popular Memory', *Radical Philosophy*, No. 11, Summer 1975, pp.24–29

—— *Discipline and punish: The birth of the prison* (trans. A. Sheridan), Vintage Books, New York, 1977

—— 'Politics and the study of discourse', *Ideology & Consciousness*, No. 3, Spring 1978, pp.7–26

—— 'The eye of power', *Semiotext(e)*, Vol. III, No. 2, 1978, pp.6–19

—— 'My body, this paper, this fire', *The Oxford Literary Review*, Vol. 4, No. 1, Autumn 1979, pp.9–30

—— 'On governmentality', *Ideology & Consciousness*, No. 6, Autumn 1979, pp.5–22

—— *Power, truth, strategy* (trans. and edited by Meaghan Morris and Paul Patton), Feral Publications, Sydney, 1979

—— *The archaeology of knowledge* (trans. A. M. Sheridan Smith), Tavistock, London, 1979 (1st English edn 1972)

—— 'Introduction' to *Herculine Barbin: Being the recently discovered memoirs of a nineteenth-century French hermaphrodite* (Trans. Richard McDougall), Pantheon, New York, 1980

—— *Power/knowledge* (trans. Colin Gordon), Pantheon, New York, 1980

—— *The history of sexuality: Volumn one: An introduction* (trans. A. Sheridan), Vintage Books, New York, 1980

—— (with Richard Sennett), 'Sexuality and solitude', *London Review Of Books*, Vol. 3, No. 9, 21 May–9 June, 1981, pp.5–7

—— 'Questions of method: An interview with Michel Foucault', *Ideology & Consciousness*, No. 8, Spring 1981, pp.3–14

—— *Language, counter-memory, practice* (trans. Donald F. Bouchard and Sherry Simon), Cornell University Press, Ithaca, New York, 2nd Printing, 1981

—— 'Sexual choice, sexual acts: An interview with Michel Foucault', James O'Higgins, *Homosexuality: Sacrilege, vision, politics, Salmagundi*, Vol. 88, No. 59, Fall 1982–Winter 1983, pp.10–24

—— *The use of pleasure: The history of sexuality: Volume two* (trans. Robert Hurley), Pantheon, New York, 1985

—— *The care of the self: The history of sexuality: Volume three* (trans. Robert Hurley), Pantheon, New York, 1986

Fox, Alan, *A sociology of work in industry*, MacMillan, London, 1971

Fox, Judith, 'Duo reworks old themes to make the invisible visible', *Sydney Morning Herald*, 14 May 1985, p.12

Frank, Laurel, 'An exhibition of women's work', *LIP*, Nos. 2/3, 1976, p.83

Freiberg, Freda, 'Nothing new?—Photographs by Helen Grace and Sandy Edwards', *LIP*, 1982/83, pp.67–69

—— 'Review of *And So…We Joined The Union*', *Photofile*, Vol. 4, No. 1, Autumn 1986, pp.23–25

Freund, Gisele, *Photography and society*, David Godine, Boston, 1980

'G, Judy', 'The myth of wages for housework—and the reality of wages for housework', *Vashti*, No. 22, Autumn/Winter 1978, pp.11–14

Galbally, Ann, 'Women only? A feminist exhibition considered', *Meanjin Quarterly*, Vol. 34, No. 4, December 1975, pp.389–391

Gallop, Jane, 'Impertinent questions: Irigaray, Sade, Lacan', *Substance*, No. 26, 1980, pp.57–67

—— 'Nurse Freud: Class struggle in the family', *Hecate*, Vol. VIII, No. 1, 1982, pp.26–31

—— *The daughter's seduction: Feminism and psychoanalysis*, MacMillan, London, 1982

Game, Ann (with Rosemary Pringle), 'The making of the Australian family', *Intervention*, No. 12, April 1979, pp.63–83

—— (with Rosemary Pringle), *Gender at Work*, George Allen & Unwin, Sydney, 1983

Gardiner, Susan, 'The methodology of feminist biography', *Hecate*, Vol. VII, No. 2, 1981, pp.40–59

Garlick, Beverley, 'Interview with Vivienne Binns', *Refractory Girl*, No. 8, March 1975, pp.7–16

Garrard, Mary D., 'Of men, women and art: Some historical reflections', *Art Journal*, Vol. XXXV, No. 4, Summer 1976, pp.324–329

Garron, H., *The captive wife*, Penguin, Harmondsworth, Middlesex, 1966

Gatens, Moira, 'A critique of the sex-gender distinction', in Allen and Patton (eds), *Beyond Marxism? Interventions after Marx*, Sydney, 1983, pp. 143–162

—— 'Women, the family and philosophy', unpublished paper delivered at the Power Foundation forum on art history and the family, University of Sydney, 1986

Gay Liberation, 'Whose aversions?', *Nation*, April 15th, 1972, pp.12–15

Genet, Jean, *The thief's journal*, Penguin, London, 1971

Gertsakis, Elizabeth, 'The romance', *The Mercury*, 1/11/1986

Gillett, Judy, 'Women–liberation–revolution', *Australian Left Review*, September 1971, pp.16–24

Glazer-Malbin, N., 'Review essay: Housework', *Signs: A Journal of Women in Culture and Society*, No. 1, 1976, pp.906–922

Goddard, Julian, 'Pamela Kleeman', Catalogue Essay, *Five from the West*, Undercroft Gallery, University of Western Australia, August–September 1984

Godden, Christine, *CSR Pyrmont Refinery Centenary 1978 Photography Project*, Australian Centre for Photography, Sydney, 1978

Goffman, I., *Gender advertisements*, Macmillan, London, 1979

Goldin, Amy, 'American art has been called elitist, racist and sexist. The charges stick', *Art News*, Vol. 74, No. 5, April 1975, pp.48–53

'Golda', 'Finding oneself', *Vashti's Voice*, No. 11, Winter 1975, pp.8–9

Gorman, John, *Images of labour*, Scorpion, London, 1985

Grace, Helen (with C. Merewether, T. Schofield and T. Smith), 'Mods and Doccos', in Nickson and McGillvray (eds), *Working papers on photography*, Melbourne, 1978, pp.36–47

—— 'The lovely motherhood show', *Scarlet Woman*, No. 9, September 1979, pp.13–20

—— (with Stephen, Ann), 'Where do positive images come from? (and what does a woman want?)', *Scarlet Woman*, No. 12, March 1981, pp.15–22

—— 'From the margins: An essay on feminist art', *LIP*, 1981/82, pp.13–18

—— 'The repetition of difference', *Photofile*, Vol. 3, No. 3, Spring 1985, pp.5–7

Graham, Anne, photographs reproduced in *Praxis M*, No. 1, April 1983, pp.14–17

—— (with Alan Vizants), 'Domestic devices', performance notes, Australian Centre for Photography, 8 February 1984

—— *Mediation: Perceptual identity*, Exhibition Catalogue, Institute of Modern Art, Brisbane, May 1984

Green, David, 'On Foucault: Disciplinary power and photography', *Camerawork*, No. 32, Summer 1985, pp.6–9

Greer, Germaine, *The female eunuch*, Paladin, London, 1971

—— *The obstacle race: The fortunes of women painters and their work*, Secker and Warburg, London, 1979

Greive, Norma and Grimshaw, Pat (eds), *Australian women: Feminist perspectives*, Penguin, Melbourne, 1981

Grislam, Joan L., 'On healing the nature nurture split in feminist thought', *Heresies*, 13, Vol. 4, No. 1, 1981, pp.4–9

Grosz, Elizabeth, 'Lacan, the Symbolic, the Imaginary and the Real', *Working Papers in Sex, Science and Culture*, Vol. 1, No. 2, November 1976, pp. 12–32

—— 'Foucault, Herculine Barbin and the truth of sex', *Gay Information*, No. 8, Summer 1981, pp.16–22

—— 'Pornography and power', *Filmnews*, July 1981, p.7

—— (with Mia Campioni), 'Love's Labour's Lost: Marxism and feminism', in Allen and Patton (eds), *Beyond Marxism? Interventions after Marx*, Intervention Publications, Sydney, 1983, pp.113–142

—— 'Feminism, representation and politics', *On The Beach*, No. 9, 1985, pp.14–19

—— *Men don't make passes at women who ...* Exhibition Catalogue, Roslyn Oxley9 Gallery, Sydney, October 1985

—— 'On Irigaray and sexual difference', *Australian Feminist Studies*, No. 2, Autumn 1986, pp.63–78

—— (with Pateman, Carol) (eds), *Feminist challenges: Social and political theory*, Allen and Unwin, Sydney, 1986

—— *Irigaray and the divine*, Local Consumption Publications, Sydney, 1986

Gunew, Sneja (with Adler, Louise), 'Method and madness in female writing', *Hecate*, Vol. VII, No. 2, 1981, pp.20–33

Guthrie, Bessie, 'You can't run all the time', *Mejane*, No. 8, August 1972, pp.8–13

Hall, Barbara, 'Women and post-object art', in Brook and Sheridan (curators), *Post-object art in Australia and New Zealand*, Experimental Art Foundation, Adelaide, 1976, n.p.

—— 'Australian women photographers project', in Nickson and McGillvray (eds), *Working papers on photography*, 1978, pp.17–19

—— 'Women's images of women', *LIP*, '78/79, pp.22–25

—— 'Child's image, woman's hands', *LIP*, 1980, pp.28–33

—— (with Mather, Jenni and Gillespie, Christine), *Australian women photographers 1840–1940*, Exhibition Catalogue, George Paton and Ewing Galleries, Melbourne, 1981

—— (with Mather, Jenni), *Australian women photographers 1840–1960*, Greenhouse Publications, Melbourne, 1986

Halliwell, Kevin, 'Photography and narrativity', *Screen Education*, No. 37, Winter 1980/1981, pp.79–84

Hamblin, Angela, 'The suppressed power of female sexuality', in Allen et al. (eds), *Conditions of illusion*, Feminist Books, London, 1974

Hamon, Marie-Christine, 'Good-enough', *m/f*, No. 8, 1983, pp.32–33

—— 'The figure of the mother—A study', *m/f*, No. 8, 1983, pp.33–39

Hampshire, Carol, 'Dancing in the margins of other texts', *Photofile*, Vol. 3, No. 3, Spring 1985, pp.30–31

—— 'Pentimento', *Photofile*, Vol. 4, No. 2, Spring 1986, pp.23–24

Hanna, Bronwyn, 'Feminism and art history', IV Year Methodology Essay, Fine Arts Department, University of Sydney, 1985

—— 'Why do feminists both criticise and utilise the monography in art history?' IV Year Methodology Essay, Fine Arts Department, University of Sydney, 1985

Hansford, Pam, 'Women raid the old to bring in the new', *Sydney Morning Herald*, 20 November 1985

Hardman, Marion, *Practical dreams*, Sydney, 1981

Havana, Anna, 'The women's art register extension project', *The Women's Show conference papers*, Adelaide, 1977, p.64

Hawkes, Ponch, 'Our mums and us', *LIP*, Nos. 2/3, 1977, p.21

Hawkes, Terence, *Structuralism and semiotics*, Methuen, London, 1977

Hebdidge, Dick, 'Posing … threats, striking … poses: Youth, surveillance and display', *Substance*, Nos. 37/38, 1983, pp.82–92

Heks, Robyn (with Wayne Hutchins), *A captive audience: An analysis of the Community Mural Project, Long Bay Prison Complex, NSW, September–December 1982, Caper No. 17*, Australia Council, 1983

Helyer, Nigel, 'Anne Graham', *Australian Perspecta '85*, Exhibition Catalogue, Art Gallery of New South Wales, 1985, p.153

—— 'Balancing acts IV', *Performed and presented*, Exhibition Catalogue, Chameleon Gallery, Hobart, May 1986

Hemensley, Kris, 'Melbourne commentary: Everything or nothing', *Photofile*, Vol. 2, No. 3, Spring 1984, p.9

—— 'Photography as performance', *Photofile*, Vol. 2, No. 2, Winter 1984, pp.11–12

Hershman, Lynn, *Dream weekend: A project for Australia: 3 dream homes, Burwood Hwy, Vermont South, Victoria, September 16th, 17th, 19th 1977*, Exhibition Catalogue, George Paton and Ewing Galleries, Melbourne, 1977

Hicks, Peter (with Rick Martin), 'A process of organisation', *Caper*, No. 26, Australia Council, April 1984

Hirsh, Julia, *Family photographs: Content, meaning and effect*, Oxford University Press, New York, 1981

Hirst, Paul Q. (with Woolley, Penny), *Human relations and social attributes*, Tavistock, London, 1982

Hodges, Jill (with Athar Hussain), 'Review of Jacques Donzelot's *La police des familles*', *Ideology & Consciousness*, No. 5, Spring 1979, pp.87–124

—— 'Children with parents: Who chooses?', *Politics And Power*, No. 3, Routledge & Kegan Paul, London, 1981, pp.49–66

Holloway, Memory, 'Reel women: Narrative as a feminist alternative', *Art & Text*, No. 3, Spring 1981, pp.34–42

—— 'In the tracks of isis', *Micky Allan retrospective*, Exhibition Catalogue, Monash University Gallery, Melbourne, September 1987

Holmes, Johnathon, 'Pieces of eight', *Photofile*, Vol. 4, No. 2, Spring 1986, pp.15–17

Horne, Robert, *Eight easy pieces*, Exhibition Catalogue, Australian Centre for Photography, May 1987

Howe, Graham, (ed), *New photography Australia: A selective survey*, Australian Centre for Photography, Sydney, 1974

Hull, Andrea, 'Women in the community arts', *The Women's Show conference papers*, Adelaide, 1977, pp.62–63

Hunt, Sue, *A certain likeness: A show of portraits*, Exhibition Catalogue, Artspace, Sydney, December 1985

Hunter, Alexis, *Photographic narrative sequences* (with critical essays by Lucy L. Lippard and Margaret Richards), Edward Totah Gallery, London, 1981–2

Hunter, Ian, 'On reflection theory: Including remarks on John Docker's *In a critical condition*', *Australian Journal Of Cultural Studies*, Vol. 3, No. 1, May 1985, pp.3–28

—— 'Culture and government: The emergence of literary education', PhD Thesis, School of Humanities, Griffith University, 1986

Hunter, Thelma, 'Reform or revolution in contemporary feminism', *Politics*, Vol. VIII, No. 2, November 1973, pp.321–329

Hussain, Athar, 'Foucault's *History of sexuality*', *m/f*, Nos. 5/6, 1981, pp.169–191

Huyssen, Andreas, *After the great divide: Modernism, mass culture, postmodernism*, Indiana University Press, Bloomington and Indianapolis, 1986

Institute of Contemporary Arts, *Women's Images of Men*, Exhibition Catalogue, Institute of Contemporary Arts, 4–26 October 1980 (Director: Sandy Naime)

Irigaray, Luce, 'That sex which is not one', in Morris and Foss (eds), *Language, sexuality and subversion*, Working Papers Collection, Feral Publications, Sydney, 1978

—— 'Women's exile', *Ideology & Consciousness*, No. 1, 1978, pp.62–76

—— *Speculum of the other woman* (trans. Gillian Gill), Cornell University Press, Ithaca, New York, 1985

—— *This sex which is not one* (trans. Catherine Porter), Cornell University Press, Ithaca, New York, 1985

—— *Divine women* (trans. Stephen Muecke), Local Consumption Publications, Sydney 1986

Iverson, Margaret, 'Exhibition review: *Difference: On representation and sexuality*', *m/f*, Nos. 11/12, 1986, pp.78–88

Jackson, Sue (with Diane Otto), 'Making links: The Women's Movement and the factory floor, The Everhot Factory', *Scarlet Woman*, No. 6, October–November 1977, pp.2–9

Jacobs, Mary (ed), *Women writing and writing about women*, Croom Helm, London, 1979

Jayamanne, Laleen, 'The holey family', reproduced in *LIP*, 1981/82, pp.42–46

Jerrems, Carol (with Virginia Fraser), *A book about Australian women*, Outback Press, Melbourne, 1974

Johnson, Carol, 'Some problems and developments in Marxist Feminist theory', *3rd Women And Labour Conference Papers*, Vol. 2, 1982, pp.517–523

Johnston, Claire, 'Towards a feminist film practice: Some theses', *Edinburgh 1976 Magazine*, pp.50–59

—— 'Women's cinema as counter-cinema', in Nichols (ed), *Movies and methods: An anthology*, California University Press, 1976, pp.208–217

—— 'Myths of Women in the Cinema', in Kay and Peary (eds), *Women and the cinema*, New York, 1977, pp.407–411

—— 'The subject of feminist film theory/practice', *Screen*, Vol. 21, No. 2, Summer 1980, pp.27–34

Johnston, Craig, 'Foucault and gay liberation', *Arena*, No. 61, 1982, pp.54–70

Johnston, Jill, 'Lesbian/feminism reconsidered', *Homosexuality: sacrilege, vision, politics, Salmagundi*, Nos. 58–59, Fall 1982–Winter 1983, pp.10–24

Jolly, Martyn, 'Rupture, generation or continuity?: The 70s and 80s photography (A speech from a rostrum)', *After the artefact*, Exhibition Catalogue, Wollongong City Gallery, July–August 1984, pp.15–17

—— *Killing time*, Exhibition Catalogue, Mori Gallery, Sydney, January–February 1985

Kalfon, Dominique, 'I am expecting a baby', *m/f*, No. 8, 1983, pp.28–29

Kaluzynska, Eva, 'Wiping the floor with theory—A survey of writings on housework', *Feminist Review*, No. 6, 1980, pp.27–54

Keesing, Nancy (ed), *The white chrysanthemum: Changing images of Australian motherhood*, Angus & Robertson, 1977

Kelly, Christine (with Andrew Sisson), 'The social construction of feminist art: An exploratory study', unpublished report, submitted Caulfield Institute of Technology, 1979

Kelly, Mary, 'Post-partum document', *m/f*, Nos. 5/6, 1981, pp.124–148

—— 'Re-viewing Modernist criticism', *Screen*, Vol. 22, No. 3, 1981, pp.41–62

—— 'Woman, desire, image', *Desire*, ICA Documents, London, 1984, pp.30–31

—— *Post-partum document*, Routledge & Kegan Paul, London, 1985

Kennedy, Peter, 'Inhibodress—Just for the record', *Art Network*, No. 6, Winter 1982, pp.49–51

Kessler, Maya, 'The obscurity of sight: Anne Ferran's *Carnal knowledge* and Bill Henson's *Untitled'*, 1985, IV Year Essay, Fine Arts Department, University of Sydney, 1987

King, Ynestra, 'Feminism and the revolt of nature', *Heresies*, Vol. 4, No. 13, 1981, pp.12–16

Kingston, Beverley, *My wife, my daughter and poor Mary Ann*, Nelson, Melbourne, 1975

Kirby, Sandy, 'The Women's Art Movement in Victoria 1975–85', *150 Women*, Catalogue Essay, Australian Centre For Contemporary Art, Melbourne, August 1985, n.p.

Kleeman, Pamela, 'Drastic on plastic', *Praxis M*, No. 1, April 1983, pp.18–19

Klein, Richard, 'In the body of the mother', *Enclitic*, Vol. 7, No. 1, Spring 1983, pp.66–75

Klinger, Barbara, ' "Cinema/ideology/criticism" revised: The progressive text', *Screen*, Vol. 25, No. 1, January–February 1984, pp.30–44

Koedt, Anne, 'Lesbianism and feminism' (1971), in Koedt and Rapone (eds), *Radical Feminism*, Quadrangle, New York, 1973, pp.246–258

Kolbowski, Silvia, 'Images', *m/f*, Nos. 11/12, 1986, pp.74–77

Kress-Rosen, Nicole, 'Women's transference', *m/f*, Nos. 11/12, 1986, pp.17–26

Kristeva, Julia, 'The semiotic activity', *Screen*, Vol. 14, Nos. 1/2, Spring/Summer 1973, pp.25–39

—— (with an Introduction by Geoffrey Nowell-Smith), 'Signifying Practice and mode of production', *Edinburgh Review*, No. 1, 1976, pp.60–76.

—— *Desire in language: A semiotic approach to literature and art* (Ed. by Leon S. Roudiez, trans. by Leon S. Roudiez, Thomas Gora and Alice Jardine), Columbia University Press, New York, 1980

—— 'The maternal body', *m/f*, Nos. 5&6, 1981, pp.158–163

—— *Powers of horror: An essay on abjection* (trans. Leon S. Roudiez), Columbia University Press, New York, 1983

—— 'Approaching abjection', *Oxford Literary Review*, Vol. 5, Nos. 1/2, 1983, pp.125–149

—— *The revolution in poetic language* (trans. Margaret Walker), Columbia University Press, New York, 1984

—— 'Histoires d'Amour—Love stories', *Desire*, ICA Documents, London, 1984, pp.18–21

—— 'In conversation with Rosalind Coward', *Desire*, ICA Documents, London, 1984, pp.22–27

—— 'Interview with Julia Kristeva' (trans. Rene Gallimard), *On The Beach*, Nos. 3/4, Summer/Autumn 1984, p.8

—— 'Say nothing' (trans. by Salvatore Mele), *On The Beach*, Nos. 3/4, Summer/Autumn 1984, pp.10–14

—— 'The last word on this adventure', interview by Louise Burchill, *On The Beach*, No. 6, Spring 1984, pp.22–26

190   *Indecent exposures*

—— *The Kristeva reader*, Toril Moi (ed), Basil Blackwell, Oxford, 1986
Kruger, Barbara, *We won't play nature to your culture*, ICA, London, 1983
Kuhn, Annette (with Anne-Marie Wolpe), *Feminism and materialism: Women and modes of production*, Routledge and Kegan Paul, London, 1978
—— 'Introduction to Cixous' "Castration or decapitation?" ', *Signs: Journal Of Women In Culture And Society*, Vol. 7, No. 1, Autumn 1981, pp.36–40
—— *Women's pictures: Feminism and the cinema*, Routledge & Kegan Paul, London, 1982
—— *The power of the image*, Routledge & Kegan Paul, London, 1985
Lacan, Jacques, *Ecrits, a selection* (trans. Alan Sheridan), Tavistock, London, 1977
—— (and the Ecole Freudienne), *Feminine sexuality*, Juliet Mitchell and Jacqueline Rose (eds); (trans. Jacqueline Rose), Macmillan, London, 1982
Land, Hilary, 'The family wage', *Feminist Review*, No. 6, 1980, pp.55–78
Laurent, Eric, 'A new symptom of the woman: The mother effect', *m/f*, No. 8, 1983, pp.22–25
Levy, Bronwyn, 'Recent directions in feminist theory (North America, United Kingdom, France)', *3rd Women And Labour Conference Papers*, 1982, Vol. 2, pp.527–541
Lewens, Caroline, 'Photographs', *LIP*, 1982/83, pp.28–29
Lingwood, James (ed), *Staging the self: Self-portrait photography 1840s–1980s*, Exhibition Catalogue, National Portrait Gallery, Plymouth, 1987
Lippard, Lucy R., *Changing: Essays in art criticism*, Dutton, New York, 1971
—— *The de-materialisation of the art object*, Praeger, New York, 1973
—— *From the center: Feminist essays on women's art*, Dutton, New York, 1976
—— 'Projecting a feminist criticism', *Art Journal*, Vol. XXXV, No. 4, Summer 1976, pp.337–339
—— *Issue and tabu*, Exhibition Catalogue, ICA, London, 1980
—— 'Hot potatoes: Art & politics in 1980', *Block*, No. 4, 1981, pp.2–9
Lloyd, Genevieve, *The man of reason: 'Male' and 'female' in Western philosophy*, Methuen, London, 1984
Louden, Marcia, 'Women's estate', *Intervention*, No. 2, October 1972, pp.95–99
Lynch, Lesley, 'Greater openness?', *Mejane*, No. 3, July 1971, p.4
—— 'Myth-making in the Women's Movement', *Refractory Girl*, No. 5, Summer 1974, pp.34–38
Lynn, Elwyn, 'Paris: City of male supremacy', the *Weekend Australian*, 8 September 1987
Lyotard, Jean-Francis, 'One of the things at stake in women's struggles' (trans. Deborah Clarke, Winnie Woodhull and John Mowitt), *Sub-stance*, No. 20, 1978, pp.9–18
Macey, David, 'Review Article: Jacques Lacan', *I&C*, No. 4, 1978, pp.113–127
Maloon, Terence, 'Concept and precept', Catalogue Essay, *After the artefact*, Wollongong City Gallery, July–August 1984, pp.5–6

—— 'What's in? Kinkiness and lewedness, that's what!', *Sydney Morning Herald*, 2 November 1985

Manderson, Lenore, 'Self, couple and community: Recent writings on lesbian women', *Hecate*, Vol. VI, No. 1, 1980, pp.67–79

Marsh, Anne (with Jane Kent), *Live art*, no publishers imprint, Adelaide, 1984

—— *Difference*—A radical approach to women and art, South Australian Women's Art Movement, Adelaide 1985

Marshall, Brenda, 'Pat Brassington', *Feminist narratives*, Exhibition Catalogue, George Paton and Ewing galleries, Melbourne, June 1987, p.6

Martin, Adrian, 'Immortal stories', *Photofile*, Vol. 4, No. 3, Summer 1986, pp.11–15

Maxwell, Ailsa, ' "The lovely motherhood show"—A reply to Jenny Boult', *Art Network*, Nos. 3/4, Winter/Spring 1981, p.11

McCarthy, Sarah, 'Photo practice 2', *Screen Education*, No. 36, Autumn 1980, pp.56–68

McDonald, John, 'Dawes shares the crest of a feminist new wave', *National Times On Sunday*, 31 August, 1986, p.30

McDonald, Sharon, 'My body or my politics', *The Advocate*, No. 357, December 1982, pp.33–35

McKluskie, Kate, 'Women's language and literature: A problem in Women's Studies?', *Feminist Review*, No. 14, 1983, pp.51–61

McLeod, Laura, 'Sydney Women's Art Movement', Honours Thesis, Fine Arts Department, University of Sydney, 1980

McRobbie, Angela, 'The politics of feminist research: Between talk, text and action', *Feminist Review*, No. 12, 1982, pp.46–58

Media Education Committee, NSW Department of Education, *Women as artists: Resisting images by men*, Educational Kit, Sydney, n.d.

Melbourne University Fine Arts Department, 'A note to the Fine Arts Department at Melbourne University—Methodology and history of art and sexism', unpublished leaflet, Melbourne 1977

Mercer, Colin, 'Generating consent', *Ten-8*, No. 14, 1984, pp.3–9

Mercer, Jan (ed), *The other half: Women in Australian society*, Penguin, Melbourne, 1975

Merewether, Charles and Stephen, Ann (eds), *The great divide*, no publishers imprint, Melbourne, 1977

Merk, Mandy, 'Introduction—Difference and its discontents', *Screen*, Vol. 28, No. 1, Winter 1987, pp.2–10

Meulenbelt, Anja, Outshoorn, Joyce, Sevenhuijsen, Selma and de Vries, Petra (eds), *A creative tension: Explorations in socialist feminism*, Pluto Press, London, 1984

Miller, Andrew, 'Art, culture and radical critique', *Arena*, Nos. 32/33, 1973, pp.90–92

Millet, Kate, *Sexual politics*, Abacus, London, 1971

Milossi, Dario (with Pavarini, Massimo), *The prison and the factory: Origins of the penitentiary system* (trans. Glynnis Cousin), Macmillan, London, 1981

Minchin, Annie, 'Women in art: A fool's paradise', *The Women's Show Conference Papers*, Adelaide, 1977, pp.50–53

Minson, Jeff, 'The assertion of homosexuality', *m/f*, Nos. 5/6, 1981, pp.19–40

—— 'Reservations about sexual radicalism', in Botsman and Harley (eds), *Theoretical strategies*, Local Consumption Publications, Sydney, 1982, pp.112–126

—— 'Entertaining ethics—Review of *Les usages des plaisirs* and *Le souci de soi*', *m/f*, Nos. 11/12, 1986, pp.121–138

Mitchell, Avenel (with Catriona Moore), 'Staking claims', *Photofile*, Vol. 2, No. 3, Summer 1987/1988, pp.34–35

Mitchell, Juliet, *Women's estate*, Penguin, London, 1971

—— *Feminism and psychoanalysis*, Penguin, London, 1974

—— (with Oakley, Anne) eds, *The rights and wrongs of women*, Penguin, London, 1976

—— (with Jacqueline Rose), 'Feminine sexuality: Interview—1982', *m/f*, No. 8, 1983, pp.3–16

—— 'Femininity, narrative and psychoanalysis: Some comments', in Gunew and Reid (eds), *Not the whole story: Tellings and tailings from the ASP ACLS Conference On Narrative*, Local Consumption Publications, Sydney, 1984, pp.83–88

Mock, Ruth, *Principles of art teaching: A handbook for teachers in primary and secondary schools*, University of London Press, London, 1955

Moi, Toril, 'Representation and patriarchy: Sexuality and epistemology in Freud's Dora', *Feminist Review*, No. 9, 1981, pp.60–75

—— 'Jealousy and sexual difference', *Feminist Review*, No. 11, 1982, pp.53–69

—— 'Feminist readings of Dora', *Desire*, ICA Documents, London, 1983, pp.16–17

—— 'The case of Dora', *Desire*, ICA Documents, London, 1984, p.3

—— *Sexual textual politics: Feminist literary theory*, New Accents, Methuen, London, 1985

Montrelay, Michele, 'Inquiry into femininity', *m/f*, No. 1, 1978, pp.83–102

Moore, Catriona, 'Dangerous liaisons', *Afterimage*, Vol. 14, No. 2, September 1986, pp.5–7

—— 'Recent Australian photography', *Artlink*, Vol. 6, Nos. 2/3, June/July 1986, pp.47–49

—— *Pure invention*, Exhibition Catalogue, Parco Gallery, Tokyo, 1987

—— 'Slave girls: Welcome to the world of style', *San Francisco Camerawork*, Vol. 15, No. 1, Spring 1988, pp.12–17

Moore, David and Hall, Rodney, *Australia: Portrait of a nation 1850–1960*, Collins, Sydney, 1983

Moore, Fiona, *Putting art to work*, Publicity Works, Australia Council, 1986

Morgall, Janine, 'Typing our way to freedom: Is it true that new office technology can liberate women?', *Feminist Review*, No. 9, 1981, pp.87–102

Morris, Meagan, 'Feminist critique', *Cinema Papers*, November–December 1975, pp.207–209, 286

—— 'The pirate's fiancée' in Morris and Patton (eds), *Michel Foucault: Power, truth, strategy*, Feral Publications, Sydney, 1979, pp.148–168

Mort, Frank, 'The domain of the sexual', *Screen Education*, No. 36, Autumn 1980, pp.69–84

Mulvey, Laura, 'You don't know what is happening, do you, Mr. Jones?', *Spare Rib*, No. 8, 1973, pp.13–16, 30

—— 'Visual pleasure and narrative cinema', *Screen*, Vol. 16, No. 3, Autumn 1975, pp.6–18

—— 'Afterthoughts on "Visual pleasure and narrative cinema", inspired by *Dual in the sun*', *Framework*, Nos. 15/16, 1981, pp.15–17

—— 'The image and desire', *Desire*, ICA Documents, London, 1983, pp. 28–29

Myers, Kathy, 'Fashion 'n passion', *Screen*, Vol. 23, Nos. 3–4, September–October 1982, pp.89–97

—— 'Towards a feminist erotica', *Camerawork*, No. 24, March 1982, pp.14–16

—— 'Pasting over the cracks', *Desire*, ICA Documents, London, 1984, pp.35–38

Nemser, Cindy, 'Forum: Women in art', *Arts Magazine*, February 1971, p.18

—— 'Art criticism and the gender preference', *Arts Magazine*, March 1972, pp.44–46

Nestle, John, 'Butch and feminine relationships: Sexual courage in the 1950s', *Heresies*, Vol. 3, No. 4, 1981, pp.21–24

Newmarch, Ann, *Projects in prospect 1982–1983*, Experimental Art Foundation, 1984

Nicholls, Jane, 'Portrait of the artist as housewife—with a review', *6 a.m. Arts Melbourne and Art Almanac*, Vol. 2, No. 2, December 1977, n.p.

Nickson and McGillvray (eds), *Working Papers On Photography*, Melbourne, 1978

Noble, Alex, 'The body politic', *Ten-8*, No. 25, 1987, pp.2–3

Nochlin, Linda, *Woman as sex object: Studies on erotic art 1730–1970*, with Hess, T.B. (eds), Lane, Allen, 1973

New South Wales Women and the Arts Festival, *NSW Women and Arts Festival Seminar Papers: The growth of women's art: From manifesto to politics*, October 1982

Newton, Gael, *Shades of light: Photography and Australia 1839–1988*, Australian National Gallery, Canberra, 1988

O'Connor, Ailsa, 'A little paper on women and creativity' delivered to the National Women's Conference on Feminism and Socialism, Melbourne University, 5–6 October 1974

O'Sullivan, Sue, 'Passionate beginnings, ideological politics 1969–72', *Feminist Review*, No. 11, 1982, pp.70–87

Oakley, Anne, *Housewife*, Penguin, Middlesex, England, 1974

—— *The sociology of housework*, Martin Robertson, London, 1974

Oliver, Margo, McMirchy, Meaghan and Thornley, Jenni, *For love or money: A pictorial history of women and work in Australia*, Penguin, Melbourne, 1985

Owens, Craig, 'The allegorical impulse: Towards a theory of post-modernism', *October*, No. 12, Spring 1980, pp.67–86

—— 'Representation, appropriation and power', *Art in America*, Vol. 70, No. 5, May 1982, pp.9–21

—— 'Honor, power and the love of women', *Art in America*, January 1983, pp.15–20

—— 'The discourse of others: Feminists and post-modernism' in Foster (ed), *The anti-aesthetic: Essays on post-modernism*, Port Townsend, Washington, 1983, pp.57–82

—— 'Posing', *Difference: Representation and sexuality*, Exhibition Catalogue, New Museum of Contemporary Art, New York, 1985, pp.7–18

Parker, Rozsika (with Griselda Pollock), *Old mistresses: Women, art and ideology*, Routledge & Kegan Paul, London, 1981

—— *The subversive stitch*, Routledge & Kegan Paul, London, 1984

—— (with Griselda Pollock), *Framing feminism: Art and the Women's Movement 1970–1985*, Pandora, London, 1987

Patton, Paul, 'More on the Foucault Effect', *Media Interventions*, Interventions Publications, Sydney, 1981, pp.105–112

—— 'Notes for a glossary', *I&C*, No. 8, Spring 1981, pp.41–48

Peace, Bob, 'Feminism and community work', unpublished paper delivered Phillip Institute of Technology, School of Social Work, 19 August 1985.

Pearse, Warwick, 'Art and working life', *Photofile*, Vol. 2, No. 3, Spring 1984, p.7

Perry, Tony, Warwick Pearse, 'Nostalgia Close To Overdose', *The Age*, 30 November 1979

Petruck, Peninah R. (ed), *The camera viewed: Writings on twentieth century photography*, Vols. I and II, E.P. Dutton, New York, 1979

Phillips, Anita, 'Fast operators—Women at the workstation', *Camerawork*, No. 32, Summer 1985, pp.12–14

Photography Workshop (eds), *Photography/politics: One*, Photography Workshop, London, 1979

The Visual History of South Sydney Project, *Pictures for cities: A visual history of south Sydney project: Aboriginal history, industrial history*, Exhibition Catalogue, Artspace, Sydney, 1984

Plaza, Monique, ' "Phallomorphic power" and the psychology of "Woman" ', *Ideology & Consciousness*, No. 4, Autumn 1978, pp.4–36

—— 'Our Costs and Their Benefits', *m/f*, No. 4, 1980, pp.28–40

Plummer, Kenneth (ed), *The making of the modern homosexual*, Hutchinson, London, 1981

Pointon, Marcia, 'Interior portraits: Women, physiology and the male artist', *Feminist Review*, No. 22, Spring 1986, pp.5–22

Pollock, Griselda, 'What's Wrong with Images of Women?', *Screen Education*, No. 24, Autumn 1977, pp.25–34

—— 'Three perspectives on photography', *Screen Education*, No. 31, Summer 1979, pp.49–54

—— 'Feminism, femininity and the Hayward Annual II', *Feminist Review*, No. 2, 1979

—— 'More than methodology', *Screen*, Vol. 23, Nos. 3/4, September/October 1982, pp.122–126

—— 'Art, art school, culture individualism after the death of the artist', *Block*, No. 11, 1985/6, p.8

—— *Vision and difference: Femininity, feminism and the histories of art*, Routledge & Kegan Paul, London, 1988

Popular Memory Group, 'Popular memory: Theory, politics, method', *Making histories—Studies in history writing and politics* (CCCS), Hutchinson, Birmingham, 1982

Prahran Neighbourhood House Women's Photography Project Booklet, Prahran Neighbourhood House, March 1985

Price, Derrick, 'Photographing the poor and the working class', *Framework*, Nos. 22/23, Autumn 1983, pp.20–25

Pringle, Rosemary, 'Sexuality and social change, an examination of Dennis Altman's *Coming out in the seventies* and *Rehearsals for change*', *Island Magazine*, No. 7, June 1981, pp.33–35

Procacci, Giovanna, 'Social economy and the government of poverty', *Ideology & Consciousness*, No. 4, Autumn 1978, pp.55–72

Radford, Robert, 'Edith Tudor-Hart—Photographs from the Thirties', *Camerawork*, No. 19, July 1980, pp.1–4

Rajchman, John, 'Foucault and the ends of Modernism', *October*, No. 24, Spring 1983, pp.41–62

—— *Michel Foucault: The freedom of philosophy*, Columbia University Press, New York, 1985

—— 'Lacan and the ethics of modernity', *Representations*, No. 5, Summer 1985, pp.50–59

—— 'Ethics after Foucault', *Social Text*, 13/14, Winter/Spring 1986, pp.165–183

Rendall, Jane, *The origins of modern feminism: Women in Britain, France and the United States, 1780–1860*, Macmillan, 1985

Richards, Barry, 'Psychology, prisons and ideology: The prison psychological service', *Ideology* and *Consciousness*, No. 2, Autumn 1977, pp.9–28

Rigg, Julie (ed), *In her own right*, Melbourne, Nelson, 1969

Riley, Denise, 'Developmental psychology, biology and Marxism', *Ideology & Consciousness*, No. 4, Autumn 1978, pp.73–92

Riley, Elizabeth, *All that false instruction: A novel of lesbian love*, Angus & Robertson, Melbourne, 1975

Roberts, Helen, *Doing feminist research*, Routledge & Kegan Paul, London, 1982

Robertson, Toni, 'Towards a feminist art', *Arena*, Vol. 7, No. 3, Macquarie University Students' Council, Sydney, 1974
—— 'Sins of omission', unpublished Honours Thesis, University of Sydney, Fine Arts Department, 1977
Robinson, Denise, *Meaning and excellence*, Exhibition Catalogue, ANZART in Edinburgh, 1984
—— 'Impure solutions', *Art and Text*, No. 26, September/November 1987, pp.5–6
Roe, Jill, 'Lesbian love', *Mejane*, No. 5, November 1971, p.12
—— 'Lesbians are women', *Mejane*, No. 3, July 1971, pp.4–5
Rogers, Catherine, *The Newtown Photographic Project*, Exhibition Catalogue, Sydney College of the Arts, March 1984
Rogers, Meredith (with Ann Stephen), 'Experiments in vitreous enamel— Portraits of women an interview with Marie McMahon, Frances Budden and Toni Robertson, *1 AM: Arts Melbourne and Art Almanac*, Vol. 1, No. 1, 1976, pp.44–50
Rose, Jacqueline, 'Dora, Fragment of Analysis' *m/f*, No. 2, 1978
—— 'Introduction II' in Juliette Mitchell and J. Rose (eds), *Jacques Lacan and the Ecole Freudienne, feminine sexuality*, Macmillan, London, 1982, pp.27–58
—— *Sexuality in the field of vision*, Verso, London, 1986.
Rose, Nikolas, 'Review, E. Badinter, *The myth of motherhood'*, *m/f*, No. 7, 1982, pp.82–86
Rowbotham, Shiela, *Women's liberation and the new politics*, Spokesman Pamphlet No. 17, 1971 (reprinted from May Day Manifesto Group, 1969)
—— *Women, resistance and revolution*, Penguin, Harmondsworth, Middlesex, 1972
—— *Women's consciousness, man's world*, Penguin, Harmondsworth, Middlesex, 1973
—— *Hidden from history*, Pluto Press, London, 1973
Rowe, Marsha, 'Noise and meaning: Feminism and writing in England', *Refractory Girl writes*, No. 24, October 1982, pp.12–18
Rubin, Gayle, 'The leather menace', *The Body Politic*, No. 82, April 1982, pp.33–35
Rule, Jane, 'Homophobia and romantic love' in *Outlander: Stories and essays*, The Niaid Press, Florida, 1981
Russell, David (with the Manchester Studies Team), 'Any old albums?— Building a people's history', *Camerawork*, No. 16, November 1979, pp. 1–3
Russell, Joan, 'Women reclaiming autonomous power', *WRAP*, April 1984, Vol. 1, No. 5, pp.3–7
Ryan, Edna (with Ann Canlon), *Gentle invaders: Women's art work in Australia 1788–1974*, Nelson, Melbourne 1975
San Francisco Museum of Art, *Women of photography: A historical survey*, Exhibition Catalogue, April 18–June 15, 1975

Sandford, Coonie, 'Women in the workforce'. Paper delivered Women's Liberation Conference, Melbourne, 16–18 May 1970, later published in *Women at work*, Words for Women, Sydney, 1971, pp.1–9

Sargent, Lydia (ed), *Women and revolution: A discussion of the unhappy marriage of Marxism and feminism*, Boston, 1981

Sauzeau-Boetti, Anne-Marie, 'Negative capability as practised in women's art', *Studio International*, Vol. 191, No. 979, January–February 1976, pp.24–29

Sayes, Janet, 'Psychoanalysis and personal politics', *Feminist Review*, No. 10, Spring 1982, pp.91–95

Segal, Lynne, *What's to be done about the family? Crisis in the eighties*, Penguin, 1983

——— 'Is the future feminine?', *New Socialist*, No. 45, January 1987, pp.7–11

Sekula, Alan, 'Photography between labour and capital', in Buchloh, Wilkie and Macguillray (eds), *Mining photographs and other pictures 1948–1968: A selection from the negative archives of Sheddon Studio, Glace Bay, Cape Breton*, The Press of the Nova Scotia School of Art and Design, Halifax, 1983, pp.193–269

Shaktini, Namascar, 'Displacing the phallic subject: Wittig's lesbian writing', *Signs: Journal of Women in Culture and Society*, Vol. 8, No. 1, Autumn 1982, pp.29–42

Sheehan, Beatrice, 'Sexism and stress in the studios', *Artlink*, Vol. 1, No. 4, September/October 1981, p.14

Shelley, Martha, 'Lesbians in the WLM', in *The second wave*, Vol. 1, No. 1, Spring 1971, pp.28–29, 32

Sheridan, Susan, 'From margins to mainstream: Situating women's studies', *Australian Feminist Studies*, No. 2, Autumn 1986, pp.1–14

——— (convenor), 'Reports: Feminism and the Humanities Year at the Humanities Research Centre, ANU', *Australian Feminist Studies*, No. 3, Summer 1986, pp.97–114

Simes, Gary, 'History and sexual categories', *Gay Information*, No. 13, Autumn 1983, pp.15–22

Simms, Marion, 'In defense of prudery', *Vashti's Voice*, No. 17, Summer 1976/77, p.7

Skirrow, Gillian, 'Whoosh!', *Screen*, Vol. 23, Nos. 3/4, September/October 1982, pp.135–136

Smith, Joan (with Kirsten Mellor), 'Reproducing the sexual division of labour', *Hecate*, Vol. XI, No. 1, 1985, pp.39–56

Smith, Margaret and Crossley, David (eds), *The way out: Radical alternatives in Australia*, Landsdowne Press, Melbourne, 1975

Smith, Terry, 'The situation now: Object or post-object art', CAS Sydney, 1971 Exhibition Catalogue

——— 'Photographic practice in the Trade Union Movement: A report', *Photofile*, Vol. 2, No. 2, Winter 1984, p.7

——— 'Representing work', *Afterimage*, Vol. 4, No. 2, September 1986, p.9

Snitnow, Ann, Stansell, Christine and Thompson, Sharon (eds), *Desire: The politics of sexuality*, Virago, London, 1984

Social Alternatives, Feminism Issue, Vol. 4, No. 3, January 1985

Soloman Godeau, Abigail, 'Winning the game when the rules have been changed—Art photography and Post-modernism', *Screen*, Vol. 25, No. 6, November–December, 1984, pp.88–102

South Australian Women's Art Movement, *The Women's Show Conference Papers*, Adelaide, 1977

—— *South Australia Women's Art Movement, 1978–1979*, Adelaide, 1980

—— *Setting the pace: The Women's Art Movement 1980–1983*, Adelaide, 1984

Sowerwine, Charles, 'Women's and family history documentaries', *Australian Feminist Studies*, No. 3, 1986, pp.173–180

Spate, Virginia, 'What ever happened to the art of the seventies?', *Art and Text*, No. 14, Winter 1984, pp.75–79

Spence, Jo and Dennett, Terry (eds), *Photography/politics one*, Photography Workshop, London, 1979

—— *Putting myself in the picture: A political, personal and photographic autobiography*, Camden Press, London, 1986

Spivak, Gayatri Chakrovorty, 'Displacement and the discourse of woman', in Krupnick, Mark (ed), *Displacement: Derrida and after*, Indiana University Press, Bloomington, 1983, pp.169–198

—— 'Criticism, feminism and the institutions', *Thesis Eleven*, Nos. 10/11, 1984/5, pp.175–187

St. Leger, Deborah, *The romance*, Exhibition Catalogue, First Draft, Sydney, July 1986

Stacey, Lorraine, and Freeman, Nicolette, *Pine Gap images*, Video Cassette, AFTS 1984

Starenko, Michael, 'The politics of interpretation', *Afterimage*, Vol. 11, No. 6, January 1984, pp.12–14

Steedman, Carolyn, 'The tidy house', *Feminist Review*, No. 6, 1980, pp.1–28

Steiner, Riccardo, 'Dora: "La belle indifference" or label(le) in différance', *Desire*, ICA Document, London, 1984, pp.9–13

Stephen, Ann, 'Understanding women's art', talk given to group of women artists, Melbourne, November 1975

—— 'At the edge of a feminist criticism: Interview with Lucy Lippard', *Meanjin Quarterly*, Vol. 34, No. 4, December 1975, pp.6–17

—— 'A female sensibility in art', paper delivered for the Women's Art Forum, February 1976

—— 'A loose conversation—Three Melbourne women who use the camera', in Sheridan and Brook (eds), *Post-object art in Australia*, Adelaide, 1976

—— 'A process of de-neutralising: A review of three Sydney Exhibitions' *LIP*, No. 1, 1976, pp.27–8

—— 'Feminist criticism', paper delivered Australian Art Association Conference, 20 August 1976

—— and Merewether Charles (eds), *The great divide*, no publishers' imprint, Melbourne, 1977

—— 'Putting art to work: Representing women', *Scarlet Woman*, 1986, No. 23, p.24

Stern, Lesley, 'Feminism and cinema: Exchanges', *Screen*, Vol. 20, Nos. 3/4, Winter 1979–1980, pp.89–105

—— 'Introduction to Plaza', *m/f*, No. 4, 1980, pp.21–27

—— 'The body as evidence', *Screen*, Vol. 23, No. 5, November–December 1982, pp.39–62

—— (with Julie Brown-Rrap), 'Stepping in', *Art & Text*, No. 29, June–August 1988, pp.8–29

Stimpson, Catherine, R., 'Zero degree deviancy: The lesbian novel in English', *Critical Inquiry*, Vol. 8, No. 2, Winter 1982, pp.363–379

Stone, Betsy, *Sisterhood is powerful*, Pathfinder Press Inc., New York, 1970

Stone, Janey, 'The biology of sex and sexuality', *Dissent*, No. 28, Winter 1972, pp.32–39

Suleiman, Susan Rubin (ed), *The female body in Western culture: Contemporary perspectives*, Harvard Press, Cambridge, Massachusetts, 1986

Summers, Anne, *Damned whores and God's police*, Penguin Books, Ringwood Victoria, 1975

Tagg, John, 'Power and photography', *Screen Education*, Autumn 1980, No. 36, pp.17–55

—— 'Power and photography: Part 2', *Screen Education*, Winter 1980/81, No. 37, pp.17–28

Taylor, Paul, 'Australian New Wave' and the 'Third Degree', *Art and Text*, No. 1, 1981, pp.23–32

—— *Popism*, Exhibition Catalogue, National Gallery of Victoria, 1982

—— (ed), *Anything goes: Art in Australia 1970–1980*, Art and Text, 1984, Melbourne

Teale, Ruth (ed), *Colonial Eve: Sources on Women in Australia 1788–1914*, O.U.P., Melbourne, 1978

The Women's Domestic Needlework Group, *The d'oyley show: An exhibition of women's domestic fancywork*, Exhibition Catalogue, Sydney, 1979

Thompson, John, O., 'Real pictures, real pleasures?', *Screen Education*, Spring 1981, No. 38, pp.89–95

Thornley, Jenni, 'Beyond defensive criticism', *Filmnews*, June 1979, pp.14–15

Tickner, Lisa, 'Notes on feminism, femininity and women's art', *LIP*, Vol. 8, 1984, pp.14–18

—— 'Sexuality and/in representation: Five British artists', in *Difference: On representation and sexuality*, New Museum of Contemporary Art, New York, 1985, pp.19–30

Trangmor, Susan (with Yve Lomax), 'Montage', *Camerawork*, No. 24, March 1982, pp.8–9

Trenfield, Karen, 'On the role of biology in feminist ideology', *Hecate*, Vol. III, No. 2, July 1977, pp.41–56

Tribe, Keith, 'History and the production of memories', *Screen*, Vol. 18, No. 4, Winter 1977–1978, pp.9–22

UNESCO, *Seminar on the professional training of the artist*, National Gallery of Canberra, June 1967–1970

—— *Art education: International survey*, Paris, 1972

Vernon, Kay, 'The impact of the Women's Movement on the commercial galleries in Sydney', Honours Thesis, Fine Arts Department, University of Sydney

Vinson, Tony, *Wilful obstruction: The frustration of prison reform*, Methuen, Sydney 1982

Vizents, Alan, 'The pleasure of the gaze', *Praxis*, No. 9, Winter 1985, pp.41–42

Walkerdine, Valerie, 'Progressive pedagogy and political struggle', *Screen*, Vol. 27, No. 5, September–October 1986, pp.54–55

Walkowitz, Judith, *Prostitution in Victorian society: Women, class and the State*, Cambridge University Press, New York, 1980

Watney, Simon, 'Photography–education–theory', *Screen*, Vol. 25, No. 1, January–February 1984, pp.67–73

Watson, Bronwyn, 'Reworking Roberts in 3-D', *Sydney Morning Herald*, 14 August 1987, p.14

Webster, Paula, 'Pornography and pleasure', *Heresies 12: Sex Issue*, Vol. 3, No. 4, 1981, pp.48–51

Weeks, Jeffrey, *Sex, politics and society; The regulation of sexuality since 1800*, Longman, London, 1981

Weeks, Wendy, 'Women and community work: Current issues of concern in women's community action', unpublished article, Phillip Institute of Technology, School of Social Work, August 1985

Weinstock, Jane, 'Sexual difference and the moving image' in *Difference: on representation and sexuality*, Exhibition Catalogue, New Museum of Contemporary Art, New York, 1985, pp.41–45

Wells, Liz, 'The words say more than the pictures: Jo Spence's work reviewed', *Camerawork*, No. 32, Summer 1985, pp.26–28

Wevleman, Emily, 'An issue of feminist materials and media', IV Year Essay, Fine Arts Department, University of Sydney, 1981

Wex, Marianne, 'Photo-essay', *Screen Education*, No. 39, Summer 1981, pp.47–55

White, Barbara Ehrlich, 'A 1974 perspective: Why Women's Studies in art and art history?', *Art Journal*, Vol. XXXV, No. 4, pp.340–344

Whiting, Pat, 'Female sexuality: Its political implications', in M. Wandos (ed), *The body politic*, Stage One, London, 1972

Williams, Anne, 'Re-viewing the look: Photography and the female gaze', *Ten-8*, No. 26, 1987, pp.4–11

Williams, Val, *Women photographers: The other observers 1900 to the present*, Virago, London, 1986

Williamson, Dugald, *Authorship and criticism*, Local Consumption Occasional Paper, No. 7, 1985

—— 'Language and sexual difference', *Screen*, Vol. 28, No. 1, Winter 1987, pp.12–25

Williamson, Judith, *Decoding advertisements: Ideology and meaning in advertising*, Marion Boyers, London, 1978

—— 'The images of woman—The photographs of Cindy Sherman', *Screen*, Vol. 24, No. 6, November–December 1983, pp.102–116

—— 'Family, Education and Photography', *Ten-8*, No. 14, 1984, pp.19–22

Willis, Anne-Marie, 'The local and the ordinary: Community photography in Caulfield', *Photofield*, Vol. 2, No. 3, Spring 1984, pp.6–7

—— *Picturing Australia: A history of photography*, Angus & Robertson, 1988

Willis, Sue, 'The politics of sexual liberation, Sydney sexual liberation movements 1969–1973', PhD Thesis, Government Department, University of Sydney, 1981

Wilson, Elizabeth, (with Weeks, Jeffrey), '1992: Two gay historians look to the future', *Gay News*, No. 243, 24 June, 7 July, 1982, pp.4–5

—— 'Beyond the ghetto: Thoughts on *Beyond the fragments—Feminism and the making of socialism* by H. Wainwright, S. Rowbotham, L. Segal', *Feminist Review*, No. 4, 1980, pp.28–44

Wimmin For Survival, *Wimmin for survival: October 1986, Wimmin's Peace Camp*, Sydney, 1986

Wishart, Barbara, 'Motherhood within patriarchy—A radical feminist perspective', *The Third Women and Labour Conference Papers*, Vol. 1, published by the Convenors, 1982, pp.23–25

Wollen, Peter, 'Counter-cinema and sexual difference' in *Difference: On representation and sexuality*, Exhibition Catalogue, New Museum of Contemporary Art, New York, 1985, pp.35–40

Wolmouth, Philip, 'Photography in opposition', *Camerawork*, No. 18, March 1980, p.12

Women and Art Group, Art School, Preston Institute of Technology, 'Self images, Central Street.... a criticism', *LIP*, 2/3, 1977, p.93

Women's Art Register, *Unfold* (WAF magazine, December 1977)

—— 1978 *Annual*, Victoria, 1976

—— *Women's Art Register, Slide Catalogue*, Melbourne, 1983

Women's Employment Rights Campaign, *Women and unemployment*, Panacea Press, Sydney, December 1979

Women's Studies Group, *Images of women in the media*, Centre for Contemporary Cultural Studies Occasional Paper, No. 31, University of Birmingham, November 1974

Working Women's Group, 'Does arbitration help or hinder the case for equal pay?', *Sydney Women's Liberation Newsletter*, September 1972

Yeatman, Anna, 'The second sex: Women's liberation', *Arena*, No. 21, 1970, pp.19–25

Zdenkowski, George (with Davis Brown), *The prison struggle: Changing Australia's penal system*, Penguin, 1982

—— Brown, David, Ronalds, Chris and Richardson, Michael (eds), *The Criminal Injustice System : Volume Two*, Pluto Press, Sydney, 1987

Zimmerman, Bonnie, 'Daughters of darkness: Lesbian vampires', *Jump Cut*, Nos. 24, 25, 1981, pp.23–24

Zucker, Barbara (with Joyce Kozloff), 'The Woman's Movement: Still a "Source of strength" or "One big bore?", *Art News*, Vol. 75, No. 4, April 1976, pp.48–51

Index

Numbers in *italics* refer to illustrations

203